S0-BAX-048

O, Georgia Too!

An Awesome Collection
of Original Writings
by Young Georgians

Volume VI

O, Georgia! Writers Foundation
Cumming, Georgia

Paul Joffe, Editor

© Copyright 2004
by
O, Georgia! Writers Foundation
A non-profit corporation

First Printing - October, 2004

Published by
O, Georgia! Writers Foundation
Cumming, Georgia 30040

ISBN: 0-9754290-0-0

Printed in the United States of America

Cover and text design by
Janet Bolton of TBI Creative Services

Cover illustration by Debrah Santini

For ordering information
Tel: (770) 781-9705
Toll Free: (877) 523-5156
Web: www.ogeorgia.org
E-Mail: ogwf@ogeorgia.org

Table of Contents

Section Two
Middle School

Section Three
High School

JIMMY CARTER

The *O, Georgia! Writers Foundation* illuminates the lives of thousands of Georgia's students and their families every year. Selection by impartial judges and the imprimatur of a recognized publication enhance the self-esteem of emerging writers.

The program also helps Georgia's young writers build the communication skills they need to become effective citizens of the world. The *O, Georgia! Writers Foundation* extends their youthful voices beyond the walls of home and school and thus exposes Georgia's young citizens to the awesome power of the written word.

As a Georgia author, I support the *O Georgia! Writers Foundation*. It is a remarkable educational resource for Georgia's schools, and I recommend that teachers and parents encourage their children to participate in this worthy program.

Jimmy Carter

THE CARTER CENTER • ONE COPENHILL • ATLANTA, GEORGIA 30307

Foreword

O, Georgia Too! What a wonderful validation of young writers in Georgia. All of us are writers, but these youths are taking a gift and using it to express themselves with creativity and intellect.

As a child, I loved writing book reports and making up stories for my teachers. I never dreamed that as an adult, writing would be a necessary life skill. My career in education could never have happened without the ability to write. Little did I know that as I struggled as a child to make my writing come alive, I was learning how to allow the reader to see a part of life through my eyes.

Thank you, writers, for sharing your gifts with us—your readers! You won't "grow up" to be writers; you *are* writers. You have made a contribution to society; you have enriched us. Thank you, Paul Cossman, for persisting with your dream of publishing the writings of these young Georgians. Each volume adds to your legacy—promoting the writing craft. Our community and state are enriched by this collection.

My wish is that each reader cherishes this wonderful compilation and that each writer continues to put pen to paper.

Paula H. Gault, Superintendent
Forsyth County Schools

Acknowledgments

Until two years ago, the O, Georgia Too! Writing Competition was operated by Humpus Bumpus Books, my own retail bookstore. At the 2002 book release gala, I announced that I was forced to close the O, Georgia! program because it was losing more money than my small bookstore could afford to spend to keep it going. The response to my announcement was overwhelming. So many people pleaded with me to keep O, Georgia Too! alive that I reconsidered my decision. Following the advice of the wise ones, I formed a nonprofit corporation so that financial donations might be raised to keep it going.

In 2003 the O, Georgia Too! program took a hiatus during which time we reorganized and started to try to raise money through charitable donations. (If I now use the first person plural, we, instead of the singular, I, it is because the O, Georgia! Writers Foundation is now a public charity of which I am the executive director, not the owner). Now, on this day, October 17, 2004, we are proud to present to you the very first edition of O, Georgia Too! to be published under the auspices of our new, nonprofit entity.

We are still a struggling, new nonprofit but have, nonetheless, found the support of sixty-three individuals who have contributed a combined total of approximately $8,000.00 to help keep the O, Georgia! Writers Foundation alive during its fledgling first year as a non-profit. These sixty-three people are listed in our Honor Roll of Donors in this volume. If it were not for these generous donors, this book would not be in your hands today.

In addition to those on our Honor Roll, we would like to thank all of the people who have contributed to the growing success of O, Georgia Too! These people include all the students who have entered their writings into the competition, as well as all the parents and teachers who supported them. We would like to thank all of the people who have shown their financial support by purchasing multiple copies of O, Georgia Too! We have a long way to go in order to become a viable, self-capitalizing organization, but we have made some brave first steps.

Many of us work long hours on a volunteer basis in order to keep costs down because we believe in the value of what we do here. Our judging panel consists of sixteen judges who spent many hours reading and ranking all the entries. Our judges are named in the Biographical Notes section in the back of this volume. Vicki Husby, a dedicated Gwinnett County educator, with her team of teachers, developed the Teacher's Guide, which supports this edition of O, Georgia Too! The Teacher's Guide turns O, Georgia Too! into a curriculum tool that makes this book an integral part of any teacher's classroom activities.

The O, Georgia! Writers Foundation is very proud to have attracted the attention of Georgia's most famous native son, President Jimmy Carter, who eagerly offered his personal endorsement of our program. President Carter's comments are at the beginning of this year's O, Georgia Too!

In conclusion, it is my fervent desire to one day see this organization endowed with enough money to keep it operating in perpetuity—this is the legacy I, as executive director, would like to leave when I eventually retire. We have a long way to go. In the meantime, we need to build an active support base of cash donors and volunteers to enable the O, Georgia! Writers Foundation to run the 2005 competitions. Can we count on you?

Paul A. Cossman
Executive Director

Section One

Elementary School

4th grade

Everyday Signs Of Courage

by Kamryn Coan

There are many kinds of courage. There are awesome kinds.
And everyday kinds. Still, courage is courage—whatever kind.

Courage is...

Getting back on a bicycle after you have fallen off—that's courage.
Practicing a dive off the diving board, even though you didn't
do it very well the first time!

Courage is doing something until you get it right!

Talking things over with Dad when you've done something wrong.
Saying, "I'm sorry," when you fight with your best friend.

Courage is making things right again.

Letting a doctor give you a shot, even though it stings—that's courage.
It's opening your mouth for the dentist so they can fill a cavity.

Courage is being brave.

Telling your mother you tracked in the dirt on the carpet—that's courage.
It's letting your dad know that the kid who tossed the baseball
through the basement window was you and not the neighbor kid!

Courage is telling the truth when you did wrong.

When you make the last out in a baseball game, courage is not
blaming the umpire! It's when you score your first soccer goal,
but it was for the other team!

Courage is maintaining your composure in competition.

It's when you have to give a speech in front of your class, and
your knees feel like jelly. Just picture them in their underwear!
You're in a spelling bee, and your word is "extravaganza!"

Courage is overcoming a fear.

Courage is trying to be the best kind of person you can be, every day!

The Changed Man

by Erin Galvin-McCoy

Once upon a time, there was a water peddler whose name was Anansi. He was very rich, but also very stingy and greedy. Now, to the beginning of the story…

It was a sunny day. Anansi hummed as he strolled along the path while a servant carried the heavy water baskets. He thought, *"The day will be very hot. Lots of people will want water. I shall sell all of it and make lots of money!"*

Once he got to the market, he found a nice spot under a ginkgo tree. Acrobats were doing acts on a stage in the market. Soon an old man came up to Anansi's stall. He didn't have a penny in his pocket, but any normal person could tell that this man was magic.

"Water peddler," the old man said to Anansi, "please give me some fresh, cool water. I have not a penny in my pocket, but I am sure you will take pity on me and give me a bottle of water."

"Go away!" yelled Anansi. "My water is for *sale*. I do not give it away to stupid old men like you."

"Fine," said the old man coolly. He started to walk away. Then suddenly he turned back. "Anansi! You may be rich, but you are hard-hearted. Soon you will find out how hard my life is." Then he turned around and walked down the dirt path.

Anansi sat under his tree, staring after the old man. After he had sold all of his water bottles, he went home. BUT a transformation had begun.

When he got to his street, all the dogs began to bark at him like he was a stranger. When he reached his house, he opened the door. A servant stood waiting in the doorway. The servant shouted, "Go away, old man. You can't steal anything from here! This is my master's house and my master is very powerful. So, get out of here before you get in a lot of trouble!"

"Did you take stupid pills? I am your master, idiot. So get out of my way before I beat your rump so hard you won't be able to sit down for a year!"

"WHAT!? WHO DO YOU THINK YOU ARE? ARE YOU CRAZY?" The servant rushed at him with a broom, shouting, "Git!"

Anansi still refused to move. The servant went berserk and actually beat Anansi with the broomstick, yelling "Git! Git! GIT! GIIIIIIIT!!!"

The blows knocked Anansi down the steps. The servant spun in a huff and slammed the door behind him.

Anansi shook his head to clear it, but it still wasn't cleared. He said, "I need some really fresh air. I'm going to go to the shore." He turned and walked slowly toward the beach.

When he got to the ticket stand for the beach, he saw one of his favorite ticket sellers (because he always let rich people get away with free admission but charged poor people a lot so they couldn't use the beach). Suddenly, he stopped. He didn't believe his eyes. There at the ticket stand was someone who looked just like him, who was being extremely generous to the ticket seller instead of accepting the free admission. "HEY," shouted Anansi, "You look just like me!"

"Sorry about the crazy old man," said the ticket seller to the fake Anansi.

"WHO ARE YOU CALLING CRAZY? I'M THE ONE WHO SHOULD BE HIM!"

The ticket seller stammered, his voice shaking with fear, "N-n-no. D-d-d-id y-y-y-ou come f-f-rom the m-m-m-adhouse, old man?"

"I am not old!"

"Take a look in this mirror."

Anansi yelped when he saw his reflection. It was not a rich young man that he saw. It was a poor, old man. He flailed his arms wildly. Suddenly he saw his old, wrinkled hands becoming young and smooth again. The ticket seller fainted.

The form that was the fake Anansi now changed back into

the magic old man.

"Be gone!" shouted Anansi, who now looked like himself.

"You see how hard the lives of the poor are?" said the old man. "You can't even get into a beach or your own house. You have to travel from place to place, never knowing when you're going to get water or food. Now, do everything you can to help the poor. Do I have your word for it?"

Anansi stammered, "Y-y-yes, s-s-s-ir." Anansi was better than his word. He gave the poor food and much beyond that.

In The Night

by Marabeth C. Walkusky

In the night, I hear the wind whistle
through the trees,
as a barn owl catches his prey with ease.
The crickets sing their song,
for the morning's light they long.

Out of my window, I can see near and far.
I can see every star.
A bat flies through the sky;
all insects will surely die.

The moon is full tonight.
Look at how it is extremely bright.
The croak of a bullfrog is a magnificent sound to hear,
but nothing to fear.

I hope I have fulfilled your delight,
For things you can hear and see
In the night.

The Magic Shell

by Gloria J. L. Mahoney

As I walked along the shore by my house, something glittered in the distance. I was curious and wanted to know what it was. By the time I had discovered what it was, my mother called me for dinner. I grasped the object tightly and neared the house quickly.

Before I went to the dinner table, I went upstairs to wash up and observe the item I had found. It was a shell, coated with shiny gloss. It had a unique look and included purple lines and blue spots.

As I treaded down the stairs, I noticed we were having fresh fish and a tossed salad for dinner. Mmmm, my favorite!

"Gloria, I made fish and salad for dinner, because I know you like it," said my mom.

"Thanks, it looks great!" I exclaimed with glee. We all sat down, said grace, and ate a delicious dinner.

That night, I went to my room early to examine my shell. While looking at it, I found out that it had been seen by another person, because it had a note in it. Some of the words written were hard to see (because the water had run the ink a little bit), but I could still make out what it said:

September 18, 2002

Dear Person Who Finds This,

Please take care of this shell. It is very beautiful, and I hope it will help me to live. I'm shipwrecked on a deserted island. When I washed up on shore, something hit my foot. I looked down and saw the shell you see in front of you. It has a perfect place to keep a note safe from the water. If it has reached you, it is truly magical. Please let my parents know that I am still alive and to please keep looking for me. I have hope that they will find me. Enjoy my gift!

Sincerely,
Nina

I couldn't believe I had found this shell from the infamous Nina! She was well known in the area because she had gone on a cruise with her family and had disappeared from the ship one night. The reports were that she had fallen overboard somehow. The police had stopped searching for her, but her parents had hired a private detective to continue the search. They had not given up.

I wanted to jump up and down with joy, but jumping wasn't allowed in our house, so I ran down the stairs to show my mother. When she saw the note and the shell, she said, "Gloria, this shell must be from the famous Nina. She was lost at sea almost a year ago."

"Mum, we need to let her parents know right away!"

My mother knew just what to do and whom to call. She started right away to make the contacts.

The next few days were a whirlwind of police, reporters, and, of course, Nina's family. Everyone was very excited about what I had found. I think I told the story more than 1,000 times!

The magic shell became the famous shell. Special people came to our beach to measure winds, ocean currents, and I don't know what else, so they could find the island that Nina was on.

I had a better idea. If her shell could reach me, maybe a message sent in a bottle would reach her, if all else failed. I got the bottle ready and wrote a note to her. Then I thought of the magic shell she had given me! As I held the shell tightly in my hand, I wrote:

July 13, 2003

Dear Nina,

I found your shell. It's so beautiful! Everyone is very excited that you are still alive. They are searching for you right now! I am a ten-year-old girl. I live on an island called Strawberry Island. I have sent my picture so you know who you are talking to. I know you will be rescued! I can't wait to meet you! Keep your spirits up. You will be found soon!

Sincerely,
Gloria

After I wrote the letter, I rolled it up and stuck it into the glass bottle. I tried to think of other things to put in the bottle. I sent some waterproof markers, some paper, and some newspaper articles that I found about her disappearance. I corked it tightly, and my mother sealed it with melted wax from a candle. Then I threw it in the ocean and made a wish that it would go to Nina. As I walked back to the house, I looked back at the endless water and didn't see the bottle. I wondered where it had gone, secretly hoping that it was headed toward Nina.

Three weeks after I sent the note to Nina, my family and I were watching television and a news bulletin interrupted the show. Nina had been found! The news showed Nina getting off a helicopter on a landing strip with soldiers and her dad. In her hand, she held my bottle!

She looked very happy, as she waved to the cameras. As I watched, very excited, they led her to news microphones. She stood there calmly as flashes went off in front of her. She started to speak, saying that she was excited to be back home. Then she started talking about me! She said that she had made a new friend who gave her hope and kept her alive during a lonely time. She said she couldn't wait to be in touch with me and was looking forward to seeing me face to face.

After that, everything was a blur. The phone started ringing nonstop, and people were knocking at the door day and night. With my parent's help, I was able to set a date to see Nina. We got a lot of publicity at that meeting! We had a great time together, even though the whole country (maybe the world!) was watching. It was as though I had known her forever. We tell people that we are sisters, because it is as though we found a new family member. We sort of look alike, as well!

Things have settled down here on Strawberry Island now, and hopefully, all is forgotten. It is not something that I will ever forget. Nina said that I could have the magic shell to keep. My mother put it in a special frame along with a picture of Nina and me. It is on my wall next to my bed. I think of Nina every time I look at it. We talk on the phone every day, and we get together whenever we can. We will always be the very best of friends.

5th grade

I'm Exceptionally, Exceedingly, Genuinely, Extremely Happy!!!

by James Madison Tuggle

I'm happiest when…
everyone is quiet,
my dad says, "Let's buy it!"
and Mom's on a diet,
when my siblings don't riot.
That's the way I like it!

I'm happiest when…
two plus two equals four,
my brother doesn't snore,
when there's no talk of war,
and I make a great score.
That's what I adore!

I'm happiest when…
others get some glory,
when I read a new story,
when things are hunky-dory,
when news stories aren't gory.
That's my love story!

I'm happiest when…
I'm as free as a bird,
I know the right password,
my vision isn't blurred,
my punishment's been deferred.
That's when I splurge!

I'm exceptionally, exceedingly, genuinely, extremely happy!!!

3rd grade

The Mysterious Monster Of The Deep

by William A. Robinson, III

"This will be a wonderful trip," said brave Raymond Davidson.

"I still think it is a bad idea," said Raymond's wife Margaret. "No ship has ever gotten to the other side of that ocean."

"Cool," said Raymond's two sons, who were twins.

"I'm scared," said Raymond's smallest and youngest child, Ashley, who was only three years old.

"Don't worry, the *Desire* is a strong ship," said Raymond.

"Well, you can't change my mind," said Margaret.

"It doesn't matter now, because the boat is leaving!" cried Raymond, running towards the dock as the large passenger ship, *Desire,* was loosening its ties at the pier. But he was too late.

"Well, that takes care of my problems," said Margaret satisfyingly.

"Not quite," said Raymond in an angry voice, because he had missed the ship.

"What do you mean, Daddy?" asked little Ashley.

"What I mean is that small rowboat over there," Raymond replied.

"Double cool" said the twins.

"You mean…that you're going in that old rowboat all the way across the sea?" asked Margaret in a puzzled voice. "It's abandoned isn't it?" said Margaret trying to convince Raymond not to go. "So it probably was abandoned for a good reason. Besides, it won't last the whole way across the ocean."

"I am double scared," said Ashley.

The Davidson family walked up to the rowboat. Margaret did not know why anybody would want to ride in such an old, abandoned, and ugly boat. She finally spoke. "Raymond, that won't last a day against the weather."

The twins looked excited. "Oh come on, Mom, it will be fun. Just think, it will be just like the good old days," said one of the twins convincingly.

"Well, I am not giving up hope," said Raymond. "Let's see if there are any holes."

"Wait, wait, wait!" said Margaret. "Now you have gone too far. You are either going by yourself, or you're not going at all."

"Margaret, please; this means a lot to me. Just let me check the…" Raymond's body went stiff as he started sniffing the air. "Do you smell that?" asked Raymond with his head high in the air.

"I don't smell anything," said Margaret, trying to smell what Raymond smelled as hard as she could. "Raymond, what is happening to your eyes? They are turning red!" But Raymond did not answer. Instead he started walking toward the boat. "Raymond, please do not do this," said Margaret desperately. Raymond kept on walking, despite what Margaret was saying. In fact, he seemed to be in a trance.

Raymond continued to get into the boat despite Margaret's protests. Raymond didn't seem to hear her. All was silent.

Then a cold, creaky voice, which seemed to come from nowhere, could be heard speaking to Margaret. "I have waited this long for a follower!" it stated. "You won't be able to take him from me."

The voice no doubt belonged to someone or something that was very old. It put shivers down Margaret's spine. In fact, she was so scared she couldn't move. When the kids heard the voice, they hid behind a rock. Raymond, however, slowly stepped into the boat and, immediately, it began to move out to sea.

The voice started speaking again. "Come, you will live with me. First, however, you must help me sink the *Desire.*"

Margaret stopped shaking. She couldn't chicken out now! What happened now would affect her whole future! Besides, she didn't want to raise a family by herself! She had to stop whatever had a hold of Raymond. But the boat vanished, as soon as the voice stopped talking.

Margaret decided to take the kids to their grandparents'

house, just in case she didn't come back. She realized that the best chance she had of finding Raymond was to go back out in another rowboat.

By the time she had bought a rowboat and returned to the pier, it was dark. The night was foggy, and the waves seemed to be giving her a warning by pushing her back towards the shore. But Margaret was determined. She kept rowing.

After what seemed like hours and when she could no longer see the shoreline, she heard the voice again. "After we destroy the ships and take control of the ocean we shall rule the land. With you I can start a new generation of giant crabs like me." Margaret listened with fright. This was bad. She had to save Raymond from the crab monster.

Margaret couldn't decide what to do. It was getting colder by the minute. She also thought of something she hadn't thought of before she left (because she was in such a hurry)—food!

The voice was quickly vanishing, and she needed to make up her mind. She kept rowing towards the voice of the giant crab. Her hands were shaking from the idea of Raymond becoming a crab. She shivered even more at the thought that she might be too late to save him as a human, and he would already be transformed into a crab. Thoughts filled her head of having to kiss a crab good night and trying to hold one of its claws without getting pinched. This made her worry even more.

When she finally caught up to Raymond's boat, she was surprised to hear Raymond speaking. "Are there more crabs like you out there?" he asked.

"No," said the giant crab in a cold voice. "The rest is a long story, but you won't have to wait too long to find out."

Margaret was puzzled about the crab's last words. What was the crab going to do with Raymond? Was the crab about to show Raymond some new place, like a hideout?

As her mind filled with questions, she realized that the fog was clearing. She could see a tall figure in the middle of the ocean. "Oh, my gosh," Margaret whispered. "It's the *Desire!*" The water started bubbling, then whirling, and then crashing against the sides of the ship.

A big, black crab, about twice the size of a man, came to the top of the water and began climbing the side of the *Desire.* When one pincer was halfway to the top of the ship, it stabbed a hole into the side. Margaret was watching with horror, as an alarm sounded and water began to fill the ship. From where she was in her boat she could see something that even Raymond couldn't see. There was a wire coming out of the crab's leg! As it scuttled down towards the side of the ship where passengers were getting into life rafts, she could make out a dent on its stomach, as though it were made of metal. She realized that this was a robot, and someone was inside of it!

Margaret quickly rowed towards Raymond. As she was rowing, she started trying to put the strange pieces of this mystery together. She couldn't believe that the crab was a fake. And how could a robot communicate or control a person without another person knowing it? What had Raymond smelled, and why did his eyes change color? Could that smell have put Raymond into some sort of trance? She splashed water in his face in order to snap him out of his trance as her boat drew nearer. She quickly told Raymond that the crab was a robot.

Raymond stared as the crab neared the passengers. He frantically jumped into the water and swam under the crab's belly, where the crab could not see him. He reached for the apron of the crab, which opens a crab's shell. Just like a real crab, the apron opened and water started to fill inside the giant crab's belly and the robot began to sink.

Suddenly, an old man desperately crawled out of the robot. Raymond quickly realized that the old man would not be able to reach the surface in time. Margaret couldn't see either one for what seemed like a very long time. When Raymond finally surfaced, he came up with the man, who was not conscious. As

Raymond pulled the body on board Margaret's rowboat, he began to explain everything.

"I met this man, named Bradley, at the drugstore." Raymond gasped, as he started heaving himself into the boat. "He told the pharmacist that he made this potion over fifty years ago to control people's brains. He said that he had 'improved it' and was now trying to sell it to the pharmacist as a medicine to cure nervousness. When Mr. Bradley opened the plastic box at the store, it smelled so bad that I coughed and sneezed. Apparently, I was allergic to the ingredients, so the pharmacist threw him out. I guess he has changed the formula some, because the only part of me that still had an allergic reaction was my eyes. That is why they turned red when I smelled the potion this time."

Margaret and Raymond propped the man up in the bow of the boat and began rowing back towards the shore. "Well, you certainly had an adventure, even if you didn't get to the other side of the ocean," said Margaret, smiling happily at Raymond. She was glad he had not been changed into a crab.

Raymond smiled back at her. "I tell you what. Once we get this fellow dropped off at the police station, I say we go out to dinner and celebrate—I am so hungry!" Raymond and Margaret laughed.

"Let's pick up the kids before we go", said Margaret. And then, with a little smile she asked, "How do you feel about The Crab Shack for supper?"

"Perfect!" shouted Raymond, and they headed for home.

Darkness Is No More!

by Stefanie Smith

Lost in dismal sadness,
Having nowhere to look,
I see a shelf in my mind,
And I opened up its book.

It says to sweep my heart,
And dust my stuffy soul.
It said to open up my brain,
And put all bad feelings in a bowl.

I listened to this little book,
It helped me out so much!
I cleaned out every part of me,
And put it in a hutch.

I threw the hutch out the window,
I don't need misery on the floor!
I am so excited,
Because darkness is no more!

The Monorail Ride

by Hannah Shaul

In a city of darkness there was a girl whose family was rude and mean to her. They really didn't care about her. This little girl was an abused child. She was seeking freedom and deeply needed help. She was not allowed to go places and did not have a clue about the world except for one thing, the monorail.

This particular girl lived in the hallways that led to the steps for this kind of transportation. The little girl had nothing to do during the day, while her parents worked at the nearby factory. When her parents came home from work they scolded her for things that she did not do, just for their entertainment. This little girl did not like her parents at all and wanted to get away. She knew that someday her parents might kill her because of the way they were.

One night at eleven o'clock, while her parents were sleeping, the little girl crept away to catch a ride on the last monorail train of the night. The monorail was headed for Boston and was going fast. When the little girl got to Boston, she found an orphanage and got a room to stay in for a while. At this place she could come and go as she liked.

She sometimes went back home to see how the city was doing, but her parents caught her one time while she was by a café, just a block away from the factory where they worked. They held her captive for a long time until the people at the orphanage started to worry. Someone was sent to find the little girl, but there was no luck. The little girl's parents put her in a hole that led deep down into the ground. They put a lid on the hole and left her inside without any food or water. She had no way out. Her parents told the police of the city there was a little girl trapped underground and she was the robber of the store nearby (which had just been robbed). The police surrounded her, and she had no way out. The one thing she had was the monorail.

The girl ran for the monorail, got a ticket and took a ride to freedom, back to Boston. The police followed her, and when she got to Boston she ran for a long time, just going in circles around the city.

Late at night, when it was safe, the little girl crept over to the orphanage and slept for the night. The next morning, the police came looking for her again and found her.

They took her to the police department in the city and asked her some questions. She told the police that her parents were mean to her and abused her and did not care for her at all. The police did some research and found out that the people that the little girl called her parents were not really her parents. They had taken her hostage when she was just a little baby. Her real parents lived in Pittsburgh. The only way she knew to get to them was the monorail.

Now, the little girl lives with her parents and is very happy. She sometimes goes back to Boston to see some of her friends at the orphanage. As for her so-called "parents," they went to jail and will remain there for a long time and will never see her again. All thanks to the monorail, the little girl is safe and happy.

Ocean And Sea

by Brittany Bodine

The ocean,
The sea,
Brings joy to me.
The life of the ocean
Gives great notion;
It is a symbol of great freedom.
The sea, the sea,
How could you be
So perfect at morning and night?
With waters so great,
How could you hate
To see such a beautiful sight?

Military Missions

by Samuel Andrew Warnke

Once there were three desert rangers. They had a mission to do. The name was "laptop recovery." What they were supposed to do in "laptop recovery" was recover a laptop from an ex-op compound.

Once they got to the ex-op compound, they used a missile shooter on top of their Humvee to shoot a hole in the gate. Then they used the hook on the front of their Humvee to grab the gate and pull the gate out. (By the way, did I mention that the enemy's name was ex-op?)

The ex-op guard loaded his gun. But one of the rangers jumped out of the Humvee with a gun. Once the ex-op guard saw the gun in the ranger's hand, he dropped his gun and put his hands in the air. The ex-ops who were inside the compound were startled to see that their gate was missing. Once he did realize that, he opened fire on the rangers. But he was outnumbered three to one.

Once the ex-op grew tired of firing, he finally surrendered. But the ex-op would not tell where he had hidden the laptop. So one of the rangers went into the compound and searched it. After a while, he found a safe. He guessed the code XOO7 and, to his amazement, it worked! He looked inside the safe and found the laptop. He returned back to the rangers' Humvee and on his way, yelled, "The mission was a success! The mission was a success!"

Once there were seven Falcons. They had a mission to do. The name was "satellite rescue." (Falcons are men from the Air Force.) In "satellite rescue," they were supposed to rescue a satellite from an ex-op tower.

The Falcons had a helicopter to help them. So the seven Falcons flew over to the ex-op tower. The helicopter had a hook. Men grabbed hold of the hook, and the hook was lowered to the ground below the ex-op tower.

To save time, some Falcons parachuted down to the ground.

An ex-op who was on guard on top of the tower alerted the other two ex-ops. They, too, saw the helicopter. As soon as they saw it, they opened fire on it. But thankfully, the metal on the helicopter was bulletproof. The top of the ex-op tower was a trap door. The ex-ops were outnumbered three to seven.

Once the Falcons were on the ground, they opened fire on the three ex-ops. After one or two hours of nonstop firing, the three ex-ops gave up. But they would not tell the Falcons where they hid the satellite. But the Falcons were smart and immediately knew where it was. It was inside the tower. So, a Falcon grabbed the hook and was lowered down into the tower. And as soon as the trap door opened, he saw the satellite. Once he was lowered all the way to the ground, he grabbed the satellite off a table and gave the signal for the helicopter to reel in its hook. Once the Falcons were back at the Air Force base, they were each awarded a medal.

Lime Green

by Megan Galvin

Lime green is the smell of freshly cut grass on a sizzling
hot day.

Lime green is the elegant, slender leaves on a blossoming,
pearly-white daisy.

Lime green shouts out to you like a famous pop star singing in a
rock and roll concert.

It dances to the music as you do, too.

It is the teenage daughter of Mr. Green and Mrs. Yellow.

It jumbles and squirms all over the room like a
popped balloon.

Lime green is the noticeable exclamation point at the end of
a sentence.

It is the twisted, tart taste of a sour apple's first bite.

Lime green is hot and spicy, like freshly picked green
bell peppers.

It is sweet and tart, like a jellybean right out of your
Halloween bag.

It is the color of my favorite highlighter, pointing out an
important fact on my research project.

Lime green is the thick, moist jungles filled with lively
monkeys and angry tigers.

It is the wide, luscious meadow with bright, yellow dandelions and
singing birds.

It is the color of a hungry rattlesnake's deadly venom.

Lime green is the huge, swaying leaves on a palm tree covered in coconuts.

Lime green is more than a color.

It is me.

Willie's Wednesday

by Joshua R. Dane

Wednesday was not a good day for Willie, nor was Monday or Tuesday. Come to think of it, every day was not a good day for Willie. This was because the neighborhood bullies considered Willie an easy target. He was small for his age and did not have a single friend. Having no one to stand up for him, he was completely helpless. Whenever he tried to stand up for himself, all he received were a black eye, a swollen lip, and sometimes a bloody nose. Usually, he had to watch as his backpack was torn apart and his stuff was tossed around and laughed at. His parents tried everything to help him, but to no avail.

Willie groaned and rolled over in his bed. The clock read 12:15 a.m. That meant only a few more hours until the torment would begin. Caught in his own frustration, he cried angrily, "Why does it always have to be me?" Unable to control himself, he buried his face in his pillow trying to stop the flow of the tears running down his face.

Sometimes Willie wished he were dead. Sniffling, he said to himself, "Might as well try to get some sleep." But sleep wasn't exactly easy for him. He tried reading, but that didn't help. Finally, sleep wove its spell over Willie. It was not a peaceful, good dreaming sleep, but a troubled, disturbed sleep.

Suddenly, Willie thought he must be in heaven. White, white was all he could see. This was not the kind of white you see on a new piece of paper or newly fallen snow, but a radiant light. It was like a gleaming mist swirling together. Becoming more solid by the moment, a young glowing lady took form in front of him.

As gently as a summer breeze, she spoke into his mind, "I know what is troubling you, Willie."

Mystified, Willie replied nervously, "Who are you? How much do you know about me?"

"Who I am I cannot answer, but there is much I know about you," she said gently. "The reason I brought you here is to help you."

Willie thought this over carefully. "I'm not sure how, but before you go on I need to test you. If you can tell me two things about my life I will believe you."

Patiently, she replied, "Well, I know you have a brother who never takes part in your life, and I know you cheated on your science quiz when you were in second grade, and…"

"Hold it," he said. "No need to go that far. Come on, I was only seven." Willie was impressed. "Okay, I believe you."

Smiling at him, she said, "I'm here to help you by granting you one wish. So I suggest you use it wisely."

Without thinking, Willie said hopefully, "I wish I weren't afraid. What I mean is I wish I could stand up to the bullies!"

"I understand," she told him. "But not so fast—first you must complete a task."

"Oh," he said, a little disappointed. "What is it?"

Wordlessly, she snapped her fingers. Everything around him began to spin. As his feet left the ground, he tried to cry out for help, but the whirling winds drowned out his shouts. His eyes were tearing so much he had to close them against the wind. Just as quickly as it started, it stopped.

All was quiet. He opened his eyes and blinked, to make sure he wasn't imagining things. He wasn't. Slowly, he got to his feet and stretched. "I guess that lady is some kind of enchantress," he said, impressed. "What a thing it is to be transported!"

As he walked, he found himself in his schoolyard. He tripped on something. It was the book he had been reading. As he picked it up, he noticed the bookmark was not familiar. When he opened the book there was a message on it: "Your task is to save the one who suffers from the same problem as yours, only far worse," he read.

"Well, I now know what I have to do, but I'm not sure it will be easy." Suddenly, he heard a shout of pain nearby. He dropped the book and ran towards the noise. The shouts where getting louder, and there was laughter. He began to crawl, knowing that he was near. In a few minutes, he came upon a scene that took his breath away. There stood three teenagers standing over a ragged boy about his own age. The boy was curled up in a ball on the ground. Next to him were a baseball bat and a glove. To his horror one of them had a belt. He struck the boy, who cried out. The others laughed and gave him a kick.

Willie was overwhelmed with anger and was determined to help the boy. He knew this had to be his task. He tore a strip of cloth from his shirt and fastened a sling.

Grabbing a rock, he set it in his makeshift sling. Whirling it above his head, he let it go as hard as he could. The rock struck the closest one on the back of the head, making him react with pain and stop kicking the boy. Willie never knew that knowing how to make a sling would come in so handy.

Willie realized his advantage was short-lived, as he did not see any more rocks. But rather then being afraid, he dropped his sling and charged at the one with the belt. Willie forgot about the other kid, who then tripped him. Down he went, lying there stunned. He saw the boy with the belt standing over him, ready to strike, saying, "I'll teach you, you little brat!"

Still, Willie wasn't afraid, and as he was struggling to get up, he heard a *thunk*. The boy had revived and had hit the bigger boy in the back of the knees with his bat. Slowly, the boy with the belt toppled over, and the third boy turned tail and ran off as fast as he could go.

Willie looked up to see the boy standing with a bat in his hand. "Thank you,' said Willie.

"Thank *you,"* said the other boy. "I was afraid and didn't know what to do. When I saw you rush in to help me, I suddenly wasn't afraid anymore. I felt like I knew just what I had to do."

When Willie heard that, he jumped up excitedly and started to say, "I know just what you mean; that's what happened to me." But before Willie could say the words, the scene began to fade away.

He was back in the place he called heaven. The place was as gleaming as ever.

This time the young lady stood waiting for him. “Why did you take me away?” he asked sadly. “I finally made a friend.”

“Don’t worry,” she said soothingly, “You’ll make plenty of friends when the time comes.”

“If you say so,” he said glumly. “What about my wish?” he asked.

“You granted it yourself,” she laughed.

“How?” he asked, a little confused.

Patiently, she said, “You stood up to the bullies and defeated them.”

“You’re right,” he said, recognition dawning upon him. “So what you’re saying is that this was all a setup?”

“Not exactly,” she said knowingly. “But now I think it’s time for you to return home.” Before he could answer, she snapped her fingers. This time he plunged downwards; down, down, down he went.

Suddenly, Willie’s eyes snapped open. He was in his own room again. He took a few deep breaths, savoring each one. He was glad to be home. He wondered if that dream had been a dream. After all, it had seemed so lifelike.

Somehow, Willie felt different. It was in a way he could not explain. It was as if he had changed. He felt at that moment he could do anything. Once again, he glanced at the clock. This time he was unafraid. It read 8:00 a.m. “I might as well go and face the day’s challenges,” he laughed. He got dressed and hurried downstairs. The smell of his dad’s delicious pancakes greeted him as he entered the kitchen.

The moment he reached the breakfast table, his mother nervously asked, “Did you sleep well?”

“Absolutely,” he said, remembering the previous night’s adventures.

As Willie set upon his pancakes, his parents exchanged glances. "Is there something you need to tell me?" he asked.

Unable to control herself, his mother blurted out, "We have decided to send you to a class that is guaranteed to solve bullying problems and make friends." Finishing, she waited for his reaction.

"I don't think that will be necessary," he said confidently.

"You're sure?" his father said, impressed.

"I'm positive," he said, just as confidently as before. "Breakfast was great! May I be excused?" With that, Willie got up and walked out the door, leaving his parents proud and a little surprised.

The moment he started walking towards the park he was set upon by half a dozen bullies. "You're late," said the ringleader. "And you know I hate people who are late."

"You hate everybody," Willie muttered under his breath.

"What was that?" he demanded menacingly.

"I said to let me alone!" he shouted defiantly in his face. "Is that loud enough for you to hear?"

Stunned by the outburst from Willie, the bully suddenly backed up a step. He saw that Willie was no longer afraid and that he had a very determined look in his eyes. The bully sensed that something had changed. This was not the scared little boy from yesterday. This seemed like a different Willie. This Willie seemed older. This Willie was not afraid and was going to fight back. This Willie even *looked* bigger.

Suddenly, the bully was the one who was afraid. The bully didn't want to lose face, and he didn't relish the thought of fighting Willie. It was no fun trying to pick on someone who wasn't afraid of him. So he laughed and in a loud voice said, "Okay, no problem this time, but don't let it happen again." But Willie and everyone else knew it wouldn't happen again.

As they walked away, Willie heard a voice behind him, "Hey, Willie!"

Spinning around, he saw five boys his own age approaching. They each had baseball gloves. One was throwing a ball up in the air. Willie recognized him as the boy from his dream. "Do you want to play?"

"Sure!" Willie called, as he ran up to join them.

Growing

by Shannon Mewes

Everybody needs some time to grow—
        time to get ready.
Time to know what they are.
        And where they belong.

Caterpillars are like an
Unfinished work of art.

No one is ever quite finished.
Everybody should have a chance to grow.
We are all growing.

I Am The Earth

by Alyx White

I am the earth. From far away, I look white and blue. I have a round shape, but I am small compared to most planets. I have one moon and one sun. All around me there are stars. I think I am the only planet with people.

When you get closer to me, you can see the lands and waters. I have islands and seven oceans. I have seven continents, too. I have mountains, valleys, deserts, canyons, and nature. There are many different types of people and animals, too.

But some people cut down the trees I have. Then there's not much oxygen. My feelings get hurt when people do that, because people and animals need trees. Without trees, everything would die. My feelings also get hurt when people are not careful with my water. When people dump chemicals in my water, the creatures that live there can get stuck or die from it.

I also like all the animals that live on me. Sometimes, people kill or injure the animals. I wish those people were nicer to my animals. I wish that people were more careful with my air, too. Sometimes, people build large factories that puff out smoke, and it is hard for all to breathe.

But, I still have faith in my people. A lot of people are trying to keep me healthy. I want my people to be safe. I want to go on forever.

When I Am Mad

by Gemma Kim O'Connor

When I am mad
I don't feel love,
I don't have or make peace,
and I don't see the light shining above.

When I am mad
I sometimes slam my door,
I would feel like crying,
or make a loud roar.

When I am mad
I would go on my new computer,
or watch a video,
or play on my scooter.

After I am mad
I finally relax,
I can finally smile
and maybe play Korean jacks.

After I am mad
I can enjoy my day,
I can bear to face people,
and with my sister, play.

After I am mad
I can handle things with care,
be more patient,
and maybe be able to share.

After I am mad
I can put on a smile.
I can enjoy myself,
I can probably even walk a mile!

Why I'm Thankful To Be Alive

by Austin T. Smith

When I was five years old, my grandfather, Jack Powell, passed away. I never really knew him or remember him because I was so young. The only way I know about him today is because my grandmother told me stories about him. One story amazes me. I hope it amazes you.

It was World War II. The Germans were trying to take over European countries by the German dictator named Hitler. He believed in a superior race and was killing Jewish people. The United States and other countries joined together to fight against Hitler's German army.

In July of 1943, my grandparents got married in Shawnee, Oklahoma. After they had been married for a few months, my grandfather and a few of his friends volunteered to be in the United States Air Force.

He went to training classes in Texas, Oklahoma, and Nebraska for the United States Air Force. He was trained as a waste gunner on a B17 Bomber. The B17 Bomber usually had approximately twelve men. There were two pilots, a bombardier, a navigator, a nose gunner, a tail gunner, two wing gunners, and two waste gunners. After his training, they called him Sergeant Powell.

My grandfather was a waste gunner. My grandfather's and the other gunners' jobs were to protect their plane from getting shot down. The navigator's job was to tell the pilots where to go. The pilots' job was to fly the plane, and the bombardier's job was to drop the bombs by using a high-tech instrument they called the Nordic Bomb Site.

The Nordic Bomb Site was very important to the war. This instrument allowed the bombardier to drop the bombs more accurately. This instrument was the bombardier's major priority. He was to protect it from enemies' hands with his life.

My grandfather was assigned a tour of duty in 1943 and was stationed in Italy. His tour of duty was to carry out several missions to bomb German ammunition plants. These German ammunition plants were located in Germany, Austria, Hungary, and Yugoslavia.

Now, here is where everything is very interesting. In 1944, my grandfather had a mission to fly into Yugoslavia from Italy. While flying over the mountains of Yugoslavia, his B17 Bomber came under attack by the Germans. While his crew was dropping bombs and the gunners were trying to fight off the Germans, his plane was struck by enemy fire.

As the B17 was losing engine power, the crew decided to jump out of the plane before it crashed into a mountain. This was a very scary time. As my grandfather jumped out of the plane, he hit his head on the tail wing right before he pulled his rip cord to deploy his parachute.

As they were landing in the trees and on the ground, their plane crashed and blew up. The noise brought attention to the Yugoslavian people in a nearby village. These people were known as Freedom Fighters. They came to rescue my grandfather and the rest of the crew by cutting them out of their parachutes, which were tangled up in the trees. One of the crew members drifted too far away and was captured by the Germans.

After this event took place, the United States government sent my grandmother a telegram, notifying her that my grandfather was MIA (Missing In Action). My grandmother was sad, but she had faith that he would be okay. My grandmother and her friends all supported each other. They talked all the time about the reports they heard on the radio and read in the newspaper. They did not have television back in those days.

The Yugoslavian Freedom Fighters took care of my grandfather and his crew by giving them food and medical attention. Fortunately, one of my grandfather's crew members knew how to speak the Yugoslavian language.

The Freedom Fighters were communicating with the British to help get my grandfather back to the Air Force base in Italy. It took three and a half weeks of secretly moving my grandfather and his crew to a British naval ship in the Adriatic Sea.

Once my grandfather made it back to the Air Force base in Italy, the United States sent my grandmother another telegram. She was very happy to hear the good news. However, my grandfather had to complete his tour of duty by finishing several more missions. Thankfully, he was successful on the rest of his missions.

In 1945, my grandfather finished his tour of duty. After he retired from the Air Force in 1946, my grandparents moved to a small town in Indiana.

There are many reasons why I am thankful to be alive. I am thankful for the Yugoslavian Freedom Fighters and the British Navy who rescued my grandfather. If he was killed or was not rescued, my dad would not have been born, and I would not have been born.

If all that was not amazing enough, I was born on Thanksgiving morning 1993, the day we give thanks in the United States. This was almost fifty years to the day that my grandfather volunteered to go into the Air Force.

Brother Against Brother, Father Against Son

by David S. Bailey

Bang! The first gun has been shot!
The blue and grays, oh how they fought.

It was the war to end slavery,
How the many men fought bravely.

The Civil War began in 1861,
The president at the time was Abraham Lincoln.

He was against slavery in the South,
The Union was to be saved without a doubt.

There was the March to the Sea,
The South did not flee.

The Union army tried to break the rebels' will to fight,
But they could not, for the Confederates had great might.

Lee surrendered and the war was done,
Brother against Brother, Father against Son.

My Greatest Joy

by Christina Nicole Abreu

My greatest joy is when I see my mother healthy, vibrant, and enjoying life. Allow me to explain what I mean. When I was at the age of four, my mother told me that she would be going to the doctor's office for a checkup. In my head I was thinking, *"Okay, just a checkup."*

My mother took my sister and me to preschool and then left for her checkup. When preschool was over, my sister and I waited for my mother to pick us up. We decided to color as we waited. I turned around and saw my dad waiting for us to hug him.

"Hey, Daddy!" my twin sister, Catherine, said. We both went and hugged him. I stood there wondering where Mommy was. I waited until we got into the car to ask.

"Daddy, why didn't Mommy pick us up?" I asked, as we were headed home.

"Mommy gets to have a sleepover at the hospital tonight. Isn't that nice?" my dad said. He sounded scared and worried. I looked at him and smiled. My sister and I looked at each other, and I could tell that Catherine was scared, too. Daddy didn't want us to worry, so I acted like I thought that my mom would be having a great time.

We got home and my daddy went to make a phone call. He went into his room and locked the door. He was talking in Spanish and at the time I understood perfectly. This is what he said:

"I'm scared. I love Raysa, my beloved wife." My dad started to cry. "I don't want her to die. I don't!" I realized that he was talking to my grandparents, my mother's parents. I got very scared and turned pale.

Catherine walked up the stairs and looked at me. She asked if I was okay, and I said no. We went into the small room that we shared, and I told her what I had heard. Catherine gasped and we hugged each other.

We went downstairs until my dad finished talking on the phone. I could see his face was still wet from tears. I asked my dad, "Is Mommy okay?" Unfortunately, I got an answer that I didn't want to hear.

"No, honey. Mommy isn't okay." We sat down on the couch to talk about Mommy, and in no time we were all in tears. Catherine and I didn't understand all of it. He wouldn't tell us all of it. What he told us was that mommy was sick and she would have to be in the hospital for a while.

My daddy worked every day, so my mom's mom came to live with us so that she could take care of us. My grandfather still worked in a little town called Milledgeville. My grandfather would come to visit us on weekends and would go back on weekdays. It went well for a while. We went to the hospital to visit my mom every day, and my grandmother played with us a lot. But soon things got worse.

Thanksgiving came, and my mother was still in the hospital. I was getting worried again, and Thanksgiving wasn't the same. My mother came home a few days after Thanksgiving. I thought that everything would be great! Too bad that it wasn't great.

Three days before Christmas, my mother went back to the hospital for her first surgery. It was a shame, too, because Christmas was very close. What a way to spend Christmas, right?

Christmas came and my mommy wasn't with us. My dad cried the morning of Christmas. I wasn't very happy either. Catherine and I got lots of gifts that we couldn't wait to show Mommy, but my daddy said, "The best gift is the gift of love, and right now our family is missing someone that we love." My grandfather and grandmother said a nice prayer.

Later that day we went to see our mom. She was happy to see us happy. She was worried because we used to be afraid of hospitals, and we never wanted to enter. To be honest, I faint in hospitals but I never did when I went to see my mom. My mom looked pale, and my dad told her that he would sleep at the hospital that night with her.

Soon, Valentine's Day came, which meant one month until my sister and I got to turn five. March was getting closer and we wanted our mom home for our birthday. She had missed everything else, so how could she make it to our birthday? My mom kept saying, "I'll be home for your birthday. I will be home." Catherine and I wanted her home and, sure enough, she was home. She had missed Thanksgiving, Christmas, New Year's, and Valentine's Day, but she would be home for my birthday!

My birthday was a small party at the house, but it was the best birthday ever because my mom was better and healthy. We had to help her get her strength back but now she's doing fine. She won an award for surviving such a great struggle. She got to travel a lot and help a lot of people who have her illness—Crohn's Disease.

Now my mom's fine. She has a great life even though she had almost died. That's why I'm happy to still have my mother. Now do you see why? I have her now and that's all that matters.

Orange

by Alex Stenhouse

Orange is fall-colored leaves sprinkled on the ground.
Orange is pumpkins carved with scary faces all around.

Orange is the blazing campfire that warms the autumn night.
Orange is the raven's squeal as he takes his first flight.

Orange is creepy stories told to give you a scare.
Orange is the goblins, ghosts, and ghoulish costumes that meet you with a stare.

Orange is the fun you have when trick-or-treating door to door.
Orange is the way your stomach feels when you can eat no more.

4th grade

Shadow And Nicole Save The Day

by Ariana Fouriezos

One Friday afternoon, I was brushing my horse's sleek, black fur. My horse's name was Shadow. I had gotten him for my tenth birthday. After I had finished brushing him, I said, "Shadow, I have to go now." Shadow stood there and stared at me; then walked up to me, and I gave him a last pat on the head and left.

The next morning, I woke up to the smell of bacon and eggs. I walked down the steps and stepped into the kitchen. I sat down at the table and then I noticed that my mother was crying.

"What's wrong Mom?" I asked.

My mother was only able to force out the words, "Your brother is missing."

"What are you talking about?" I asked anxiously.

"I went to wake him up this morning and he wasn't there," my mother choked out. "I want to go look for him, but it's hard for me to walk around much." Mom was about to have a baby and had not been feeling well.

"I will go and ride Shadow and find him," I assured her.

"But, Nicole, you might not be able to find him, and what if you got hurt?" my mom said with a worried look.

"I think I know where he is, and I will be really careful," I told her.

"Okay, but come back soon," she told me.

I ran upstairs into my room and put on my riding boots. Then I ran downstairs and opened the fridge and took out some drinks and made a few sandwiches. I also took some apples. Before I left, I hugged and kissed my Mom and she told me to be careful again. "I will," I assured her.

I walked out of the house and across the street and into the barn. Then I opened Shadow's stall and walked in. Shadow was standing near the end of the stall eating some hay. When I walked in, he lifted his head and walked towards me. "Hey boy," I said, "We have to go on a little trip." He neighed. Then I put the saddle and stirrup on Shadow. Soon, when I was finished putting on Shadow's things, I said, "Come on, Shadow, it's time to go." Shadow just neighed and neighed. Then I remembered that I needed to get Shadow food. So I stuck some hay in my bag. Finally, I hopped on Shadow's back and I was ready to go.

"Let's go now, Shadow," I whispered to my horse. I tapped his back with my foot and we were off. Then I tapped him again and he went faster. I suddenly felt the wind soaring through my hair. I was a good rider, so I could make Shadow go really fast.

After a little while, I decided to stop Shadow and have some lunch. "Whoa, Shadow," I said. He stopped and I tied him to a tree. I pulled out some hay and stuck it by his legs. Then I pulled out a soda and a peanut butter and jelly sandwich. After I finished eating, I untied Shadow and hopped back on him.

Once we had started up again, I started to think about Timmy. He was only seven, and he was out there by himself. Then I realized that since I was heading towards the lake, I needed to go a little more to the east. I couldn't stop thinking of Timmy. Suddenly, I heard a noise near the lake. I walked towards the edge and looked at the restless water. When I was turning around, I heard a sound. I turned around and I saw Timmy! "Timmy, I found you!" I exclaimed.

"Nicole! Nicole!" Timmy yelled out. Timmy was all the way across the lake, and it looked like it must have taken him a long time to walk around.

"I'll get you somehow," I assured him. I walked up to where Shadow was. I started to think of some way to get Timmy. Then Shadow neighed and I had an idea. "Shadow, I need you to swim across the lake and get Timmy." Shadow neighed and shook his mane. "I know you don't like water, but you have to." I untied him and brought him down to the lake. "Timmy, I am going to send Shadow down there and you have to get on him and he will bring you to me," I told him carefully.

"Okay, Nicole." said Timmy.

Shadow jumped into the water and swam across the silent

lake. The lake was not that wide, so Shadow got across pretty quickly. Timmy hopped on his back and hung on to him tightly. "Come on back, Shadow," I called.

Once they got back, I fed Timmy some sandwich and gave him soda. "I am so glad that I found you!" I said happily.

"I'm so glad that I was found!" Timmy said.

"How did you get here, anyway?" I asked.

"I was pretending to be an explorer, and next thing I knew I was lost," Timmy told me.

"Well, we better get home to Mom," I told Timmy.

We headed home and before we knew it, we could see the barn. We went to drop off Shadow and I said, " Good job, Shadow, you saved the day and Timmy!" Then I hugged him and we walked up to the house.

My mom saw us coming up, so she ran out the door and hugged and kissed us. "You are both safe!" She exclaimed happily. She couldn't stop asking questions, so we told her everything about our journey. She was so amazed and happy. "Congratulations, Nicole, you saved the day!" said Mom.

"With a little help from Shadow!" I said.

Mounting The Beam

by Amanda Marie Boyd

I stand next to the beam waiting my turn.
I'm feeling excited, scared, and nervous.
Listening to Renee's pep talk, I feel more confident.
I'm wondering if I'm going to fall.
Will I make my leap?
Will I hold my handstand?
What will be my score?
Now it's my turn.
I salute the judge.

Soaring In The Sky

by Jim Acee

Today, I woke up. It was a nice day outside. I went to stretch downstairs and decided to go flying for the day.

I started flying after a mysterious man gave me a ruby and told me it had magical powers. I didn't know what that meant until one day when I jumped off the slide and started to float! I was so afraid. But I discovered that I could move forward by moving my arms and legs like I was swimming.

But that was a long time ago. Now I travel all around the world. Today I thought I would visit the countries where my grandparents were born.

I flew until I reached Lebanon. The warm air blew on my face. I passed Beirut and saw a ton of things such as birds, people, and fish. I smelled bread baking.

I passed Austria. It was kind of cold there. I saw a huge fish and a fisherman, too.

Next, I dropped by Lithuania. It was so nice. I smelled flowers when I swooped down. I passed Vilnius, where there were a ton of people singing and dancing.

Next I dropped by Chicago. I saw the Bears play against the Dolphins. The Bears won. It was a good game, but it was so windy there it was hard to fly.

Finally, I went to Hollywood, California. I passed the mountain with the big Hollywood sign. I went to Friday's because I smelled great food.

I was very tired after my busy day, so I went home and went to bed.

5th grade

Baseball Is Fun…

by Joe Carnaroli

When I round the bases,
and see all of the excited faces.

When the game is on the line,
and I feel like I am on cloud nine.

When the pitcher throws the ball my way,
because the batter will be blown away.

When the fly ball is caught,
when the game is hard fought.

When I block the plate,
preventing that run feels incredibly great.

When my team works hard to beat the rest,
when I play the game I love the best.

I have only begun my baseball quest!
I have yet to master this tricky test.

Each season I learn some more,
that's what makes baseball more than just a score.

4th grade

Madam Sticklefrutz's Big Escape

by Allie Elizabeth Dean

Once, in a faraway kingdom called the Castle of Cheddar Cheesecake, there lived Madam Sticklefrutz. She was an adventurer. However, she was never allowed beyond the palace walls, for there were birds and giant alley cats who could scoop her up in one bite and she would be dinner! For a mouse her size, she would have no chance of survival out in the forest alone. In fact, she would be a snack within thirty seconds!

Oh, how she dreamed the world was perfect, with sweet alley cats that were nice, especially to mice. But the world was only like that in her dreams. In the real world, alley cats were nasty creatures who drank and ate the blood of mice and small rodents such as guinea pigs. *"Such a harsh world,"* thought Madam Sticklefrutz.

One night, Madam Sticklefrutz got up her courage and sneaked secretly out of the palace in her nightgown. She seemed so small compared to the trees that towered high above her. *"They must touch the sky,"* she thought. She yawned wearily, just now noticing how far away from the palace she was. She was too tired to walk back, so she found a soft patch of grass and fell asleep instantly. That night she slept under the stars.

When she woke up the next morning, she was starving. The sweet scent of cheese seemed to be coming from deep in the forest. *"Cheese!"* she thought one minute. But then she thought, *"Nah!"* But her legs couldn't resist. She shot towards the forest like a bolt of lightning. She ran to the edge of a cliff and didn't notice it. She ran right off the edge and into a net. Then a huge paw came and snatched the net with Madam Sticklefrutz in it.

"Dinner!" said the cat, smacking his lips and carrying her deep into the forest.

"Mom!" called the young kitten, who had seemed bigger before to Madam Sticklefrutz.

"Now, cat," she said politely, "if you take me back to my castle—I mean 'home'—I will give you all the catnip you want." She did not want to tell him she was a queen, because then he would eat her!

"Okay," said the cat. "I'll go," he said purring. So Madam Sticklefrutz jumped on the cat's back and they were off.

That night they set up camp and rested. It would be a long trip home. The next morning they were up at the crack of dawn and on the way to Madam Sticklefrutz's castle—I mean "home."

Once they were at the castle, there was a great celebration. There were flowers and little mice who were throwing little candies. The cat was awarded the title "Super Mouse Finder." Madam Sticklefrutz gave the cat seventy pounds of catnip, as he had been promised. From then on, Madam Sticklefrutz never had to worry about being lost again. She could explore the forest as she had always wanted.

Boys

by Kate Drummond

Boys are weird.
They're hard to
Understand.
But in the end,
You walk
Hand in hand.

Goober Mania

by Sarah Ann Evans

It was a beautiful spring day. The flowers' perfumed fragrance filled the air, and the trees hung heavy with colorful blossoms. Everything seemed perfect except for one small thing—I WAS STUCK INSIDE! Not that I did not like school. I had a lot of friends, and the teachers were nice. But what kid in their right mind wouldn't rather be outside playing? It was so hard to pay attention. I found myself looking out the window and daydreaming the hours away. School was so boring!

Near the end of the day as my class was heading back from music, I suddenly remembered that I had forgotten my recorder. I asked my teacher, Mr. Chamberlain, if I could go back to the music room. He said I could but to hurry since it was almost time to catch the bus for home.

Home! Boy, did that sound great! I couldn't wait to jump on my bike and enjoy this beautiful day. I took off running as fast as I could toward the music room. I grabbed my recorder and flew back out into the hall. I tried to turn right, but there was a huge double door with two men guarding the doors. I looked to my left, and there was nothing but a solid wall. What was happening? I knew this school like the back of my hand. Those doors were never there before!

I pulled on the sleeve of one of the guards and asked for directions back to my classroom. He glanced down at me and said, "The only way back to your classroom is through Goober Land."

I screamed, "What's a Goober Land? You must be kidding me!"

"Now calm down and just follow me. I'll lead you through," said the Guard. "By the way, my name is Bubba. What's yours?"

"Sarah," I replied.

"Put on these glasses and grab a bat." The glasses looked like something I once saw at a costume shop. Bubba said, "When we go in Goober Land, stay behind me. The Goobers will throw jello balls at you. Wherever it hits you, that part of your body will fall off and you'll grow a different body part."

"WHAT?" I screamed in a panic. "Are you telling me I could end up with four noses and three legs?"

"That's exactly what I'm telling you." responded Bubba.

"Why do we need the glasses and the bat?" I asked Bubba.

"You can only see the Goobers through the glasses. Otherwise they're invisible. The Goobers are pink with bright yellow eyes. They are so cute you'll be tempted to pet them—but don't be fooled. You'll need the bat to block the jello balls and to hit the Goobers. It will be hard to hit something that looks like a sweet little animal. If you don't, they will just keep throwing jello balls at you until you are defenseless. Then they will take you away, and you'll have to live in Goober Land forever!

Bubba opened the doors, and I followed quietly behind him wearing the goofy glasses and holding my bat tightly. Out of nowhere, I saw three Goobers! Jello balls of all colors were flying everywhere! I ducked behind Bubba. He blocked ten jello balls and hit about five Goobers with his bat. All of a sudden, Bubba was hit! His ear fell off, and he grew an extra eye. This was too weird! I knew I had to help. I came out from behind Bubba, screaming and swinging my bat with all my strength!

Finally, all the Goobers had disappeared. I grabbed Bubba's hand, and we started running through Goober Land hoping to make it out with all our parts. Bubba yelled, "I can't leave without my ear!"

"How do you get your ear back?" I asked.

"The Goobers have some ointment they keep closely guarded in a purple and green room. I have to get it, or I'll have to live the rest of my life with one ear and three eyes!" responded Bubba sadly. "The way out is through those orange doors straight ahead. You'll be safe. Now run!" yelled Bubba. But as much as I wanted to get out, I couldn't leave Bubba to face those horrible little Goobers alone.

Bubba and I ran around frantically looking for the purple and green room. Bubba's extra eye helped out. Finally we saw it, but it was locked up tightly. We took our bats and beat the doors as hard as we could.

The doors flew open and three huge Goobers charged towards us. They threw big blue jello balls at us. Bubba's nose fell off, and a finger grew in its place. One hit my hand as I was trying to strike one of the Goobers. My hand disappeared, and a foot grew in its place. Now, I only had one hand to use against the Goobers. A big blob of jello landed on Bubba's stomach, and he grew an extra mouth! Bubba screamed with both of his mouths, "Watch out!" as the next jello ball landed on my hair. My hair fell out, and four legs grew out of the top of my head. Bubba hit one of the Goobers, sending it flying across the room into the other two. All three disappeared! Bubba grabbed the ointment, and we ran toward the orange doors.

We busted through the orange doors into the parking lot. My classmates were lining up to get on their buses. They all screamed, "MONSTERS! MONSTERS!" Bubba grabbed the ointment, and we started rubbing it all over our extra legs, ears, feet, noses, mouths, and fingers. Our extra limbs disappeared, and our bodies returned to normal.

Ever since that strange day, the music hall has been locked up, with Bubba guarding the door. The cafeteria lady decided it would be a good idea to take jello off the lunch menu. I know one thing for sure—I'll always keep my glasses and bat not too far away, and I'll never again think school is boring!

I Am

by Caity Hodge

I am a sturdy willow tree, graceful and unique.

I wonder why day is day and night is night.

I hear the ring of happiness from a far-off land.

I see prejudice destroying the meaning of freedom like poachers destroying the lives of animals.

I want to make a difference like Christopher Columbus, daring to find something new.

I am a sturdy willow tree, graceful and unique.

I pretend that I am the greatest gymnast in the world, flying through the air.

I feel the wind dancing all around me as if it were some kind of party.

I touch the hearts of loving people who are there caring for me every second.

I worry about people living and dying on the streets without food, shelter, and education.

I cry when I see people taking advantage of the poor.

I am a sturdy willow tree, graceful and unique.

I understand that the world is not perfect.

I say giving up never brings success.

I dream about what the future will bring.

I try to see that everyone is happy.

I hope people are judged by the inside, not the outside.

I am a sturdy willow tree, graceful and unique.

The Boy Who Liked School

by Marshall Hahn

Once upon a time, a boy named Marshall went to elementary school. He liked it and decided to stay. He enjoyed preschool, kindergarten, and first grade, but he really enjoyed second grade.

He especially liked math because he liked the problems. Addition and subtraction problems were like puzzles to solve, and word problems told stories. It was fun.

Marshall liked to read books about science and found them to be very interesting. Reading seemed to be important in all his schoolwork, so he learned to read well.

Lunch, he wasn't too sure about. Sometimes it was good, and other times it was "yucky!"

Recess was really fun, and he enjoyed friends and playing.

Marshall had a wonderful and pretty teacher. She helped him every day to learn. He knew that school was important, and learning was like a building block. Each year, he needed to know everything from that year to use for the next year. Even second grade is a building block on your way to college.

He knew tests were important, and he studied hard to get good grades. If he needed help, he would ask his teacher. She was always ready to help him and wanted him to do well.

Homework was not fun, but it was needed to make Marshall smarter. Reading homework was good for his brain, and AR tests were, too. If he couldn't read, he couldn't do much in life. It was the first step to building a good education!

You see, Marshall is really me, the writer of this story. I wanted to write this story to let you know that I think you need a good education to have a good life. We all need to learn all we can!

Please Pray

by Leandra Houston

We are all God's children,
He loves us all the same.
Praise the Lord above,
Let's praise his holy name.

Take a little moment and
Think about your ways.
Take a little moment
Just sit down and pray.

Cause God is on your side
He'll love you till you part.
You play a role inside
Of his humongous heart.

So take a little moment
And think about your day.
And if it's going wrong, just
Take the time to pray.

Say it loud or say it clear,
So the Lord above can hear.
So praise so you can one day be
One of God's servants with me.

The Magical Place

by Claire E. Sullivan

"Do any of you know what the capital of Arizona is?" asked the teacher. No one knew. "Katherine, go get some staples out of the closet; we are going to write about Arizona and its capital."

"You mean the one that says "Off Limits?" I asked in surprise.

"Yes, it's perfectly fine," answered the teacher.

I went out of the classroom, down the hall, and to the closet. First, I checked that no one was looking; then I pulled open the closet doors, pulled out the staples, and then did the most stupid thing I could do at that time. I took a closer look.

I saw what the box of staples was sitting on. It was a machine of some kind! It had a chair next to it. I sat in the chair and pressed the green button that read "GO." Then, the machine said, in the way that robots talk, "Press any button." I pressed the blue button, and everything around me became blurred. I felt like I was going up and down all at one time. I felt like I was going to explode! I shut my eyes tight and waited.

After what seemed like forever, I stopped feeling weird. I opened my eyes and nothing looked blurry. I got out of the closet and shut the doors. I was really scared!

All around me were flowers. There were creatures making a circle, and in the circle was a beautiful lady. She wore a beautiful gown, and on her head she wore a wreath of flowers. "Welcome to Delinarita," she said. "I've heard many things of your healing powers. I need you to heal one of my unicorns."

I did not know what she was talking about. "Me?" I asked. Just then I found myself back in the machine and without doing anything, it started up!

Again, just like before, I found the room around me getting blurry. Then I could hear the mysterious lady saying, "You are not the one. You know nothing of the healing powers."

I did not want to leave that magical world. I blinked and found myself reaching for the staples again. I took them out, and ran to my classroom. Everything was like it was before.

"Thank you, Katherine," my teacher said, as she took the staples. I sat down and looked at her, searching for a questioning look on her face of why I took so long. She smiled and winked at me and then I knew she also knew about the machine. *"That must have been a time machine,"* I thought to myself.

I wanted to go back. Just then the bell rang for lunch. I dashed out of the room before anyone else had moved. I ran to the special closet, pulled open the doors, and jumped in. Just like before, I pressed the green button. I tried to press the blue button but my hand slipped and I pressed the yellow button instead.

Everything became blurred, and the weird feeling crept over me once again. I shut my eyes tight and waited for the feeling to stop. When it did, I opened my eyes and jumped out of the closet. I looked around and saw a crowd of people. I went over and saw a dying unicorn lying on the ground, with a puddle of blood surrounding its head.

I tried not to cry. All I could do was watch helplessly. Suddenly, I had a weird feeling that I should cut off its horn. I reached into my pocket and pulled out my pair of scissors. The horn was easy to cut, just like cutting a piece of paper.

Once I got it off, I asked myself, "Now what?" Everyone was yelling at me in a different language! I was surprised that no one tried to hurt me. Then I heard that mysterious lady's voice saying, "You are not the one!"

For the second time, I felt really scared. Then my mind told me to put the horn in the unicorn's chest. I closed my eyes and stuck it in its chest. Just then, he got up and galloped away; his horn disappeared from his chest and reappeared on his forehead. I had cured him.

Then, just like before, I found myself in the time machine, and it went back to my world. I got out of the closet and went to lunch. I will always remember my journey. But I never went back because I was scared of the people who saw me cut off the unicorn's horn. I planned to tell my teacher someday, but I silently promised myself that I would never, ever tell anyone else about my adventure.

My Favorite Pet

by Jacqueline G. Mahoney

The pet I love most is a snake.
It is not an animal you should bake.
I feed him and clean him and take him for walks.
Why, sometimes we even have long talks!

When I go to a party,
He is quite a big hit.
He comes along with me
As my pretty bracelet!

He is great for a trick
or to make someone sick.
Don't make us mad,
Or you won't be glad.

He escaped from his house!
That's when he caught a mouse!
I think he's great,
My mom thinks he's grouse.

I once thought it would be incredible
To own my very own Pterodactyl!
I'd saddle him up and ride through the sky…
But I don't think that this would be practical.

No, my snake is the best pet.
So we are all set,
I call him Spot
And I love him a lot!

Roboid XII And The Robot Rebellion

by Luke Richerson

One afternoon, the scientist James Harrison was working on a computer-controlled satellite called Roboid XII. He was programming on the robot's brain when the robot awakened and shot a laser at Dr. Harrison. The lightning blue laser whizzed by Dr. Harrison's ear and plunged into the dartboard behind him, destroying it completely. Then Roboid XII shot a fury of lasers at Dr. Harrison. Some of the lasers hit the scientist and some didn't, but one thing was definitely true—Dr. Harrison was dead! The robot left to conquer the galaxy.

The next day Dr. Harrison's friend, Michael DeSoto, came to his house. He stepped inside—the door was already open—and was shocked and disgusted by what he saw. Dr. Harrison's body was lying on the floor in pieces. DeSoto thought a serial killer had killed Dr. Harrison.

Soon an investigation team of five people was looking for clues to figure out who, or what, killed Dr. Harrison. The robots (not including Roboid XII) were still in Dr. Harrison's laboratory. The search team was stumped with this case, because whatever had killed Dr. Harrison left no evidence—not even DNA!

Meanwhile, Roboid XII was recruiting robots to form an army. He had already convinced Roboid I, II, III, and IX. Now, he was trying to get some of the droids who were used by Zexal the Conqueror when he took the fortress of Vuyink. He was trying to get every robot or droid in the universe to fight for him.

The investigators had now determined what killed Dr. Harrison. They had discovered that he had been shot with a laser, but they still didn't know who did it. Lasers were very expensive and had just been released for the public to buy. The technology used was the most up-to-date laser technology available, and from that information the investigators determined that Dr. Harrison had committed suicide.

After a couple of weeks, the robot army was 55,000 strong and had 550 battalions, 100 robots per battalion. The leaders of the army were training robots of all different shapes and sizes. There were even some intelligent creatures in the army who had agreed to help demolish humankind. The army was ready to fight.

Meanwhile, the investigators were beginning to realize that many of the robots were missing. They began to think that one, or many robots combined, had killed Dr. Harrison. Michael DeSoto was helping to figure out the case, too. He was also trying to find the missing robots. Although he wasn't very successful, he did spy a strange glint of metal and some lasers being shot. Even so, he didn't think that it was of much importance.

The next day the robot army attacked and took the small town of Karoog. The investigators and Michael were informed immediately, and Michael regretted not reporting the strange glint of metal he had seen on the outskirts of town the day before.

The investigators interrogated some survivors of the attack and found the answer to who, or what, murdered Dr. Harrison. The rebels' own leader, Roboid XII, had said, "Dr. Harrison was the first to go. You will be next." The investigators also discovered the strength of the robot army and started putting an army together to fight this evil rebellion.

The next week the armies clashed. One human survivor said that it might have been the most catastrophic battle of the modern age. The humans had begun with 36,500 men. The rebels had 49,500 men. The robots fought long and hard and killed many troops, but finally retreated. After the battle ended, the humans were left with 29,768 troops; the rebels had 24,375 troops.

The rebels knew another loss would ruin them, so the two armies agreed to have a ceasefire for a week. By the end of the year, the humans had 156,000 troops; the rebels had 120,000 troops. The reason the rebels had fewer troops was that it took about ten hours to make each replacement robot. The rebel leaders had to enlist people from their own planets, who wouldn't arrive on earth until March.

The next week another great battle was fought at the same place where the Americans had fought the bloodiest battle of the Civil War—Antietam Creek, Maryland. The destruction was total. The robots had a slight victory, winning by 1,000 troops.

The human generals all agreed that eventually they would be destroyed if they kept having huge battles like this one. They decided to use ambush and sneak attacks with small numbers of men until they totally outnumbered the rebels, then lead an all-out attack against the rebel forces.

The first of these sneak attacks came the next day. The humans used 935 troops. One rebel survivor said he saw the glint of metal in the tall grass but thought it was just a rebel practice. The humans had 235 casualties that day; the rebels had 2,256 casualties.

The next day the humans only sent 257 troops, but the casualties for the rebels went up to 2,584 casualties. The humans lost only 163 troops.

Five days later, the humans were attacked in Europe at the site of the Battle of the Bulge during World War II. As the rebels advanced, 2,436 troops were wounded or killed. The fighting stopped frequently so the wounded troops had time to crawl to safety.

The battle was brutal and deadly to many, and so it was put into history as the biggest battle ever. At last, the war ended. The 457 remaining robots were deprogrammed and put on the walls of a memorial to the human soldiers who had served in the war. Thus ends the story of the robots and their rebellion, which had begun with Roboid XII's decision to murder the human who had created him, Dr. Harrison.

I Don't Understand Why…

by Erica Sheline

I don't understand why people get killed, or why this world seems to be made for war.
I don't understand why there is such thing as prejudice when everyone is the same on the inside.
I don't understand why people say "Cool!" when they see pictures of bombs and devastated people.

I know that you've taught me all that you could, but I want more knowledge, as most people would.
I know that you think that I am just like the rest, going through life as if it were a test.
But what you think is not what I am, I am full of questions, always on demand.

I wish that peace could stay in the land that we live, but my wish may never come true.
I wish I could be president, and stop all this fighting, even with children, kicking, screaming, and biting.
I may still be young, but that is all for the good, now I have more time to be understood.

I still don't understand why people need to fight, or why some think that putting others down is all right.
I know that I will never learn all that there is to be learned, but I cannot help being curious.
I have many other questions, and many other things I want to know, but
I will go out in this big world, and find them all on my own.

Another Spirit Of Warren Taylor Hawks

by Ryan Waznik

Last year the strangest thing happened to me. I think I met a ghost, sitting on a log, named Warren Taylor Hawks. I helped him find a treasure chest with my dog, Samantha. I wonder if it was just a dream? Maybe I should go back to the log to see if he is still there.

I decided to go back to the log where I first met Warren with my dogs, Samantha and Charity. When we got to the log nobody was there. We waited for a long time and even called for him. I was starting to think I was dreaming and even tried to wake up. Just as I was about to go home, Warren came racing out of the trees to tell me something! I was so excited to see him, and I knew I wasn't dreaming.

"I've got to tell you something," said Warren. He seemed very upset, like something was really bothering him. I asked him if he was okay. Warren said, "Something has gone terribly wrong, my gravestone has been stolen! I saw the thief run away with it in a wheelbarrow. I tried to grab him, but he was too fast. I couldn't identify him because he had a hood over his head. All I got was a piece of his pants!" Warren loved his gravestone because his family left a poem on it for him. The poem read:

Our Father in his wisdom called
The boon his love had given
Though on earth his body lies
The soul is safe in heaven

I felt so sorry for Warren, and all I wanted to do was to help him. Samantha, Charity, and I made a plan to find the thief!

"Here, take the part of the pants," said Warren.

"See you soon, Warren, and I hope I…" He was gone!

Samantha, Charity, and I were off. I let the dogs sniff the pants, and they both ran off. While they were gone I looked for the thief myself. I didn't see anybody in the woods or on the road. One time I thought I saw something move, but it was just the wind. I didn't hear anything from the dogs yet. After what seemed like forever, I heard Samantha and Charity barking. I ran as fast as I could to them. They had cornered a scary looking man holding a wheelbarrow with Warren's gravestone in it!

The thief was tying to run away, but he tripped over a tree root and fell straight in the mud. I ran over to him and asked, "Why would you take someone's gravestone?"

"Warren always beat me in the spelling bees in school and I wanted to get him back," said the thief.

"Well that's a silly reason; you're going to the police!" I put the thief in the wheelbarrow and told the dogs to guard him! Now, I needed to go find Warren.

I went back to the log to try to find Warren. When Warren saw me, he asked, "Did you find my gravestone?" I told him that some crazy guy who was a bad speller took it!

"Barry!" laughed Warren. "Thank you for finding my gravestone. I always thought he was a bad sport." Warren chuckled.

"Well you shouldn't thank me, you should thank the dogs. Warren, I better go to get the gravestone because the dogs are guarding Barry, and I don't want him to get away," I said. I told Warren I would be back in a few minutes after I had given Barry to the police.

When I got back to Samantha and Charity, the police were already there. I told the police what had happened, for their report. When I was starting to leave I heard a big *whoosh* in the woods. All the police were wondering what it was. I raced back to the log and Warren was gone! All he left were two dog bones and a note that read:

Dear Friend,

Something has gone very wrong again. I need your help. Oh no, I have to go!

Warren

While I was reading the note, my mom rang the dinner bell. I was walking home and kept wondering if Warren was okay. At the dinner table my mom asked me what I did today. I said, "Oh, I just played outside with the dogs."

After dinner I had to go upstairs to bed. I was wondering if I would see Warren again. As I was lying in bed, the dogs were next to me, chewing their bones. All of a sudden I heard Warren call for help. Next thing I saw was Mom standing by my bed asking me something. Was it a dream or not?

5th grade

How To Be Abraham Lincoln

by Philemon M. Yoo

Be the tallest president of the U.S.A.
Promise, if ever given a chance, to hit slavery, hit it hard.
Come from a log cabin in the country.
Be one of the greatest abolitionists in the history of the world.
When elected president, cause the deadliest American war so far.
Do a revolutionary act,
Sign the Emancipation Proclamation, which freed the slaves.
Promise to reunite the North and the South.
Be a very inspiring American leader to the nations of the world.

Super Honey...Comb?

by Grant Weigel

This is a story about my amazing dog, Honey. She is a Labrador Retriever. We got Honey when she was only eight weeks old, and she seemed pretty normal. She ate, slept, fetched, and was very good. She was bigger than most dogs, but she was a big scaredy-cat, except around squirrels. She liked to chase them. The only problem happened eight months later. Now, let me tell you all about it.

One day when I was eating Strawberry Blasted Honeycombs cereal, I gave her some. I am not sure who crunched them louder, Honey or me. When she finished, she could actually talk! Now she could tell us what she wanted to do and when she wanted to do it. She told us when she wanted to take a walk, if she needed to go potty, and what she wanted to eat. She usually wanted to eat Honeycombs! When she ate them with milk, she was able to swim like a speed boat.

Once there was a little squirrel who fell into the river and drifted downstream. When Honey saw this, she dove into the river, swam to the squirrel ,and safely rescued it. She brought it back to the house and my mom screamed. Then Honey asked for some Honeycombs for the squirrel so that it would feel better. We weren't so sure this was a good idea, but Honey thought so. My mom said okay, but said that the squirrel had to eat outside. When they came back inside, my mom said Honey had to take the squirrel home. They could not find his home, so they came back to my house to live. Honey and the squirrel became good friends!

The Ocean At Night

by Meghan Cooley

The sun, a burning ball of light.
The moon, a diamond in the night.
The stars, you love them, no?
I am here, with the palm trees, a brown and green light.
The moon reflecting off the waves, a rolling ball on the sea.
The sand cold under my bare feet, soft pebbles cold and weightless.
I jump in the sea, like ice-cold water, but where is the ice?
My body numb, piercing knives all in my body.
My breathing shallow, the shore and my breathing are alike, are one.
I hop out of the sea to dry, a fish nearby does the same.
I run over and let it live.
The sun gone, the sky, many lights in the dark.

Remembering Grandpa

by Taylor Coan

"Are you sure?" was all I could say when my parents told me that my Grandpa had died. He battled cancer for a long time. I couldn't believe that I would never see Grandpa alive again. It helped to talk to grownups about my feelings. My parents and I hugged a lot. My father and I looked at pictures of Grandpa.

At the funeral I read a poem that I wrote about all the funny things I remembered about him. I especially remember how much he loved chocolate. One time when he was visiting, my Mom asked him to go to the store and get some milk, bread, and eggs. He came back with chocolate milk, chocolate ice cream, chocolate donuts, and a chocolate Hershey Bar! He ate them all in two days!

After the funeral, I kept Grandpa alive in my mind by talking about him all the time. I was afraid I might forget him. I told everyone he died. Then I realized there were other ways I could remember him.

My family planted a tree in our backyard in honor of Grandpa. We raised money for the cancer research foundation by getting pledges for a walk-a-thon. We donated a favorite book, which my Grandpa would read to us every Christmas, to the library in his honor.

My Grandpa used to sing me the song, "Yankee Doodle" when I was younger, so I asked my piano teacher to teach me to play that song—it's always in my head now. The stars made me feel good, too. I chose a star in the sky and pretended it was Grandpa looking down.

Before long I was working hard in school and having fun with my friends again. Then one day a friend of mine told me his Grandpa had just died. I talked to him about how he could keep his Grandpa alive in his memory by doing special things.

I can't remember everything about my Grandpa, but every once in awhile someone or something still reminds me of him. I always look out my window at night at the stars. Maybe they are not stars, but openings in heaven where the love of our lost ones shines down to let us know they are with us.

Art!

by Sarah C. Hoynes

Art, art, it's all about art!
What can I do to stop all this art?
Painting, coloring, drawing in books!

Art, art, it's all about art!
I just see too much art!
Art museums, art contests, everywhere I look!

Artists'...to artistic,
They paint on everything they can find;
Paper, books, covers of books,
On blocks, on locks, even on clocks!!!

Art, art, it's all about art!
Concentrating, concentrating, and thinking what to draw,
What to do with the drawing, where to put the drawing,
Hang it up, frame them up,
I think I'll throw up!!!

Guess what?
I think go I'll paint a masterpiece of me!!!!

The Dancing Planets

by Jessica Brooke Lively

Once, when the planets were orbiting the Sun, Jupiter said, "Why don't we just get out of orbit?"

"Yeah! Let's get out of orbit and move around in space," said Saturn.

(Well, they all got out of orbit. The planets will tell you the rest.)

"Hey we're out of orbit," said Mars.

"Yeah! It's cool, huh?" said Jupiter.

"Yeah!" said Pluto. "Let's get in a line and do the cha-cha-cha."

(Well, they danced all day.)

"That was fun," said Earth.

"Hey Pluto, how did you like it?" asked Venus. "Pluto, Pluto, where is Pluto?"

"I don't see him," said Neptune.

"Let's look for him," said Uranus.

(Well, they were off to find Pluto.)

"We've been looking all day," said Mercury.

"I know, but we have to find Pluto," said Uranus.

"Hey, let's all look here at the Milky Way," said Jupiter.

"Pluto, Pluto, where are you?"

"Hey, guys," said Venus. "I think I see him.

"Venus, is that you?"

"Who is it?" said Venus.

"It's me, Pluto."

"Pluto why did you run away?" asked Mercury.

"Well, I wanted to play," said Pluto."

"We'll never get out of orbit again," said Mars.

"That's for sure," said Jupiter.

(They all got back in orbit and stayed there.)

(P.S. You will not find this in an encyclopedia because this is not true.)

5th grade

My Favorite Color

by Matthew Williams

Green is the pain that shoots through you as lemon juice
hits your eye.

Green is the calming spring breeze on a tropical island.

Green is the bitter taste that slaps you as you eat
unripe fruit.

Green is the color of water on a sailor's quest.

Green is the color of a wave breaking over your boat.

Green is the color that jumps up and surprises you when
you're in a war.

Green is the soft cushion on the fairway that catches balls.

Green is the colorful barrier that dazzles you as a peacock
opens its tail.

Green is the color of a happy ending.

How The Cow Got Its Moo

by Jennie M. Pless

A long time ago, there was a brave explorer named Smile. They called him that because he was always smiling. He explored while he traveled to help grumpy people smile.

He had a black-and-white cow named Cow. She was a very humble cow. However, she was just like any other two-eared, four-legged, grass-eating, silent cow. Because Cow was silent, she had no way to tell Smile that she wanted to go with him. But she got lucky one day, and she changed history forever.

"Cow, you have been chosen to come with me on my trip to make a sad man smile," Smile said, as he stroked Cow's fur. Cow jumped and danced with excitement. This humble cow was so happy that she could barely think.

The next day Smile rode Cow to a faraway place. It was a long journey and although Cow got tired, she kept on going. As they grew closer, it became colder and colder, and soon it began to snow. As the snow got deeper, Cow was getting weaker. They continued on and finally reached the hut.

Knock, knock! pounded Smile on the door of the hut.

"Come in," said a sad and moaning voice. Smile went in while Cow waited outside.

The sad man in the hut wore a huge frown on his face. So Smile acted funny, made faces, and helped solve the man's problem. Once he got the man to smile, they had tea.

Meanwhile, Cow was so happy that she was on an adventure, she was using her last bit of energy to run in happy circles. Unfortunately, she was so tired that her eyes were closed, and she ran into a tree. Tons of snow piled on her.

Now, she was really tired, and no matter what method she tried, she couldn't break out of the heavily packed snow.

"Bye, Smile," said the man as they both stepped out the door.

"I'm sure that Cow will be glad that you gave her this tea, warm hay, and blanket," said Smile.

This made Cow hungry, thirsty, and even colder than she was before. She wanted the gifts, but she was too weak to get out of the snow. She had to make a sound!

"MOO, MOO, MOO, MOO!" yelled Cow.

Smile heard the sound from under the snow and thought it was a beast.

"MOO!" Cow screamed again.

"It is Cow; we have to save her," said Smile.

They dug Cow out of the snow, gave her his gifts, and warmed her. Then they said goodbye and journeyed home.

Cow and Smile lived happily ever after. And to this day, cows still moo.

God

by Laura E. Stringer

No one can live to match God's love.

You know his symbol is a dove.

It stands for peace, harvest, and rest.

So it's okay to give the dove your best!

Antonio Sedran: A Biography

by Katie Garmon

Antonio Sedran has shown a lot of courage in his life. He is an Italian immigrant who had a dream to come to America. Here is his amazing story.

Antonio Florindo Sedran was born on October 22, 1937, in Cosa, Italy. His parents were Maria Teresa and Ricardo Sedran. They provided him with love and care. He had three sisters, two of whom died in childhood. His living sister is named Sylvana. When World War II broke out, the Sedrans lost many of their possessions such as money, food, and clothing.

After World War II, Antonio was sent to Switzerland for schooling. His parents were working in Switzerland, and his sister, Sylvana, was living with relatives. While in Switzerland, Antonio received a postcard from the Empire State Building from a friend. He decided that if he ever went to America he would go to New York City. Antonio carried the postcard for many years.

When he finished school in Switzerland, Antonio moved to Lausanne, Switzerland, to go to a hotel school by the name of Hotel de la Paix. He graduated at the age of eighteen and kept in touch with his family back in Italy. Upon graduating, Antonio decided to go to Germany. He wanted to get a job in Berlin, but the Great Berlin Wall was in his way. To get to Berlin he would have to get shots and papers and go through many other hassles.

Antonio decided to stay in Hamberg and to get a job there. Unfortunately, Antonio's new job was miserable for him because his boss would only speak German. Antonio did not understand his boss's commands. He had a very rough time. As it turned out, his boss had known how to speak Italian the whole time, but had wanted Antonio to learn how to speak German. Antonio did learn to speak German and many other languages in his life.

After his difficult job in Hamberg, Antonio moved to London, England. While in Europe, he also got the opportunity to work at the World's Fair in Brussels, Belgium. From Europe, Antonio moved on to Bermuda, where he worked in hotels and restaurants.

Then, in 1962, Antonio went to visit America. The first place he went to was New York City. He saw the Empire State Building, just like he had dreamed. After that, he went to New Orleans, Louisiana, to work at the famous Brennan's restaurant. In New Orleans, he learned to speak English. He also served in the U.S. Army Reserves in order to get his green card.

In 1967, Antonio decided to become a U.S. citizen. He had to take a written test to gain citizenship. After becoming a citizen, Antonio worked at the Lake of the Ozarks resort in Missouri.

A few years later, he moved to St. Louis, Missouri. He married Trisha Kokorudz and had three children. Jennifer was the oldest, then Marc and Michael. He had fun with his children and also worked with them. Antonio's children often helped him in his restaurant career. For example, all three children worked with him at 103 West restaurant in Atlanta, Georgia, at one time.

Today Antonio Sedran owns and operates Renaissance Classic Caterers. Michael, his son, works there with him. His daughter Jennifer is a teacher. His son Marc used to work in the catering business but has moved to Arizona.

Antonio now lives in Dunwoody, Georgia, with his wife Trisha. He enjoys spending time with his four grandchildren: Kendall, Olivia, Logan, and Katie. Antonio has a pool in his back yard where he enjoys parties with his children and grandchildren. Every Christmas Eve, Antonio cooks delicious lobsters for the whole family. Antonio's mother, Maria Teresa Sedran, comes from his sister's home in Australia each summer to spend time with Antonio's family. They speak Italian together.

Antonio Sedran is a good dad, husband, grandfather, brother, cook, and son. He has had a good life in America and has worked very hard. Antonio is a wonderful guy and a great American.

My Best Friend

by Grace Lifer

My best friend is like no other,
Not my sister or my brother.

My best friend is always there to say
The narrow gate is the right way.

When I am down he makes me feel better.
I have always wished I could send him a letter.

He knows what I am thinking before I do.
He also knows what I am going through.

My best friend is more than I can say;
He watches me every day.

Can you guess whom I am saying?
Tonight to Him I will be praying.

The Magic Box

by Audrey Cate Vasina

I was walking through my front lawn on a dark, cold day when suddenly I saw it—an unusually large black box in the middle of my lawn. This is when my adventure started.

I darted toward the box—could it be the motor scooter I ordered off the Internet? Or maybe it was the late Christmas present that Uncle John had promised me?

As I got closer to the package, I was anxious to see who had sent it. But wait; there was no name or return address. That's weird. I didn't care. I was excited to see what was inside. I ripped the package open, and there were what seemed to be a thousand layers of tissue paper. As I tried to get to the bottom, I lost my balance and fell headfirst into the box.

It seemed like I traveled a thousand miles before I hit ground. When I finally did, I tried to open my eyes, but the sun was too bright. Wait—the sun—how could that be? I stood up and looked around. Where was I? How did I get here? This was definitely not my front lawn. I was a little scared, but I decided to explore anyway.

While exploring, I first found a nice, warm cave. I decided that it would be a great place for me to stay the night if I had to. Suddenly, I smelled a wonderful smell. I looked around and found that it was coming from a big bush of honeysuckle. They were the prettiest and most wonderful flowers I had ever been around. I also noticed that there were several neat animals in the area. I saw two monkeys playing in the trees and a bunch of colorful birds.

Just as I was beginning to get comfortable in my new surroundings, I heard a voice say, "Chloe." It was my Mom. I began to run towards her voice, and the next thing I knew I was back on my lawn staring into the box.

"Chloe, you forgot your English book," shouted my Mom, "and hurry or you'll miss the bus!" I guess I'll have to save the rest of my adventure for the weekend.

The USA

by Sarah Helms

The USA is my home as it's always been
Raising my mind as its own kin.
I love it, I do, the red, white, and blue
The USA is my home.

So I shout, "The USA is my home!"
Sure, it's grown, but it remains my home.
The USA stays one mind, body, and soul.
The USA is my home.

I see the eyes moving around this place.
Then I think, "Do they see what this place really means?"
The red, white, and blue, you are my home.
A solid place where the buffalo roam.

Clashing swords, people and soldiers
Rage at war along large boulders
To make the USA our home.

So remember when you reach the Golden Age
To preach the patriotism,
To keep our hearts ablaze
With the USA.

The Poisonous Seed

by Lydia Rutland Barnes

One day, Parsnip and Duckweed, two field mice, were out in the field picking daisies. All of a sudden they saw what they thought was a big rock falling from the sky.

"Parsnip, get down!" Duckweed exclaimed, as the rock fell to the ground. There was a big crash. It landed on a big hill near the cliff.

"Do you think it's safe to get up?" asked Parsnip.

"Probably, but I'm not moving until I'm positive," Duckweed said quietly. They waited awhile and then got up and started home. When they got there, they were caught in a huge crowd of mice.

"What's going on?" Parsnip asked the nearest mouse.

"Didn't you hear? A giant seed bigger than the tallest tree has just fallen from the sky! Or, at least that's what I was told," said the mouse.

"You mean you haven't seen it?" Duckweed asked.

"Nope," said the mouse, as he turned back to the crowd and began talking to the mouse next to him.

"Meet me here tomorrow at sunrise," said Parsnip to Duckweed.

It was a while before Duckweed's parents would get home. Duckweed made his own dinner and went to bed.

The next morning, Parsnip got up bright and early. She went into her mom's room to leave a note saying that she was going to the big hill where the seed was. When Parsnip got there, her mom looked very pale, and so did her father. She ran out the door in horror. "Duckweed," she cried, as she reached the seed. "My parents are sick!"

"I know, so are mine," Duckweed said. "I asked if they ate anything weird, but they told me all they ate was a few bites of the seed!"

When Duckweed finished saying this, they both looked up at the giant seed in terror. "Then that means everyone who ate from the seed is going to get very sick!" said Parsnip.

"The worst part is, everyone ate the seed except us!" Duckweed said, only making Parsnip feel worse. They split up and searched the town to see if anyone besides them was still healthy. It was no use. Everyone was sick.

"We have to do something. There has to be a cure," said Parsnip.

"We have to get rid of that poisonous seed," Duckweed said. And that's what they set off to do. Parsnip started searching for a cure to save the mice, and Duckweed tried to think of a way to get rid of the seed that caused it all.

Duckweed and Parsnip were on their own. There was no one to help them. The doctor was too sick to move, and the rest of the mice were so weak they could barely lift their paws. Parsnip and Duckweed were determined to save the town.

Parsnip spent all her time in the field and kitchen gathering and mixing together different plants and foods to make medicine. She tried out her various potions on her parents and siblings, but unfortunately all her attempts failed. "There has to be something around here that will make them better!" she sighed. Parsnip didn't know it, but she was right.

Meanwhile, Duckweed wasn't doing any better. *"How on earth am I supposed to push a huge seed 500 times my size off a cliff?"* he thought to himself as he was losing hope. He pushed, and pushed, and pushed, but the seed wouldn't budge.

Duckweed went home that night depressed. He went into his parents' room to check up on them. "Are you feeling any better?" he asked. The only response was a small groan.

Duckweed poured a bowl of cheese puffs for dinner. He put one on his spoon and catapulted it off, flinging it across the room. "That's it!" he shouted. "I'll make a catapult and fling the seed off the cliff!"

Even as Duckweed was having his brainstorm, Parsnip was

busy gnawing on a willow tree. Her head hurt from all the thinking she had been doing. Then she remembered that willow bark contains aspirin. The pain in her head awakened another memory of a day with her father in the apple orchard. Her father loved apples. That day he picked a shiny red one for her saying, "If you eat one of these apples every day, you'll never get sick."

"That's it! I'll mix apples with aspirin and make the medicine that the town needs!" Parsnip yelled with joy.

The next day, Parsnip and Duckweed set to work. Parsnip got a big pot and began chipping away the bark of the old willow tree. She gathered apples and chopped them up. Then she mixed the apples and the bark together in the pot. She scooped the medicine into bottles.

Duckweed gathered sticks and mud and started building the catapult. He slowly dug a hole under the seed. As he dug away the dirt, he pushed the end of the catapult under the seed. Then Duckweed started sawing down a huge oak tree that stood nearby on the hill. He had to saw the tree in the exact place so it would fall on the handle of the catapult and send the seed soaring off the cliff. He worked and worked.

Finally, Duckweed sawed down the tree. It fell with a bang, and the seed went flying. Even Parsnip stopped her work to watch the flight of the seed.

Duckweed went to help Parsnip feed everyone the medicine. Then they went to sit on a boulder by the cliff to wait. Finally, after an hour had passed, they heard voices off in the distance. The whole town was running to them! The mice were all better!

"Mom, Dad, you're back!" Parsnip yelled, running to them. Duckweed ran to hug his parents.

The whole town named Duckweed and Parsnip honorary heroes. Each of them got a medal. The catapult went to a special museum that was dedicated to Parsnip and Duckweed, and there was a big party for the grand opening.

Everything was back to normal. The town was saved, and the mice were happy, all thanks to two very brave mice who never gave up.

Golden Retriever At My Side

by Jenna Hoffman

This golden retriever at my side
Fills my life with happiness and pride.

The young dog with chestnut brown eyes,
He grows and grows, my, how time flies.

Just like in marriage, till death do us part,
When he died, broken was my heart.

Golden retriever in my heart, not at my side,
Filled my life with happiness and pride.

The Very Scary Forest

by Paul Fouriezos

An eight-year-old boy, Paul, and his six-year-old sister, Maria, were taking a walk in the forest. As they walked, it got darker and darker. Before they knew it, it was the middle of the night and they were lost, so they decided to stop and sleep by a tree. In the morning, they tried to find their way home on the other side of the forest, but they kept walking in circles.

After a while, Paul and Maria came upon a Friendly Ogre. The Friendly Ogre gave them directions to the other side of the forest and decided to go with them. Then they came upon a Beautiful Fairy. The Beautiful Fairy said, "I wish I could help you, but the Evil Witch stole my powers. Anyway, the other side of the forest is not too far away. I'll go with you."

So Paul, Maria, the Friendly Ogre, and the Beautiful Fairy walked up to a door. They knocked and out came a Very Smart Wizard. The Very Smart Wizard said, "Come in, come in. I hear you need to get to the other side of the forest. Just follow the trail of doors."

So Paul, Maria, the Friendly Ogre, the Beautiful Fairy and the Very Smart Wizard followed a trail of doors. On the way, they sang, "We're on the way to the other side of the forest!" and that made them feel better and not so scared.

Finally, they came upon an old, scary-looking house. The Very Smart Wizard said, "That's where the Evil Witch lives. Come on, let's sneak past." Suddenly, shrieks of terror could be heard all around. The Evil Witch came flying out of the old house. They all ran out of the forest and—suddenly—Paul woke up!

Fairness

by Alex Wilbourne

Fairness is a word that is hardly ever spoken.
It is a lonely word sitting in a dark valley
with no one around to be its friend,
because the world is unfair.
Fairness is a word that is hardly spoken.

The Mystery Suitcase

by Amelia Hays

One day, when my mom was taking my brother, my brother's friend (Matt) and me to run errands, I looked out of the window and saw a large black briefcase. I yelled, "Briefcase! Briefcase! Mom, there is a briefcase on the side of the road! Pull over."

"We still have to run the errands, and if it is still there on the way back we can go look at it," my mom said. We all groaned after she said that.

Everyone had a different, crazy idea of what could be in it. I said it could be ten million dollars that fell from the sky out of an airplane. That would be awesome.

My brother said, "It could be a suitcase of a clown that ran away and joined the circus at the age of sixteen and married the big, fat, singing, bearded lady and moved to Alabama in 1916 and opened his own circus called 'Clown Town,' then died at the old age of 96 because of a lion attack." Whew!

My brother's friend, Matt, said, "It could be the hands of a dead criminal killed by the mob, who had just gone to an old wicked witch's house, taken all her money, and killed her dog who was already sickly. The rest of the body floated down the creek and is in the ocean now!" Yuck, it's just like a boy to come up with that!

Mom said, "It could be a stolen knife, baked into a cake which was on the way to the jail to help someone pick the lock and make his escape."

We all came up with about a dozen other scenarios. We whined and complained, imagined and guessed for the next half-hour until we could head back. We all ran to the car and got in and drove to the briefcase. Then my mom got out and picked up the briefcase and gave it to me to hold. She made us wait until we got home to open it.

When we got home, we turned into the driveway and opened the briefcase to see that it held nothing—but the memories of a sixteen-year-old clown who ran away and joined the circus; the invisible hands of a dead man killed by the mob; ten million stolen dollars you couldn't see; a nonexistent stolen knife; the see-through clothes of a traveling man; the silent CDs of a rapper; and the stitchless sewing machine of an old sewing woman. Even though it was empty, it sure made for a full afternoon!

Who Am I?

by Kirsten Carella

Who am I?
A wistful thinker,
A curious poker and seeker.
Like a hound dog,
Always looking.
Like a monkey,
Very playful.
Like a hyena,
Always laughing.
I'm a mouse,
Thinking I'm a lion.
A sister, a daughter, a lover.
Who am I?

Smoltzie Adventure 1

by Jacob Randall Walker

One day my dog, Smoltzie, was eating his bone. My crazy dog said to me, “They should make a new type of bone for me.” So, this man delivered us a big, juicy, peach bone. My dog loved it. He gave me some kisses for a thank-you.

Then Smoltzie met a new puppy named Snoopy. They had lots of fun together. One day Smoltzie was playing with Snoopy. Smoltzie had an idea. First, Smoltzie got the chickens. Then, they had a race to see who could catch the chicken first. Since Smoltzie was faster, he won and got Snoopy’s golden bone. So my dog now has two bones.

Smoltzie went to a bone factory. He saw a machine and put both bones in it. Then, both bones were fused together to make a golden, peach bone. It was perfect for Smoltzie. So that’s the end of the story. Tune in next time for Smoltzie Adventure II.

I'm Happy When…

by Stephanie Pool

I'm happy when I act in plays.
I'm happy when I have good days.

I'm happy when I'm at the pool.
I'm happy when there is no school.

I'm happy when kids don't do drugs.
I'm happy when there are no bugs.

I'm happy when it's Christmas time.
I'm happy when I say a rhyme.

I'm happy when I go to camp.
I'm happy when I am the champ.

I'm happy when I jump in leaves.
I'm happy when there are no thieves.

I'm happy when I build a fort.
I'm happy at the basketball court.

I'm happy when I play with friends.
I'm happy when I get new pens.

I'm happy when I'm at the beach.
I'm happy when I eat a peach.

I'm happy in a lot of ways,
But mostly when I get all A's!

Dream Or Not

by Octavia Lynette Benson

Let me tell you about a dream I had. No, it was real...no, it was a dream...oh, I'm confused. You'll find out while reading the story. Okay, here's how it goes:

My parents won a two-day trip in a submarine for us. They let me swim in a scuba suit to explore the reef. While I was exploring, I heard a strange voice saying, "Help me, please." Before I could answer, an odd-looking fish came out of nowhere.

"Please help me," said the fish. I was so surprised I couldn't speak. The fish continued, "My name is Marely. I'm not a fish; I'm a mermaid."

"How did you become a fish?" I asked.

Marely replied, "The evil sea witch, Evilana, took my magic stone and combined its power with hers and turned me into a fish. With all that power she could turn the ocean into a horrible place. I know where my stone is, but without hands I can't hold or turn the silver key to the treasure box it's in. So please help me; you won't regret it."

"What do I get in return?" I asked.

Marely replied, "Being able to breathe under water so you can play with me."

"Okay, I'll help you," I replied.

We were on the way to the house of Evilana. Suddenly, a dolphin named Sandy appeared and said, "I can give you two a ride to your destination."

"We're headed to Evilana's house," I said.

Halfway there, we had to get off Sandy because she had to go up to the surface. But it was just our luck that a friendly group of sea turtles offered to give us a ride to Evilana's house.

Once we got to Evilana's, we thanked the sea turtles and waited behind some rocks. When Evilana went out, we went in. Marely showed me where the key was. I took it to the treasure box and took the stone and put it on Marely. Then all of a sudden Marely turned back into a mermaid. It reminded me of "The Ugly Duckling."

Marely said, "You've kept your promise. Now it's my turn, but before I keep it we need to hurry. Evilana will be coming back soon." So we hurried out as fast as we could.

"Now that we got out, you are now able to breathe under water. Take off your scuba gear," she said.

"Oh, no! I've got to get back to the submarine before dark," I said. It was just then I saw the sun going down over the water.

"Don't worry, I can teleport us back," said Marely, and Poof!

"Wow! Back before dark?"

"Have a nice vacation," said Marely.

"I can't wait till next vacation here at the beach."

We remained friends forever.

So now can you tell me if it was a dream or not? I'm going crazy trying to figure it out!

1st grade

The Red-Nosed Christmas Present

by Rachel I. Pless

If I could choose the best Christmas present, it would be something with hooves and a red nose. It would be Rudolph. I would fly with Rudolph. He would be my new pet.

Every Christmas, he would go back to the North Pole to help Santa. Every January, he would return to me, and we would spend New Year's together.

5th grade

My First Race

by Kyle S. Cristal

It was my first race driving my Ford Taurus in the Winston Cup, and my team was hoping for the best. Quite a few people doubted me because I was a new racer. The engine was roaring as I pulled my car up to the starting line. The race was about to start.

3…2…1…the green flag waved, and I was off with the pedal to the metal! The jolt was so strong I could hardly breathe, and it pushed me way back into my seat. Everyone was weaving, trying to get his tires warmed up. It took a few seconds to put the car into third gear.

Another racer cut me off, and I was tempted to spin him out. I did, but I got a penalty of one more lap. I had to start lapping the other racers if I wanted to catch up, and it took me about twenty minutes to finally catch up and get rid of the penalty.

After the long pass, I started running out of gas and got a flat tire when I ran over some debris on the track. I had to get to the pits as soon as possible. As I pulled in, my pit crew put gas in my car and changed my flat tire.

The speed limit coming out of the pits is 45, and as I was accelerating back onto the track, there was a car moving about 200 heading right towards me. *SMACK!* I was slammed on my right side. Luckily, I wasn't hurt.

The tow truck came to get me, and I was towed to the pits. They taped up my car with some heavy-duty tape, replaced my wheels and tires destroyed by the impact with new ones, and I was back on the track. The car didn't drive as well as it could have, but I was driving a half-wrecked car.

With twelve laps to the finish line, I was in eleventh place. I wanted second or first place, so that meant that I would have to start speeding up. I had to be more aggressive and more focused. When the race got to eight laps remaining, I was in sixth place. More and more racers started speeding up. Before I sped up, I went into the pits to get some gas so fuel wouldn't affect me for the final few laps. By the time there were three laps remaining, I was in fourth place and ready to win. I pushed the car faster and faster until I was at 227 m.p.h. I thought that was the fastest that car would ever go.

With two laps remaining, I was in third place, and all I could think about was winning. The two cars in front of me seemed to slow down a bit, so I took advantage and took the lead. When I looked down at the speedometer I was going 231 m.p.h. The speed scared me, but I didn't slow down at all.

About a half-mile to the finish line, I felt a bump in back. There was a racer trying to get around me, so I started weaving. Twenty feet from the finish line, I felt the bump harder while I was weaving. Five feet from the finish line, the car clipped me and pushed me over the finish line in first place. I lost control and slammed the wall.

The tow trucks and fire engines came out to see what had happened. They got me out of the car and got me on my feet. I had a few scratches and bruises, but I was okay. I had won my first race, The Daytona 500.

My pit crew carried me to victory lane with my car being towed behind me. All of a sudden, my back was wet. Somebody was pouring champagne all over me. That was the beginning of the celebration. I was so excited; I could feel my heart pounding through my chest. I knew then what I had accomplished. I couldn't wait for the next race!

5th grade

Hot Pink

by Lucie Gourdikian

Hot Pink is the sweet smell of peaches and a
juicy watermelon.

Hot Pink is the ecstatic feeling I get when I'm in a
joyful mood.

Hot Pink is the loud rock-and-roll music I listen to when
I'm in my room.

Hot Pink is the friend I can tell my deepest, darkest
secrets to.

Hot Pink is the craziness that lives inside my head.

Hot Pink is the ring of fire that my world and courage will
have to jump through.

Hot Pink is the bright, rocky road that will lead me to
my future.

2nd grade

The Magic Car's Wildest Adventure: A Day With Dinosaurs

by Kyle Oreffice

Once upon a time, there was a boy named Ryan. He lived on Dunhome Street. He liked reptiles, amphibians and playing marbles, but his favorite thing of all was the magic car. It could take Ryan anywhere—even back in time! The magic car works by putting candy in its gas tank.

One day Ryan decided to travel back in time to when the dinosaurs lived. When they got there, Ryan saw more dinosaurs than he expected. He saw a T-rex, Triceratops, Pterodactyl and an Iguanodon. They looked really cool.

Some of the dinosaurs were playing, some were fighting, and some were eating. They were about eighty feet tall! None were chasing Ryan. They were doing what dinosaurs love to do: play, fight, and eat. They had soft skin, sharp teeth, sharp claws, and their skin was red, green, black, brown, and blue. Their teeth were as big as your hand!

Ryan was not afraid. The magic car protected him with an invisible shield so that if the dinosaurs tried to eat him, it would be like running into a brick wall for them!

Ryan needed to go home because it was getting dark. After enjoying a day of fun, he went home. His dad is a paleontologist. Ryan told his dad about his adventure.

Tropical Crash

by Laura E. Stringer

Allen was a nine-year-old boy with brown eyes and brown hair. His mother was a farmer, and his father was an airplane pilot. They all lived in a small house in a neighborhood called Barning Street, in the state of Alabama. It was called that because all the people who lived there owned a barn. Allen loved horses. He had his own horse he named Abbey. His friends, Valerie, Gabby, Maggie, Alison, Patrick, Andy, Shay, and Skyler, went horseback riding whenever they could on an old trail they found in the woods.

One day, Allen had to go on a trip (on his dad's plane) to a small island 59,980 miles away from the coast of Florida called K-lorp Island. On the day of the plane's departure, Allen said goodbye to all of his friends. At least he got to take Abbey with him. Once he saw that Abbey was safe and comfortable in the back of the plane, he found a seat, buckled up, and watched his friends waving goodbye until he could see them no more.

While they were flying over the ocean, the airplane started wobbling. Allen called to his dad, "Stop! You're scaring me!"

"Allen, grab a parachute!" was the response.

"No!" thought Allen. *"The plane couldn't be crashing!"* He felt the plane going down. He grabbed a parachute. But it was too late. The nose of the plane crashed into the ground, and Allen knew no more.

When he woke up, Allen found himself lying on a sandy beach. Beside it was a tropical forest. His head hurt, but he looked around. He saw Abbey drinking water from the ocean! He tried to figure out how she survived, but that only made his head hurt more. When she saw him, she trotted over to him. Then he saw something that made his heart jump. The saddle pad, the saddle, bridle, and girth were all in a pile! But his smile faded. Where were his parents?

Two things caught his eye. One, the emergency food was lying on the ground with a canteen of water! Two, there was a white piece of paper stuck on a branch of a nearby tree. Allen could tell it was not blown there by wind. The top of the paper had a branch through it, and the very end of the branch was bent up so the paper wouldn't blow away.

First, he grabbed the food, and then he went over to where the piece of paper was. He noticed his dad's writing. Had his parents written the note? His heart was beating very fast as he pulled the note off the branch. It said:

Dear Allen,

We hope we haven't worried you too much. We couldn't find you, so please do not feel mad at us for not waking you up or something like that. If you find this note, we have gone in this direction. (There was an arrow pointing north.) There are people on this island that are very nice. Do not be afraid of any person on this island. If you meet a person, tell him your name is Allen. They will take you to the city.

From,
Your Mom and Dad

P.S. You know to go north, but you do not know this: DO NOT TURN AND GO ANY OTHER DIRECTION; YOU WILL NOT FIND US IF YOU DO!

After Allen read the note from his parents he felt better. He put the letter in his pocket and sealed the pocket with the Velcro that was sewn on it. Heading toward the pile of riding stuff, he saw his saddlebags lying on top of the saddle. Those would be useful.

Allen caught Abbey and saddled her. He attached the saddlebags to the saddle and, after checking for even the smallest of holes on them, he put the food inside, filled the canteen, and put that inside too. Then, heading toward the spot where the note was, he got onto Abbey and started north.

After about an hour of riding, Allen and Abbey stopped for a drink at a stream.

"Hey!"

Allen jumped; he was not the one who made the sound. He looked at where the voice had come from. He saw nothing but a tree. But then the tree moved. *"Wait,* he thought, *"that isn't a tree!"* He was right, too, for what he had thought to be a tree was a boy.

When he came closer, Allen saw that the boy was in his late teens. "By any chance, is your name Allen?" the boy asked.

Remembering his parents' letter, he answered a mere, "Yes."

A smile formed on the boy's face. "Your parents are looking for you. They're in the city where I live." He said, "Come on, I'll show you the way!"

Allen smiled too. The people *were* nice! He got back on Abbey.

"Oh yeah, I forgot to tell you this," the boy said. "My name is Jason."

As Allen followed Jason into the forest, he saw what looked like a small mountain; but as he got closer, he saw that it was a city! "Is this the city you live in?"

Jason nodded. Abbey neighed to two people standing and waving to him. There was a woman and a man. He wandered who they were. He knew who he wanted them to be, but he wasn't sure they were.

The closer he got, the outline of the people became clearer. "No they couldn't be… But, yes they were! The people were his parents!

"Mom! Dad!" He jumped off Abbey and ran toward them. They both hugged him.

"Hello, Allen!" said his mother and father at the same time. They looked very happy to see him. Allen noticed Abbey was beside them. She looked happy to see his parents too. "We were staying in the city over there. It is called Feolyn. We are going to stay there for the night, if you don't mind."

"Okay," Allen answered.

Allen's parents showed him around. Feolyn was a nice city.

At 8:50, Allen's parents showed him where they were staying. It was a big hotel called the Feolyn Inn. In Allen's room there was a large bed with a table beside it, a TV, and a dresser. It was a very nice room. His parents were sleeping in the room next to him. Abbey was in the stable. Allen lay down on his bed and fell asleep almost instantly.

When Allen woke up the next morning, his parents were already up. Allen got out of bed and went into his parent's room. "Morning, Allen," said his mom.

Just then a man from Feolyn came inside his parents' room. "Come," he said, "we have something to show you."

We followed him out the door. Allen felt like a bomb blew up inside him. They were saved! A brand new airplane was outside! After putting in some fuel, Allen, his mom, his dad, and Abbey were inside the airplane and ready to go.

After saying goodbye, they took off. After what seemed like twenty hours, they got back to Barning Street—safely!

The Bucket

by Connor Wadsworth Clark

When I am eight, I am going to buy a bucket. The next time I go fly-fishing with my dad, I'll tie the bucket to my line and cast it out into the middle of the river. The bucket will fill up with water and sink to the bottom of the river.

I'll yell, "Dad, I think I hooked a big one!"

My dad will run over and say, "Let me help you."

I'll say, "No, I've got it!"

And he'll say, "C'mon, let me help!"

I'll say, "Okay," and I'll give my rod to my dad. He'll pull, and pull, and pull. And when he reels it all the way in, it will only be a bucket! Won't that be funny?

Ginga

by Jackie Yarbro

For centuries, the Great Wall of China lay unfinished, gaps roaring like the open mouth of a dragon. The soldiers that guarded this yet-to-be-finished, mighty wall rested the fate of their country, China, on their skills to guard the gaps from intruders.

The underground mines near the Wall were places no one dared venture. Ginga, a feared and respected dragon, rested in those mines until summoned. Rumors said that anyone who dared enter would be attacked by Ginga's little ones. The caverns were said to have been carved by Ginga's great body, twisting and winding like a maze making you dizzy. No one knew the truth, because truth be told, there was not one soul brave enough to enter the underground mines.

Ginga was one of the truly beautiful creatures to ever walk this earth. The length of Ginga was an uncountable measurement. Her scales protected her like armor and shone out like deeply colored moons which overlapped in a graceful manner. Her little ones took on her same look, so when they all moved in unison it looked like a great river and one giant wave overshadowing them all.

The people of China had once offered their mines to Ginga, saving her and her little ones from certain death. Hostile people did not understand her nature and that she was not a threat to them. Therefore, Ginga felt in debt to them and swore her loyalty to the Chinese.

One night as the weary soldiers rested, a sneak attack planned by the Chinese rebels was put into action. Ginga, who was wandering, heard them finalize their plans and immediately sprang into action. She hissed her forked tongue in the manner of a snake, summoning her little ones. The little ones flowed over the hill like a river. As they crested the hill, Ginga let out a huge puff of smoke that moved towards the rebels, clouding their path. The only warning the rebels had of the upcoming danger were the chilling red eyes of Ginga.

Her eyes gleamed like red-hot coals, dancing in flying red sparks. The rebels fled in fear of the smoke that was now becoming fiery red. As the rebels retreated, Ginga's eyes turned the natural fiery blue that contrasted so well with her shiny silvery scales. The soldiers, awakened by all the commotion, fell to their knees, some weeping, because they knew Ginga had repaid the debt by saving their lives.

As Ginga strutted proudly over to them, the decision was made to be a permanent guardian of the people. She and her little ones, with a great gust of wind, formed a whirlwind like no one had ever seen! With a final shake, a mighty roar could be heard, and the gaps that were in the wall were filled and the stone reinforced, twice as high. The soldiers looked down, awed at the sight of the now-finished Great Wall of China. Ginga and her little ones will forever watch over the people of China.

Section Two

Middle School

Da Vinci's Smiling Girl

by Taylor Hartley

What do you hide
Lovely maiden
Behind that clear, bright smile?
A lonely heart
An anxious mind
A life that's not worthwhile?
Perhaps a secret love you share
With someone quite divine
Who waits to kiss
The silent lips
Of the beauty no one can define.
Your long, dark hair
Sits around
Your lovely, long white face
And in your eyes a sorrow
No one can erase.
The secrets that you keep from us
Lie in your piercing stare
Mona Lisa, sweet Mona Lisa
The girl Da Vinci had to share.

8th grade

The Great Snowball War Of 2002

by Will Partin

February 8, 2002—Fraser, Colorado

The winter wind blows on my face, and the sun is high in the sky. I am in the driveway of my friends' (Riley and Roger's) grandparents' house. My brother comes out of the house ready to begin what will be eventually the greatest snowball war ever. Riley and I face off in front of Roger and Thomas. We shake hands and then walk away from each other.

The second they are out of sight we start digging snow tunnels in a huge heap of snow. An hour later, an intricate web of tunnels has formed. This is the snow base belonging to Riley and me. On the other side of the street, Roger and Thomas have created their own base.

It is time for the snowball wars to begin. I climb up to the berm on the edge of the street and look at the other side. A berm, for those who don't know, is slang for the area that is created in the winter when snowplows push the snow to the side of the street.

In my intelligence-gathering mission, I see that Roger and Thomas have created a large wall instead of a web of tunnels. On the wall there are multiple cardboard slabs. I reason that these are holes from which the cardboard is removed when one wants to throw a snow ball, and put back when one is under attack. I climb back down and relay my findings to Riley.

We decide that in order to break past the wall we must throw many snowballs and try to knock away the cardboard. We split up and go to opposite sides of our berm.

We take aim and fire. The shot I throw moves at an amazing speed—seeing as I am a pitcher—strikes the wall and...nothing happens. The wall is so well-packed that the snowball bounces off and falls uselessly into the street. Suddenly, a head pops out of the bottom of the wall. It is Thomas. He retrieves the snowball from the road, using a lid as a shield from my fire. He runs back inside his fort, but not before I hit him in the back with a snowball.

I look over to see if Riley is doing any better. He is not. He has launched several volleys, but all have been retrieved by Roger the Scourge! Riley yells to me, suggesting we meet in the fortress. I crawl down and go into the fort. We converse and decide that in order to break down the wall, we need to throw with very high velocity. We need a high-velocity-snowball-catapult-machine-thing. Riley runs inside to collect components to make such a device.

In the meantime, I crawl back up to the ramparts and hurl a volley at the wall. It hits a cardboard slab on the bottom of the pole, which knocks it over. Inside, I can see that a stick is holding the tunnel together. This gives me an idea. I grab another snowball and throw it at the stick supporting the hole. My plan works perfectly. The stick is knocked away; the tunnel collapses on itself. A small dent appears in the once invincible wall.

Riley returns with a box of bungee cords and a napkin. He says that he can create a catapult from these. Just then, a snowball hits me in the face. And another. A relentless volley! I risk a look over the berm and I see snowballs flying from all parts of the wall. A larger snowball hits the entrance to our snow citadel. A small snow slide occurs and the entrance collapses. In retaliation I hurl an ice ball, which blasts through a cardboard slab and hits Roger in the chest. I hear a *thump* as he falls over from the force of the blow.

I laugh with triumph and feel even better when Riley returns with his snow catapult. He fits a snowball onto the napkin, and we pull back on the elastic cords. After we feel the tension we release at the same time and the ball flies across the street into the wall, knocking the affected part down. Yes! We are finally on the offensive.

Our snow catapult wreaks havoc on the wall until darkness

begins to fall. As the mountain begins to cast shadows across the street, Riley and I look over the berm to see what destruction our catapult has caused. The wall seems to gave been destroyed. What was once a ten-foot berm is now a three-foot pile of rubble. Snow trash lines the edge of the street, and pieces of cardboard dot the snow.

Riley and I think that it is safe to enter their base and take it once and for all. We hop over the berm and run headlong towards the wall. We jump over it, expecting a hail of snowballs but nothing happens. The base is empty.

Riley and I look at each other, and suddenly comprehension dawns in our minds—ambush! We dive just in time to avoid a slew of snowballs. We can't see where the snowballs are coming from. We duck and begin to crawl into the snow. The snow that we are crawling through is previously untouched. I look over the snow. It is a white sheet except for one part, a trail leading behind the house across the street from Riley's grandparents' house. This must have been where they went.

I think of something. They probably know that we would see the path, follow it, and then set an ambush on it. This is why Riley and I decide to go around the other side of the house. We come up on the back of the house, and I look around the corner. Roger and Thomas are looking straight at the path from where we would have been coming.

On the porch they have a small snow base set up. In order to win this battle, we must plant a flag in this heap. I tacitly signal to Riley to come out and bring snowballs. Once we have snowballs in both hands, we take aim and fire. The moment that they are hit seems to last forever. They both recoil and slowly turn around, only to be hit by another round of snowballs.

It is a glorious victory. They stand no chance. They are totally annihilated. They run away towards their destroyed fort. Riley and I pull out our flag (my orange mittens and his black ones, all tied together with a white string) and plant it into the heap. Victory is sweet. We walk back triumphantly to the warm house. Although we may have won the first battle, we may not win the war. But for now, I am the victor.

I will never forget the great snowball fight that we had that day. We have had many since, but none have ever come close to the epic battle that took place in the snow-covered landscape of Colorado.

A Child's Memories

by Joshua Cohen

The summer swing, swaying in the heat,
The gentle summer breeze
Blowing through his sandy hair.
The sound of chains creaking in the breeze,
And laughter traveling through the summer sky.

As the leaves start to change,
The colors fill the air like a dazzling painting.
The excitement of school starting for another year.
Then as the days continue,
The leaves fall and start to turn brown,
Along with the memories of summer.
The child's pile of leaves grows,
Waiting to be jumped through.
Laughter and new friends fill the fall air with happiness.

The delicate, white snow,
Falling like a baby's blanket, covering the earth.
A snowball fling into a child's face,
Laughter filling the cold wintry air with joy.
And as the holidays arrive,
The unwrapping of presents,
Along with the children's smiles so broad.

As the flowers start to bloom, the sun shines with glory.
The days grow longer for more playtime and joy.
April showers bring their flowers,
Along with the laughter of the new season.

The Creation Of The Cloud

by Joshua Evans

In the beginning, the sky above was a realm of infinite blue and black. There were no other colors in the upper world except the blue of day, the black of night, and the yellow of the sun. These were the only hues to be found in the entire world when one would look up at the sky. One day a female sheep with her mate climbed up into a cave in the side of a mountain for shelter. As they rested, a sudden landslide skidded down the mountain and covered up the entrance to the cave. The sheep were trapped inside the mountain and were positive that they were destined to die.

The other animals of the forest at the base of the mountain had seen the catastrophe and were desperate to take action. The squirrel, with his excellent climbing and leaping abilities, seemed a perfect match for the job of scaling the mountain. "I shall go and save them!" he exclaimed.

The valiant squirrel leapt from rock to rock with amazing agility. He was one rock away from the entrance of the cave when Wisima, the wind goddess, began to whistle her sweet tune. Although the squirrel was a daring and muscular mountaineer, his lightweight body made him a perfect victim of the goddess' gust. She caught hold of his tail and threw him off the edge of the mountain with the greatest of ease. Luckily, the brave animal was able to grab hold of a tree branch just seconds before he was sure to hit the ground. The hair on his tail still stands on end to this day.

The optimistic squirrel was not about to give up hope so easily. He called up to the bald eagle's nest on the side of one of the mountain's lower cliff faces. "Oh great and powerful eagle, will you not come to the aid of these helpless creatures in their hour of need?" he cried.

"I will uphold my duty as guardian of this land!" he responded. The mighty eagle dove down from his nesting spot in the cliff face and then flew straight up into the heavens. But as he looked up to try and spot the cave, the sun blinded his eyes and bleached his face snow white, as white as the light of the sun itself. He fell from his graceful ascent and had to take shelter in a dark wing of the forest until his eyes could recover, the duration of which would be a hundred days and a hundred nights.

The squirrel saw this horrible and shocking event and decided to turn to his last chance, the faithful mountain goat. He sprinted across the forest until he came upon the trusty goat basking in the sun. "Horse of the mountain, I call to you in a time of great peril. I ask that you take advantage of the powers that the earth has awarded you and save these pure and innocent beasts," he pleaded.

"I shall do as you ask, oh bold and courteous squirrel, for your tail is as big as your heart, and who am I to refuse such a request?" So the goat leapt from rock to rock up the mountainside. He made jumps so courageous and daring that any human would have fallen to his knees in awe.

The powerful goat was soon at the cave's entrance. Lowering his horned head, the great creature charged at the cold hard stone. *Crack, boom, shcrchhhh,* the rock went. Time after time the rock cracked a little more, and time after time the goat would charge and batter it, until at last every single rock blocking the mouth of the cave was in shambles!

The sheep, being so startled and overjoyed by the sight of light, darted out of the black hole and flew right off the side of the mountain. At that very moment, Wisima began to blow, and her breath lifted the precious animals into the heavenly realm of the gods, and their fleece was left behind at the border between mortality and eternal life to lace the skies with their white beauty until the end of days.

The Stone Angel

by John Henry Boger

My body and mind hung there
In the place where war and suffering are but a thought
A shadow
And I can lose myself there
If only I close my eyes
And let my soul wander
But this heaven
This utopia
Can be shattered; interrupted
By the most basic of forces
"Wake up! Wake up, you men you soldiers!"
"Wake up!"
"For there are battles to be fought and wars to be waged"
"So roll out of your cozy bunks and get on your gear!"
"Cause we're the 101st Airborne and can be deployed far and near!"
"So wake up now,"
"Wake up!"
The sergeant's voice was loud and clear
And induced moans from every throat
But we got out of bed and put on our gear
"All right boys! We're going to France today
to a little ol' place called Bastogne!"

The plane rattled and shook
Like the men inside from fear
(and the cold, they'd insist)
They were scared sick of dying
But
Someone had to die, so that many might be free
We knew someone would die today
So looking around at our brothers
Our best friends
At all the young, innocent faces
Everyone asked the same silent question:

Who is going to be left here, on a bed of snow
in the cold winter air?
Whose mind and soul will walk the stairs to heaven,
Leaving his bloody and broken body behind?
And it gathered strength, that question did
Until it became a prayer
And slipped out
Unseen
Into the cold winter air
To fly and dance amid the clouds and sky
And then to reach an untold height
To climb Heaven's Gate and whisper in the ears of angels:
"Somewhere, far below
above a land all covered in snow
Some men and boys sit in courage and fear
Waiting for an order to be called
And then to fall from the sky
Like so many stars
To fall among their enemies
To die and fight in frozen throngs
For this thing called freedom
And for liberty
So dear angels please remember them
And help their troubled spirits
Make it home again"

The guns that were aimed at the sky
At us; our sky
Were in the hands of boys and men like us
Just in different uniforms
And on different sides
O, why is war so cruel?
And while those guns tore holes in my friends
I landed in France
And thought of my home
And what we were fighting for

And I cried "For Liberty!"
For that was my well of courage
In which I dipped today
The other men roared as well
"Liberty! Liberty! Liberty!"
We ran on to Bastogne

My tears fell down towards the white Earth
Down like burning planes
Like fallen soldiers
And all round me
Fallen soldiers lay
Our ticket into Europe had been punched with the blood of paratroops
The blood of American boys
And German ones
I felt the Earth underneath my boots
And Mother seemed to say
Run, my children! Flee from this carnage and go away! Fly back!
Sobbing, I silenced the Earth and ran on

Shells rained down on us
Like so much deadly hail
The scream of a German shell is like nothing else in the world
A banshee's cry of death and destruction
That is the song of the shells that pelted us
Killed us
And still, we plunged on
Through the screams
Through rubble fields littered with men
Past medics trying to save some poor boy's life
We always stopped here and there, to help
Through the whine of bullets, killer angels flying through the city
Through the roar of field guns
Smelling gunpowder
The sounds and smells and sights of that day I will never forget

Never
But now was not the time for deep thought
Men who stop to think get a bullet in the belly
So now the men of the 101st Airborne Division plunged onto their commander
The god of the 101st
We loved him and trusted him
“Well boys, I’ve got some bad news,” he said
“The Germans have enclosed the city
And Allied help is miles off
We can hold ’em off
If we seize that church, over there with the golden dome”
“We’ll do it, commander,” yelled a thousand men
“We’ll fight to the Golden Dome and back again”

So now thousands ran
Jumped
Shot
through a city of ruins and dead
And the Golden Dome loomed closer and closer
Until we, the 101st US Army Airborne Division
Stood at the foot of marble angels at the Golden Dome
And in front of countless German muzzles
The fight raged all around
No one winning
Just dying
Until paratroopers started jumping on grenades
So no others would be hurt
Leading machine guns so their brothers could silence them
And the tide turned
And it was over

Americans stood in silence in the churchyard
Crying, staring
Shocked to be alive
When gunfire came from inside

And the tired, bloodied boys stumbled in to find a desperate knot of Germans
Despair was on their faces
They had lost, mind, body, and soul
But they gathered for one last stand
Grenades flew
And bullets cracked
And amid the clouds of dust and smoke
A grenade landed, lazily, at my feet
A soldier leaped on the bomb
And all I felt was a shock
But inside, I felt much more
Why did that boy die for me?
What drove him to dive on a deadly object to save the life of a man he didn't know?
And then I knew, from the deep recesses of my soul
Courage
Raw courage that sent men to jump out of planes, run through a forest, invade a city, and fight through to a church that had little importance in the overall war
It was then I realized this
Signs of courage surrounded me all my life
But I had never noticed
Until another life was lost for mine
Until a man killed himself for me
And so
I fell to my knees in front of the stone angel
Who beckoned with outstretched arms and wings
My name is America, and I am a soldier of liberty

Travel Not Into The Night

by Kaitlyn Klucznik

A soft breeze blew through the open balcony doors, causing the curtains to flutter. Muffled sunlight fell upon the floor, causing the room to brighten a tad. Two pale feet fell upon the cold, stone floor and found their way into slippers. A pale blue night dress swished about the feet of a young maiden. Her raven hair fell in a braid upon her back, though a few loose tendrils fell over her grey-violet eyes.

With spidery, delicate fingers she tucked the tendrils behind her ear. She paused as she passed the balcony doors to stare at this dreary day. Tonight would be a sad All Hallows Eve, for no moon would light the sky, amongst billions of stars. A knock upon the door soon startled her. Closing the door to the balcony and heading to open the other door, she frowned, causing her brow to wrinkle. Grabbing a nearby robe, the maiden thrust her arms into the sleeves and strode the last few steps to the door. A young maid stood there in a brown working garb.

"Hello, Gladria," she sighed in relief that it was neither her father nor the sensei.

"Your Highness, your father wishes your presence in the Great Hall immediately," Gladria replied, bowing her head.

"Fine, get up and tell my father I will be down shortly. You are dismissed," she stated flatly as she turned and shut the door.

She glided over to her wardrobe and glanced through. Finding a velvet dress in a color of deep midnight, the maiden placed it upon her bed to find the shoes that went with it. About ten minutes later, she had her hair done, makeup on, and was dressed. Arriving in the Great Hall, she noted her father was in a meeting with his councilmen. Most of them were about her father's age, though there were a few of about her age. They normally nodded in greeting to her, yet today they ignored her like everyone else. Gliding over, she stopped about fifty paces from her father.

"Father, you wanted to see me?" she inquired, her voice soft and gentle as music.

He looked over at her, startled for a moment; then realizing it was only his daughter, he relaxed. "Yes, my dear, I did," he replied softly. "Saria, I must speak with you in...private." He turned to his councilmen and said a few words. They soon departed; the men of roughly her age dipped their heads as they passed.

"Father, what is it? What is wrong?" Saria asked. Worry was seen in her eyes, for her father looked weary and ill.

"Dear, it is about your departure tonight. I cannot let you leave. There is something amiss in the woods, and I am afraid I will not have you traveling through that." His eyes showed weariness, for he was tired from facing problems every day which seemed to become too much for him to handle.

"What? Why not? Father, you know this trip means everything to me, and I must leave tonight, the night of All Hallows Eve," she pleaded with him.

An hour later, after pleading with him and getting no results, she left. It was time that she took this matter into her own hands. She would leave and ignore her father's warnings. It would be easy and wouldn't matter if she left or not. Saria's father only remembered about her on important days such as this; otherwise she was hidden in her brothers' shadows.

The sun set early that night, Saria leaving through the kitchens as it set. She had a small bundle with her, nothing too big—just a few clothes and a warm cloak. The door creaked slightly as she crept through. It was dark now, and there was no steam or bustle which normally filled the kitchens during the day. All was quiet. She smiled slightly to herself and crept even more carefully, so as to not bump the pots hanging from the ceiling. The back door was just in sight, and her hand reached out to meet it when her head bumped a group of pans, knocking them to the floor with a loud crash. Feet were the last thing Saria heard as she ran out the door.

She was into the forest half an hour later. The moon was bright now; the clouds had disappeared during the course of the day. She sighed and sat down upon a tree that had collapsed. Mud was splattered upon her clothing, and her hair was full of twigs.

Suddenly, a rustle was heard, and a shadowed figure was seen at a glance moving through the woods. It moved gracefully, with much agility. Eyes of burning red flames looked out at the unsuspecting maiden. A hand shrouded by clothing reached out to touch the maiden but withdrew as she stretched and stood slowly. He was soon obscured by the leaves of brush sitting and waiting in the darkness.

Saria started to walk onward, away from the land she had called her home for the past nineteen years. It was her past, a home she wished to forget. There were no pleasant memories there, just lonely memories of being ignored. All the memories were sad, depressing ones, telling of a life she would put behind her.

The creature sat glaring at her from its spot in the brush. It was a small spot, only big enough for a rabbit, yet he fit comfortably into the area. It waited, quietly looking at the maiden. It was hungry, hungry for the life that stood in front of its red eyes. The creature, a pale white vampire, had been in the wood for three days looking for food. Now, food stood right out of his grasp, just gazing out at the trees.

Saria looked around one last time and walked onward. Her dress got caught upon the brush, and he stared at her. Smiling, he jumped out and bit her upon the neck, feasting upon the royal blood. She screamed in pain as she fell to the covered earth. Her neck bleeding, she felt weak, so weak she could not move from the spot upon which she lay. Soon she was enveloped by darkness so complete, she felt as if she had died. In fact, she had died, though in a way incomprehensible to a mere mortal. She lived, yet she didn't, for she had no soul now, a creature of the dark.

He stood above her for a moment, looking at her. During the next three days, days full of pain, she would go through her transformation in sleep to wake upon the third night. She would wake before that but not to her recollection. He bent down and picked her up, carrying this royal maiden into a cave where she could rest in peace among the shadows during her transformation.

The next three days were terrible, as she writhed in agony. Saria was becoming one of them, a creature of the night. Screaming, her soul was torn from her body at last, causing tears to fall down her eyes. They burned and dried as soon as they fell. The tears ended two minutes later, taking the last of her humanity with them.

Waking as the sun set, Saria looked out, her eyes wild. Those eyes no longer showed love and kindness, they showed terrible power and a merciless hunger. Her hair blew on a nonexistent wind, showing that she was no normal vampire, but a great sorceress as well. Saria had all of the strengths of a vampire, yet none of their weaknesses.

The sun had set by the time hunger struck. It was a sharp pain at the back of her mind before it even came to strike her in the stomach. Running out into the dark, she bumped into a man, a guard from the palace.

"Good evening, your Highness. We have been looking for you." He reached out a hand to assist her home, but she refused. His eyes looked over her, noting that she now lacked her cloak, and her sleeves were torn.

"Thank you for your offer, good sir, but really I would rather it if you left me be," she hissed, her long pearly fangs showing through her ruby lips.

He looked up to see them and turned to run, getting no farther than one step before she was in front of him. She smiled and tilted her head, a finger resting upon her check.

"Where are you going? Don't you want to play with me?" she asked, imitating a young child.

The guard looked at her, a look of fear plastered on his face. She bit him before he could scream, causing yet another body to fall to the forest floor. The other vampire stood against a tree, his face hidden by dark locks of hair.

"Well done, m'lady, well done." He clapped, coming out to reveal his glowing red eyes.

"Who are you sir?" Saria snapped, eyeing him.

"I am, Asmurus, one of shadow and darkness," he answered her simply.

"It is a pleasure, Asmurus. Now may I be so bold as to inquire why you are in this sacred wood?" Her reply came strong and demanding. She stood taller, looking at him.

"I live here…" His sentence was unfinished, for at that moment a group of villagers came, waving torches. The priest held a cross and had a bottle of holy water with him, the rest carrying stakes.

"Monsters! Kill them!" The group yelled in chorus, as they came upon Saria and Asmurus.

"Come with me, m'lady," he commanded as he grabbed her hand.

They ran on for an hour, the villagers keeping pace. A cliff was in sight, and Asmurus headed straight for it. It was time to fly on to a land where they could feast and go unnoticed. Earth crunched underneath foot as the boots of all thudded heavily upon the ground. Twiggs snapped, and a few rocks fell as Asmurus jumped over the edge of the cliff with Saria holding tightly to his hand. They fell for a few hundred feet and soared back up into the night. Flying high over the lands, they headed north towards the shadow lands, a land where vampires ruled.

The villagers witnessed it all and soon started back to the wood to kill the other victim and set his soul free. After this task was done, they set out toward the palace and the new duty of telling the king.

The king took the news with a heavy heart. The daughter he had loved, yet never seemed to show how he cared, was now undead, one of the monsters that had inhabited the forest. He sent the villagers away and called upon her brothers, grieving and weeping heavily. The kingdom had lost the guidance of a female, a young wise mind. Her mother had died when she was young. Now it seemed her fate was to live the rest of her days as a tortured soul, trapped between worlds.

A Sea Of Blue

by Noah M. Levine

Gazing ahead at a pile of presents
wrapped in different styles of blue,
it might be a sea of blue.
"Which one's mine?"
"The blue one's yours."
"Which blue?
The blue of the grass,
The oceanic cyan, blueberry blue,
sad cobalt or purple blue?"
A bunch of blue!
"Is it the tint of the sky,
or the shade of the water
calm at noon or perhaps..."
A stream of blue!
"Search no more, it's this one here."
He reaches behind
his postured back and pulls out a gift
dark, shining
light, gleaming
in different hues.
A drop of blue!
with elegant ribbon
dark, like dripping water!
A hint of blue!
My hand leaps, uncontrolled,
and seizes it, grasping it,
removes the tie,
releases the wrapping
onto the floor: A sea of blue!
From inside I pull a sphere,
a sapphire sphere.

A large, round sphere of darkest blue,
and lightest too,
in fact, together they are swirling
those two blues and more too
swirling as: A sea of teal!
Through it I can see the floor
glistening bluer than before:
sea on sea.
Two regal seas of royal blue!
no red, no yellow,
no green, too
just a sphere
and room of blue,
of cerulean,
aquamarine, and azure.
peering closer at the sphere
an inscription appears
etched in navy, are the words:
"A sea of blue!
Everywhere,
around the room, the town,
around the sky, the world, ..."
It surely is a sea of blue!

8th grade

Tony Buka And The Family Business

by Trey Roberts

Tony Buka. What can I say about Tony Buka? Some would say he was a cruel-hearted man with no emotion. Others would say he was loyal to The Family and The Family Business. Tony was not the average man of The Family. He was built like an ox, and he was deadly with a tommy gun.

His mischievous, dark black eyes were misgiving for his never-ending loyalty and passion. Now I don't know about you, but I have never seen Tony's hair. He wears a white-striped, black semi-top hat everywhere, maybe even to bed. He's the kind of guy who sleeps with a knife under his pillow and never leaves the house without his cream-lined black silk suit.

Now I must warn you, don't you ever say nothin' about Tony Buka's scar. You know it kind of distorts his face. I don't even want to talk about what happened to Chubs when he asked about it. The story still haunts half of the southside after a year. But that is enough about the "Southside Tommy." His dramatic, near-death story is what has brought you here.

Buka woke up in his small, Spartan, two-room apartment early Wednesday morning. He sat in disgust at his secondhand, wooden table while reading in the Times how the Yankees had lost to Babe Ruth and the Red Sox. He always had sugarless Cheerios and pulp-free orange juice, and it never changed. His arrival time was always the same as well—8:30 on the dot.

He was Mr. Bambino's right hand man, and that job was very important and vital to the Family Business. The boss was the advisor for all things that happened. The wise man made the decisions and gave orders to Buka and, with no questions asked, he always carried them out. The Family believed in respect, honor, class, and dignity, with a strong uniting emotion. They lived on the southside of town and kept to themselves. But because of the gang's devotion to each other and because of the Grisochi boys, they almost killed themselves and their reputation.

Tony strolled into the dark lounge with a serious, but straight look as usual. He was surprised to see the boss there, because his arrival time was normally later. Buka knew that things weren't right when the schedule had changed. He also was alarmed to see Mr. Bambino's deep, green eyes turn to a red, watery look.

"Tony, my son, my son, things are not good. Please have a seat." Buka grabbed an old stool and eased down. "The Grisochi boys are at it once more." The boss had to stop to let the reality take its toll. You could tell the feelings were deep for what had happened, and Buka was anxious to hear the disaster but didn't show it. Once Mr. Bambino got himself together, he continued, "They got Jr., Tommy Jr.!"

Buka was shattered with the news and he couldn't help showing it. He felt total rage, yet merciful sadness at the same time. The Northerners had gone too far. They had taken the life of an innocent juvenile, a young gentleman of just twenty years of age. Tony loved that boy, his close nephew. He bestowed care and affection onto the humorous kid as if he were his father. Buka could barely get out one word, "Why?"

"Well, Jr. was meddling around with Silver 9 and his fellas. You know how any disagreement will make Antonio pull the trigger, but Tommy didn't. We may never know the true reason why 9 shot him." Mr. Bambino rubbed his unshaved chin and mumbled a few whisper-like swears.

Buka sat in confused silence, but his mind was in an uncontrollable anger. Silver was the head of the Northside Bronx, the Grisochi boys. His real name was Antonio, but no one called him by that anymore. Silver 9 came from his deadly silver chrome, 9-millimeter pistol. It is said you can see the reflection of the body on the silver surface. I only see the red blood that comes from the curse of a man. "Have you told G?" Buka muttered quietly. G was Giovanni, Buka's young brother and best friend to Tommy.

"No, I figured you might want to inform him of the catastrophe," the godfather replied. Buka nodded silently and then stood up, clutching his knife in his pocket. "You know what this means? G and I are gonna have to find some answers tonight. The hard way or not, Mr. Grisochi will make that decision," Buka stated with authority.

"Yes, yes, I know. Just please, no more bodies. I can't take any more losses today," the godfather stated, even though it wouldn't make a difference. Buka gave him a brief stare and then a family hug. Tonight, people would stay inside with doors locked. Tonight would be deadly, and the whole Bronx knew it.

That night it was hair-lifting chilly with a full, silver moon. Buka wore a large trench coat over his silk suit. G wore the same over his Gucci suit, with a pistol-filled holster underneath. They hopped in the black Caddy and were on their way to the unforgiving showdown. G was infuriated more than ever. Earlier, Buka had told him the devastating news. It hit him so hard it even brought tears to his soft, indigo eyes. But now those eyes were hard, grey ones ready for payback.

They parked a block away and loaded their weapons. When finished, they looked each other deep in the eye. Buka started, "Forever Family..."

"...Family Forever," G finished. They gave the family salute, two chest beats and a point to God, the Father, and then slammed the door behind them.

They marched the silent block to the one story building. The brothers allowed themselves into the smoky office to find the three Grisochi boys puffing on Cuban cigars. Silver 9 was lying back in a comfortable chair with his feet propped on the desk. The other two hoodlums leaned against some boxes in the corner. The only light in the room came from a small lamp on the desk.

"What the heck is wrong with you?!" escaped G's mouth without hesitation. The Northerners chuckled and glanced at each other.

"Ahh, Mr. G, Mr. Southside Tommy, we've been expecting you, so glad you could make it," Silver 9 said sarcastically.

Buka nodded at G to let him know he would take care of it. "Antonio, I don't have much patience, and we need to find some answers!" boomed Buka with a deep voice.

Silver smiled and gave his cigar a quick blow. "Yes, your buddy Tommy. Did you know he cries like a little baby when you give him a shot in the gut?"

This was too much for G. He impulsively yelled, "Oh, you're askin' for death, aren't ya?"

Silver shook his head and set down his cigar. He pulled out his legendary 9-millimeter, and began to spin it on the desk. Buka turned and stared at G. A faint timing connection was mentally set.

Buka leaned on the desk and began the confrontation. "Listen up, we need some answers, and you're either going to give them to us or not!"

Silver 9 got real close to the two brothers and stated the wrong answer. "What's done is done, what's past is past."

Buka gave him a brief second before he said, "No. What's done is done, who's dead is dead."

Immediately, the Buka family ripped out their guns and gave the Grisochis no mercy or time. G gave two quick knee cap shots unto the slick Antonio. A gut shot from his own silver 9-millimeter from G finished him off. At the same moment, Tony was dispatching a living hell from his tommy gun upon the two followers. The mass of bullets created a puddle of cold blood in which the bodies lay.

The two brothers turned around in unison and walked slowly to the door. Before they reached it, Buka heard a moan from the desk. He flipped around and powered the trigger back. All that was heard were the gunshots of both men, Buka and Silver. Buka, thinking his business was finally over, was wrong. Knowing that Silver 9 was dead, he turned to his brother. All he found was another murdered man at his feet. Another body, another family member, another loved one.

People say the moon had a red tint to it that night. Don't ask the "Southside Tommy" about it because he decided it's not necessarily about the business, but rather about the family. With tears in his eyes, sirens in his ears, and a dead brother in his arms, he changed his ways that cold night. So ask yourself, "Is Tony Buka a cowardly, coldhearted man, or just a protective, loving family member?"

A Rose In Hand

by Stephen Nix

Escaped from her blazoned prison
Never noticed
Never cared

Abandoned, sad, and lonely
Never noticed
Never cared

Trampled by leather beasts
Never noticed
Never cared

Sleeping on the concrete fence
Never noticed
Never cared

She was dying after she was dead
Never noticed
Never cared

Picked up by one and dropped by another
Never noticed
Never cared

Forgotten beauty on ugly roads
Never noticed
Never cared

Death came close but never scarred her
Never noticed
Never cared

One loving her out of many
Always noticed
Always cared

Raven's Gift

by Alice Johnson

Raven delicately placed her fingers on the black and white keys of Carnegie Hall's grand piano. Adrenaline pumped through her veins as she searched in her memory to find her piece. Beautiful music streamed out of the piano as Raven pushed down the keys. Rhapsody and Blues quickly changed from largo and piano to allegro and fortissimo. The large crowd, who had come into the enormous concert hall, rapidly reacted to the many changes to tempo and dynamics in the song.

Raven finished the song off with a bang. She smiled at the thought that it was flawless. Raven stood up to the crowd, which was roaring like a lion. Bending over slightly in the bowing position of a professional pianist, Raven flashed the audience a smile and smiled to herself once more. As she gave the cheering crowd a final wave, she let in a huge gasp. That was the best concert she had ever had.

"Awww! Look at Little Raven," said Aunt Jacqueline. Little Raven Wiesler reached out with her chubby, tiny baby fingers. Aunt Jacqueline stuck her finger in one of Raven's open palms, realizing she had made a mistake after the baby closed her fingers around it. Raven's aunt grimaced, slightly overcome with the small girl's strength. "Oh my gosh, Melinda! This baby has some strong fingers! Ouch!"

"Yes, I know," replied Raven's mother. "If I didn't know better, I would say that she is going places music-wise, but I don't say it because neither me or Job are musically inclined."

"Well, I know better and I still I do say that she will go places!" argued Aunt Jacqueline, looking around. "And not just in the future. You should be watching your kid, Melinda! She's crawling on a straight course to your Baby Grand."

Melinda whirled around and glanced over at the piano just to see Raven pulling herself up by the bench. The girl stretched out one of her chubby fingers and pressed it down on one of the delicate keys. A "G" tone strove to get out of the back hood of the Baby Grand piano.

"Melinda," Jacqueline whispered in awe, "your baby is not just any baby. There is an old saying that goes: 'If first played a G, the greatest they shall be.'"

"Jackie!" Melinda shouted, "I am surprised at you! That is the largest amount of flimflam I have ever heard anyone say!" However, even as Mrs. Wiesler was saying this, she saw Little Raven's eye twinkle. Not with the normal twinkle a baby gives, but a twinkle of greatness. Raven's mother thought about what her sister said. Could it actually come true?

"Again, Raven," Raven's new piano teacher, Ms. Wingfield, lulled. "You need to get it right every time you sit down to practice." To Raven, no matter how many times she played her piece, Fantasia in E Major by Beethoven, it was never correct. "Try using dynamic level and maybe those accents on the third page. Raven, I remind you repeatedly about these things. Now, play it beautifully."

Raven lightly sighed and turned to the piano while making a mental note about the dynamics and accents. As her fingers pressed and released the keys, Raven closed her eyes, feeling the soft music in her soul. She felt one with the piano, and the piano keys seemed to flow under her fingers. Raven's inner being ached as she came close to the end, never wanting to stop. Although the song was only a few minutes long, the piano-loving girl felt as if she were enjoying hours of the music's sweet essence coming from her own fingers.

Silence. Not a sound was heard throughout the whole house, besides the steady click of the cuckoo clock. "Ms. Wingfield,"

Raven whispered, "was that better?"

"Raven Wiesler," Raven's baffled piano teacher stated, "that music gave me chills like I never had before, not even at a professional concert. You have something special, Raven. I will try to make you work to your full ability. You are going somewhere, Raven. I know it."

Raven sat on the hard piano stool bewildered. She never thought a piano teacher would ever understand her talent, let alone Ms. Wingfield. "Thank you very much," Raven mumbled self-consciously. Getting such a compliment from an ex-professional piano player was scaring her out of her wits!

"Enough with Fantasia!" the excited teacher exclaimed. "We are moving on to much harder things." Raven could see the unexplainable joy radiating out of Ms. Wingfild's eyes and knew she was not joking. They were moving on to things she had only dreamed about! Raven was moving one more step into becoming famous. She was going to accomplish her dreams.

"Raven!" her mother cried out, "That was amazing! The music gave me chills." After her mother had kissed her on both cheeks, Raven said thank-you and returned to her accompanist (depending on the song), Leo Peregrin. The immensely handsome man walked up to her and gave her a hug. "Fantastic job, Raven! I don't know anyone who could have played it better."

"Thanks, Leo," replied Raven. "Hey! I'm going out with some family tonight. Do you want to come?"

"Gee, Raven. Thanks for the offer, but I'm busy tonight. I have a business meeting with a possible employer for a halftime job. I'll talk to you later, though."

For the fourth time that night Raven smiled to herself, but it quickly turned upside down when she saw newspaper and magazine reporters heading towards her. Raven quickly tried to slip away where no one could see her in her dressing room, but she failed and the press caught up with her.

Cameras flashed as Raven answered routine questions about her life and her career. Raven started to shoo away the crowd, but one single journalist with a small memo pad and a pencil (who, to Raven, could not have been over seventeen years old) remained to ask one final question.

"Hi, my is Laura Benson, and I'm on the Jerome High School Music Newspaper, and I just wanted to know what it was that made you have such a strong passion for music."

Raven had to think about that question hard. Was it the crowd? No. The money? Definitely not! The lights, the stage, the popularity? None of those were it either. Then the answered appeared in the pianist's mind as clear as daylight, and she knew it was the right one.

"I had to think about that one, Laura. Let's see. I would have to say that it is the best gift I have ever received."

Things Aren't As They Seem

by Ashley Ryckeley

People like to pretend the world is good and well
but really
that's not how it is

How can it be
at least for me
when I'm fourteen and my face is covered in oil
my hair never fixes quite right
and I always seem to be in trouble
but really
that's not how it is

My head is full of trash
and I'm constantly thinking
what if
with a world full of rock stars
and pop stars
why can't I be like them
but really
that's not how it is

With school
who needs it
all it does is waste your time
with dorks
and geeks
and punks
and freaks
but really
that's not how it is

When the boy I obsess over
doesn't know I exist

and acts like such a jerk
when I'm doing badly in social studies
and science too
when I live in a world so busy
and hopeless
but really
that's not how it is

With violence
and murders
with friendships
and break ups
with love
and hate
and the passing days
but really
that's how it is.

Sleeping In A Cabin

by Chelsea Kephart

"Mom!" Sally Hanson yelled, "He is just like any other guy I have dated."

"No he isn't, Sally," Mrs. Hanson argued. "I know there are other boys who are more suitable for you. What about that Lewis Driver?"

"He is Mike's best friend and mine, too. It just wouldn't be right. I just don't understand why you don't like Mike?" Sally questioned.

"You won't understand until you have kids of your own. I'm afraid he might take advantage of you."

"How can you say that? You don't even know him, and you don't trust me!" Sally said smartly.

"Don't give me lip, young lady! Just march right up to your room before you say something you'll regret. We will talk about this later!" commanded Mrs. Hanson.

"No problem!" Sally stomped up the stairs, making sure her mom heard each step on the staircase as she steamed to her bedroom.

She flopped down on her bedspread, picking up her favorite teddy bear and the phone. She called her best friend, Lewis. Lewis helped calm Sally down and told her she needed to get some sleep. Sally took his advice and cried herself to sleep.

As the night went on, Mrs. Hanson tried to fall asleep on the cold, hard couch, but it was impossible. She went into the kitchen to make some coffee and think about the events that had happened earlier that night. Next thing she knew, she heard someone rumbling around upstairs. She thought it was Sally and how it would be a great opportunity to take up some cookies and milk and apologize to her about the argument they had.

She walked down the quiet hallway towards Sally's room. She put down the tray on a table and knocked on the door. There was no answer. Mrs. Hanson then just welcomed herself right in. "Sally, I brought you up some cookies and milk. I thought that we could talk about this Mike guy."

No one responded. Mrs. Hanson set the tray on the nightstand. She turned on the lights and found no one! She started to panic as she called for her daughter. She looked in Sally's closet and ran down the hallway, looking in all the other rooms. Where was her daughter? She went straight for the phone and called the police.

"Hello, Hello! I just went to go check on my daughter and she isn't in her room. I don't know where she would be this late at night. We had a fight earlier, and I think she could have run off. Could you please send over one of your officers?"

"Yes, ma'am. Just give me your name, address, and phone number, and our officers will be over right away," said the operator calmly.

While Mrs. Hanson paced around the room waiting for the police officers, she called her husband. He was overseas on business. She told him everything that had happened—the argument about Mike, how they didn't really make peace before both of them went to bed, where Sally would go, and what they were going to do.

Mr. Hanson said, "I probably won't be able to make it back in town until the weekend is over, so just sit tight and call me *when* you find her."

They were interrupted by the doorbell. Mr. and Mrs. Hanson both said good-bye. She quickly hung up and ran to the door.

"Wow, what took you so long?" Mrs. Hanson shouted out because she was out of breath.

"We're sorry, ma'am," one of the officers said politely.

"I think this is more important than just some patrol duty! Come in so we can get straight down to business," she said as she welcomed them.

"Hi, I'm Officer Pete Woodwind," he said while he shook Mrs. Hanson's hand. Another officer introduced himself as Officer Joey McDonald. They were both strong, serious, well-built men.

Officer McDonald said, "We have to ask you questions and

fill out paperwork before we can start looking for your daughter."

They talked about the fight, Sally's relationship with Mike, where they could find Mike, had she done this before, where would she go, and what the plan was for looking for Sally. Mrs. Hanson patiently answered all of their questions. After all the paperwork was done, she asked, "So, where are we going to look first?"

"I think we are going to find our best result wherever Mike is." Officer Woodwind radioed into the station to find Mike Reeves' address. Once they received it, they drove straight to Mike's house.

Mrs. Reeves opened the door to two police officers and a mom who looked beat. "Yes, can I help you with anything?" she asked.

"Is your son home?" Officer McDonald asked.

"No, is he in some sort of trouble?" Mrs. Reeves asked, panicked.

"Yes, he is. We think he might have run away with Sally Hanson. Have you ever heard your son talk about her?" Officer McDonald replied.

"No. I don't talk to him much. He's always at parties. He's at a college party now," Mrs. Reeves said.

"Maybe if you could keep track of your son we wouldn't be having this conversation!" Mrs. Hanson blurted out.

"Don't tell me how to raise my son!" Mrs. Reeves yelled back.

"Ladies, Ladies! Calm down!" Officer Woodwind yelled out. "Mrs. Reeves, do you know where the party is and when your son is coming home?"

"I don't know where it is, but he's coming back on Monday."

"Thank you. Could you contact us when he gets back?" Officer Woodwind asked.

"Sure, so you can find out that my son isn't guilty!" Mrs. Reeves said smartly and slammed the door in their faces.

The weekend went by slowly for Mrs. Hanson, waiting for news about her daughter, her husband coming home, and anything the police dug up about Mike. Finally, Mrs. Hanson got a phone call from Officer Woodwind saying that they had Mike in custody. They wanted Mrs. Hanson to be down there when they questioned him.

Mrs. Hanson grabbed her purse and ran out of the house. While she was driving over to the police station, her husband called and told her that his flight just got in. She filled him in, and he said that he would meet her over at the police station.

Mr. Hanson got there before the questioning. Officers McDonald and Woodwind couldn't get what they wanted out of Mike. He said he didn't know where Sally was, but they didn't believe him. Finally, they got some leads. They had the whole town searching—Sally's friends, the whole Hanson family, and people who didn't even know Sally.

The Hansons were beginning to give up hope, because it had been months since Sally ran off. One late October evening, a search group went to Beaverhead Forest to look around Mike's cabin. Some friends had told the police about the cabin, because Mike used to throw parties there. Officer Woodwind split the search group up into sections. After thirty minutes, he heard a cry from behind Mike's guest cabin. The group quickly rushed to that spot.

"Mrs. Hanson," Officer Woodwind said on the phone. "We found Sally up at Beaverhead Forest by Mike's cabin, and we would like you to come to the hospital."

She and Mr. Hanson screeched out of their driveway and drove up to Southwest Hospital. While Mrs. Hanson went in to visit Sally, Mr. Hanson talked to the doctors.

Mr. Hanson walked into the hospital room and saw Mrs. Hanson holding on to Sally's hand. Mr. Hanson walked up to her and put his hand on her shoulder. "The doctor said that Sally is in a coma right now. It is going to take some time before she regains consciousness," said Mr. Hanson.

Mrs. Hanson just nodded her head. Officers Woodwind and McDonald walked in the room.

"Thank you so much for finding Sally," Mr. Hanson thanked them.

"We were just doing our job," Officer Woodwind said. "We still have to find out who really did this to her. The fingerprints on Sally's clothes were not Mike's."

"What?" Mrs. Hanson asked.

"They were some guy's named Lewis Driver. Plus, we still have those witnesses from the party who said Mike was there the whole time the night Sally disappeared," Officer McDonald interrupted.

"Did you say Lewis Driver?" Mrs. Hanson asked astonishingly.

"Yes, why, did you know him?" Officer McDonald asked.

"He is Mike's best friend and Sally's, too. I brought him up the night of the argument," Mrs. Hanson said.

"Wow, then we need to talk to this kid!" Officer Woodwind said.

"Also, ask Mike about it because it is going to take Sally some time before she remembers anything," Mrs. Hanson started to cry.

Mr. Hanson whispered, "Thanks, gentlemen."

"Sure," whispered back Officer Woodwind.

"Thank you guys, for everything," Mrs. Hanson said.

"Sure," both officers replied as they walked out.

Back at the police station the officers were tough with Mike. Mike remembered Lewis saying something about liking Sally and how he couldn't have her because Mike was dating her. Sally just thought they were friends and didn't want to date Lewis. That was hard for Lewis.

When they were done with the questioning, the officers went to get Lewis to bring him to the station. Lewis wouldn't talk inside the confession room. Officer McDonald slammed his hand down on the table and got right in his face. "Lewis, we already know that you did it. We have your fingerprints on Sally's clothes, and people have told us that you have had secret emotions for Sally. So, you better confess, now!"

Lewis got the point and started right from the beginning. "Okay! Sally called me right after she and her mom had a fight. She told me how her mom didn't want her to date Mike and all of that. I did what any best friend would do, calmed her down and told her that she needed to go to bed. She called me up again and was saying how she just couldn't fall asleep and needed to talk to someone. Since she couldn't talk to her mom about it, she wanted to talk to me. We both decided to meet at Mike's cabin, because he said that anyone is welcome. We met up in Beaverhead Forest. When we were walking up to the cabin, she was walking behind me and all of a sudden she screamed and hit the ground, hard! I quickly turned around to see that she tripped on some vines that grew on the path, and hit her head. She was knocked out. I carried her all the way up to the cabin and laid her down on the bed in the guest cabin. I tried to wake her up, but she was knocked out for a long time. Finally, she started talking about all this weird stuff. I was really worried about her! I put her under the covers and told her everything was going to be okay. Then I heard something, so I got the key and locked her in. I got out of there as fast as I could. I thought she'd be okay."

"You never even thought to tell us about her being up there?" Officer Woodwind asked angrily.

"I thought I'd let you guys do your job," Lewis answered smartly.

"Do you think we did it well?" Officer McDonald replied.

"Yes, but it did take you awhile to catch the right guy," Lewis said deviously.

"So you admit it?" Officer McDonald said.

"I got to visit Sally every day. I took really good care of her, and had her for *myself* finally! Those were the best months of my life."

“Sorry Mr. Driver, but you are under arrest for kidnapping,” Officer Woodwind said.

Life As A Teenage Girl

by Rachel Menter

Life as a thirteen-year-old girl
Is a roller coaster ride.
The peer pressure,
Drugs,
Cosmetics,
Aggression,
And trauma fully spirals down
From this point.
I strive to remain flawless,
Yet I utter it doesn't matter.

I keep a burden on my soul,
And I haven't fully grasped it.
There has occurred an alteration into a woman
But am I prepared for it?
I see people doing drugs,
And I say that it is wrong.
Will I sit in their spot in high school?
I don't know what to expect.

Am I being myself,
Or am I acting like them?
I have seen girlfriends alter
From pretty to way too much makeup.
That was tough to digest.
I strive not to worry and be myself,
But I am fearful
I won't have friends.

I have four years of high school to go.
They will be gone through alone.
My sister will be departing for college next year.

Although she is not always
The correct person to look up to,
Who will I turn to?

I don't want change
But change isn't always bad.
Variation is a part of life.
I am afraid to modify my surroundings.

Thoughts scatter through your head.
Actions speak louder then words,
And that isn't always for the better.
Strive to listen to yourself and your thoughts.
It will be a difficult task,
But who will be around to help us?

Streets

by Kasee Godwin

The thing that I remember most is the smell of garbage—putrid, rotting, wasting away in cheap, flimsy trash cans. Then I remember the taste of garbage—stuff mixed with junk mixed with more garbage. Sometimes, April and I would go to vomit after realizing the junk that we had just forced down our throats was a slime-covered toy or something like that. April took extremely ill after eating a piece of rotting fish wrapped in some tin foil.

The worst thing was that I did not know where to go. My mother? No, she is too high to worry about her own daughters. My father? The problem would be finding him at which casino. Now he just waits by the door hoping that some stupid tourist will have a ten-dollar bill hanging out of their pocket. My father says he only takes their money to try to get a better life for us. That's not true, because he loses the money quicker that he gets it.

No, there's no one to turn to. Marsha disappeared two months ago. Two months. It seems like more time when I see it in writing. That means it has been four months since we were thrown on the streets. That brings me to the place where our family's dilemma started.

It's my father's fault that we are here. Not ALL his fault, but mostly his. There was my mom who didn't catch her husband before he was too far gone. Sometimes I even think that we, his own kids, weren't enough to satisfy him.

The first time the arguments between my parents about gambling happened, my family and I were living in a huge Manhattan apartment. Their screams rung out and echoed in the large place.

Then our first family move took place. It was a smaller, three-bedroom apartment in New York City. We kept losing money like a hole in a fish tank. So we moved again, for the last time. It was a one-bedroom apartment with a kitchenette and a foldout sofa. Mom and dad slept in the twin bed, Marsha and baby April slept on the couch, and I was on the floor. It was that relocation to that particular neighborhood that introduced Marsha to heroin, which didn't help our funds very much. Mom worked minimum wage at McDonald's, but when that wasn't enough she started dealing drugs.

So that left Dad, April and me (who was only three). Dad still hadn't gotten the flyer that said, *"WE'RE BROKE! GIVE IT UP!"* So he went to "The New York Winner" every morning and stayed there until his funds ran out. There is NO WAY that he would stop before his money was completely gone.

I remember seeing a tee shirt once that proudly proclaimed, *"Men plan ahead by buying TWO cases of beer."* I can't help but wonder if alcohol would have been a better addiction—at least he would have a headache and an upset stomach the morning after to remind him of his selfish behavior. But there seems to be no hangover effect with the gambling addiction.

To make a long story as short as possible, my family ended up on the streets. I couldn't take it. April didn't deserve this, and neither did I. Mom should have been more perceptive in the beginning, and Marsha certainly didn't help by taking Mom's runaway cash for drugs. But Dad is to fault for so much more.

What really set me off was seeing Emerald again. I was out on the streets as usual. The day before had been April's fourth birthday; everyone forgot except me. The only thing that I could give her was a baby doll's head that I found in the dump. I remember seeing the tapes from my fourth birthday. My mom ordered a circus, and I invited my whole preschool. It was so great compared to poor, underprivileged April.

Anyway, you might be wondering who Emerald is. She was my best friend before our first move. We were called the "Princesses of Marsden Academy," even though we were only freshmen. Then, I started public school and never saw her again.

Well, there I was at my usual begging spot, a nightclub that ironically is called "The Spot." That is the type of club where only the elite was welcome. It seemed very out of character to see the Emerald I knew at "The Spot." She was accustomed to guys taking her out to fancy restaurants, not the clubby kind of girl.

I saw her, but she didn't see me. It seemed like she had new princess friends, and now she was the queen. It was at that exact moment that I made my decision. I didn't want April to live her life on the streets, and I didn't want it either.

Three days after, I set out to do something about my family's lifestyle. I wanted to get a job, but apparently there aren't many people in New York City who trust a homeless sixteen-year-old, so I did the only thing in my power: I went to church.

I wasn't raised on religious principles, but the nuns said that was okay. They gave me a list of some of the adoption homes and wished me well on my "spiritual journey." Later, I took April to the third name on the list. It was the hardest choice I ever had to make.

As I reached the doorstep, I stooped down to talk to April. I gave her the letter that told the owners to take very good care of April Ann Roberts. I also said that her sister, Carmen Marie Roberts, would be back to get her in three years (that's when I would be nineteen), so April WAS NOT up for adoption. She just needed a place to stay. Only fate controlled what happened next.

Just as I was on my knees telling April that I was sorry, the front door opened. "Can I help you girls?" A chubby woman with cinnamon brown hair was standing there peering at my sister and me with warm, brown eyes that just seemed to understand.

Instead of just saying no and going to one of the other adoption homes, I said "Yes, I would like to speak to you about my sister."

I went inside, and we sat at a long oak table. For the first time in a long time I had a decent-sized, hot meal. No one said a word as April and I anxiously slurped until it was completely gone, which was only a matter of seconds.

We smiled and said thank you. I noticed that children were running all through the house, and I only saw this one woman as an adult.

"Now, you needed to talk to me about your sister?" She smiled as if she knew what I was going to say.

"Yes ma'am, my sister and me. I was wondering if you needed some help with the children here, because I have experience with children," I finished lamely. This was partly true. Once, back in the golden days, my parents cut off my allowance for two weeks, and I babysat twice then. Also, I had been taking care of April for months.

"Your fees?" She asked.

"A room and food for my sister and me until I am of legal age." If I were my old self I would have been embarrassed to ask for anything, but this was different. I stuck my nose up and kept my eyes on this woman.

"Alright, Miss…what did you say your name was, dear?"

"I'm Carmen Roberts, and this is April." My face broke into a huge, toothy, smile. My baby sister and I went up the stairs, and that is how my nightmare ended.

Wishing On A Candle

by Ellie Schultz

Icing laces the gentle corners
Of a three-tiered treasure
The fire licks the air
Until my breath devours it

I prepare myself for all that has come:
The silently screaming applause
And the expectation of growth
But this year has given me nothing more

My body sits enveloped
In someone else's joy
Trapped inside their thoughts
Until I make a wish

Release

by Sarah Overstreet

Taylor hated the dream. Every night it came to her, dark and foreboding, wrapping its shadow around her, smoldering in its joy of predicting her doom. It frightened her, yet she didn't wish it gone. It was almost as if as long as it was caged inside her head, it couldn't wreak havoc in real life. Her friends laughed when she had first confided in them, but now they were worried. Her teachers and family noticed, too. She slept with her lights on. Her A's dropped to C's. She walked as if in a trance, and jumped when spoken to. She lived in her head, guarding the cage of her secret, her fault.

As break neared, Taylor's friends set aside their worries and celebrated. However, Taylor was anything but carefree. The break loomed over her head like the guillotine's blade, and it seemed that all it would take to bring her doom would be the snapping of a thread. What would she, could she, do? Once break came, there would be no more hiding from her concerned parents in her room. She cursed her conscience under her breath, but no one in her class even noticed. By now, they were used to "the schizo's" muttering.

Sometimes she thought it wasn't the secret that held her captive. It was her inability to share it all. Not even her truest friends knew it all. It didn't matter much; Sean and she had already broken up, but Sean was a childhood friend. She got chills to think that only she and HE knew exactly what had happened.

The break arrived, and Taylor found herself spending more and more time finding hiding places so that she could have a break from her parents. They suddenly had more of an interest in her social life than their own. They were constantly encouraging her to leave the house, to go to the mall, a friend's house, or—as they got more desperate—a club. Taylor was not interested, thank you very much. *"If only they had shown this much interest that night and stayed home instead of flying to New York for the party of one of their clients,"* she thought bitterly. She suspected they had been seeing a shrink.

One day (she didn't even know what day of the week it was and didn't care, either), she woke up to breakfast in bed, was blindfolded, and carted off for a "surprise." Taylor was a little shocked that they would shrink to bribery, but she gave it little thought and started contemplating the abyss of darkness behind her blindfold. If she'd been paying attention, she would have noticed that her parents' smiles were obviously fake, and that there was a grim absence of sound emanating from the front of the car.

They arrived, and Taylor removed to find herself in her science classroom, surrounded by her family, friends, Sean, and there—in the corner—him. He stepped forward, to her surprise, and addressed her, "Taylor, we all care deeply about you, and we're worried. For the past month you've done nothing but sit around and mutter to yourself. Are you okay? We told your parents about the party, and they don't blame you."

Taylor spun around, with a question in her eyes, demanding a reply from her parents. When the answer was not immediate, her eyes grew large, and tiny droplets gathered on her eyelashes, giving her parents the answer to her depression.

"Oh, honey," Taylor's mom finally choked out. "We'll always love you, no matter what you do. You shouldn't worry us like that!"

It was as if someone had lifted twenty pounds off Taylor's shoulders. She straightened, and the cage opened, releasing the shadow into the world, where it disappeared. Taylor smiled inside. This was most definitely not how her dream had progressed.

But there was still one small lingering darkness. She cast a tentative glance at Sean. He smiled and gave her a hug. Almost imperceptibly, he whispered in her ear, "I know," and released her. It needed no more explanation. He then announced in a stage whisper for all to hear, "Follow your heart, and remember, no one can hold you back but you."

She hardly spared a grateful smile before launching herself into his arms. Taking the cue, Taylor's parents exited with her, offering rides to all. No one noticed Sean stop for a split second in the doorway, a mysterious smile on his face.

Life

by Anderson Wathen

The struggles of life that we endure,
The hits we take, the sacrifices we make
The pains life makes, the way it aches
And the losses of those you love
Will make you think you can take it no more.
But be strong and God will help you through each day.
Walk into the darkness and become the light.
Life is beautiful—the ones you'll love
And the lives you'll touch along the way.
Reach out for your dreams
With great diligence and persistence,
Follow your heart, ignore those who doubt.
Spark upon your new existence
Once you have achieved your goal,
You'll stand on top and you shall say,
"The best part of it was not achieving my dream
And being where I am today.
It was the ones I loved
And the lives I touched along the way."

Mary

by Gwen Pierson

I sighed as I opened yet another of the cardboard boxes that filled the tiny apartment. The never-ending buzz of traffic drifted up from the busy New York street below. I threw wads of crumpled packing paper behind me and reached inside the box. I pulled out a dusty photo album and quickly flipped through the yellowing pages, but one picture made me pause. It was a picture of Mary. She had been my best friend for, well, for forever. But that one terrifying day will never leave my memory.

We met in kindergarten at the schoolhouse in the small town of Cullman, Alabama. We clicked right away and were instant friends. In the years that followed, we were inseparable. I remember how we would put on our mothers' fancy dresses and play tea party. "Mary, would you like another tart?" I would ask.

"Oh yes, they are scrumptious," she would reply in the best British accent. These conversations were always followed by a fit of giggles. I can never remember laughing so hard.

During our teenage years, Mary became very beautiful. She had wavy black hair that shone like a blanket of diamonds and a smile that was as contagious as a thousand laughing children. We branched out and made other friends but still remained as close as ever.

In high school, we barely saw each other but still made the extra effort to keep in contact. Then there was the night at the railroad tracks that changed everything.

We sneaked out one night to meet some friends at the old train tracks not far away. The tracks were old and shaky but still in use, and were also a popular hangout spot. I had a sinking feeling that something was about to spin out of control. Mary sensed my fear. She squeezed my hand and smiled, "Don't worry, Kell, nothing can go wrong."

"Of course not," I replied with fake enthusiasm in my voice, but inside, my stomach was still doing flip-flops.

After that, I recall very little. I remember a flash of light and hitting my head, but the next thing I knew, I was lying in a hospital with two broken legs, a few cracked ribs, an unbelievable ache in my head, and a group of people standing around me. What was going on? I tried to sit up, but the pain in my back forced me back down.

My mother stepped forward and took my hand. "Kelly, honey…there has been an accident." She paused and took a deep breath. "That night at the train tracks, you were standing on them, and a train came. I guess you didn't hear it coming, but by the time you noticed, it was too late. Mary jumped in and pushed you out of the way…she saved your life." I tried to digest all that she was telling me.

"I would like to see her now," I said. It hurt to talk.

"I'm afraid that won't be possible," my mother's voice trailed off, and she did not try to hide the tears in her eyes. Suddenly, I became alarmed.

"But she's okay, right…Mom, she's okay…isn't she? Mom! Answer me!" I was practically shouting now, and a nurse came in and shushed me. My mother swallowed hard as if the words were stuck in her throat.

"Kelly, Mary has gone to a better place. She is dead."

After the accident, my broken bones healed and my bruises faded, but the mental scars stayed with me forever. Tears still trickle down my face when I think about it today, fifty years later. Even though I am an old woman now, sixty-five to be exact, I still don't know why what happened, happened. But, everything happens for a reason, and God must have kept me here because he has some greater purpose for me here on earth. Mary was the best friend I ever had, and I will never forget her. And, I know that when my time comes, and I pass on, she will be standing there at those pearly gates waiting for me.

Spring

by Lauren V. Muller

Of all of the seasons, I like spring the best,
Robins adorn the skies with bright red chests,
Tulips and daffodils peep up from the ground,
Basking in the warm sunbeams that they have found,
The woods come alive in blossom and bud,
After a cool rain the streets are dappled with glistening mud,
An intense new sun appears over the crest,
These are the reasons I like spring the best.

Worn Leather

by Marissa Nicole Duhaime

I was born in a leather-working shop that smelled of sweat and burning rubber. Four days after my birth, I was shipped out to Fort Gordon with my brothers and sisters. I am a pair of brown, sturdy Army boots. I was assigned to a nervous, but buff private by the name of Benjamin Gordon. His friends and family called him Ben. He worked very hard and worked me equally hard. Soon it was time to leave boot camp and go into World War II.

Ben had a wife who was two months pregnant with their first child. He also had a cousin named Rosy. He had known her since she was one hour old. He was twenty-one and she was thirteen. They were so close that she could sometimes read his mind. When he told her that he was going off to WWII, she did not understand. You see, he had enlisted, not been drafted, and she had not wanted him to. She spent the night with him and his wife, Diana, the night before he left. All night she cried.

"But why do you have to go, Ben?" Rosy asked over and over again.

"Because it is my duty, Munchkin," he said soothingly, using his pet name for her.

"I don't care about duty; I care about you!" she cried defensively.

That night, Rosy cried herself to sleep, thinking about all the horrors that Ben would see and have to endure. She dreamed about the Nazis capturing and torturing her precious cousin. She dreamed of his ship sinking. She also dreamed of him being pelted with machine gun bullets. No one in the Gordon household slept well that night.

The next morning, it was time; time for Ben and me to embark for Europe and the terrible war that lay there for us. He kissed Diana tenderly.

"I love you. Send me a telegram when the baby is born," he said, choking on his words.

"I will. Please come home safe," she begged.

"I will try," he said, turning away so she could not see his emotions.

Ben turned to Rosy. She threw herself at him, hugging him with all her might, not wanting to ever let go.

"Don't leave me," she sobbed.

"I don't have a choice," he said, trying to be a man and not cry. He failed that mission terribly.

They all hugged and kissed until it was time to go. He walked away from them and climbed aboard the old, dirty, smelly bus. He waved goodbye through a dusty window. The bus suddenly lurched around a corner, and too soon he couldn't see them any more.

The ship ride over was cramped and gloomy. Men didn't know what to expect. The media did not truly cover all the horrors in WWII, so people did not know what to expect. Ben and I thought that we would see no bloodshed or people on their deathbed. Boy, were we ever naive.

We landed and marched through the beat-up roads that were really the paths to the gates to Bergen-Belsen. The camp raged with typhus. Ben was exploring the camp when an elderly woman fell out of a tent. Ben bent down to help her up, but stopped short. The woman had fallen because she was dead. He was not ready for this kind of tragedy, and many a tear fell down upon me. That period of time felt like an eternity. He gently put the woman down and continued on. That is just one of the many horrors we experienced those long days. He saw many dead and many who wished to die. One man called him a saint and fell to his knees. There was another boy he took a liking to and sat beside his bed all afternoon. He held his hand while he left this world. George was only thirteen, the same age as Rosy.

When Ben came back after eight long years, Rosy had just finished college and was engaged. She was the first one who saw him and ran to him.

"Well, well. Look here. I guess you're not a munchkin any more, hey?" he said with tears in his eyes.

The teenager he had left was now a lawyer and about to marry. His wife came up to him with seven-and-a-half-year-old Ben Jr., a young, bright, blue-eyed, sandy-brown-haired, freckled boy. Ben's eyes welled up. His own son did not know him. That would change.

Ben has no need for me now. I bring back painful memories, too painful for him to remember. He gave me to Rosy, who put me in a place of honor beside the fireplace. She has three children and one grandchild, with triplets on the way. Ben has six of his own, with ten grandchildren and one great-grandchild, who is named George and is two months old. He has not forgotten the old woman and the others he watched die, and neither will I.

Big Faucet

by Mallory Keeble

This heavenly place
So divine in unique sanctity
Water running rapidly off a skyscraping cliff
An excluded realm of beauty, this dazzling faucet
Filled with wondrous life
This heavenly place

This serene place
Little fish swimming vigorously in tiny pools
Plants growing without disturbance over
The rocky surface of this illuminating faucet
This serene place

This solitary place
A quiet calm site to reflect on thoughts
No anxieties at this immense faucet, no tumultuous clatter of city life
This solitary place

There They Go!

by Amanda Nicole McGahee

I never enjoy myself more than when I'm watching my dad, Sean McGahee, drive his #29 Limited-Late-Model racecar around the dusty, muddy, sweaty, and extremely loud track of Toccoa Speedway! He and Walter Welch (a.k.a. Squirrel) started racing go-carts quite a few years ago. Then, about three years back, they decided to start racing cars. "It's for safety reasons," they assured us. So far, racing cars has been an enormous success.

It's amazing watching the combination of man with machine speed ninety m.p.h. around a small, muddy circle, passing cars one by one while still gaining speed. The way the incredibly powerful motor sounds with a simple flick of the ignition switch makes me jump out my skin. I get that helpless-as-a-baby feeling sitting there watching and cheering him on. Even though he can't hear me through the noise of the car, he sees me through the countless clots of red Georgia mud on the thick shield of the helmet protecting his head in the small, crowded cockpit.

Suddenly, I see the left front tire come off the ground as he pounds on the gas coming out of turns one and two. I can actually see the bottom of the car from the top of the twelve-foot-tall trailer. It almost makes me think he's gonna flip over! At the last moment, he manages to steer the car down the straightaway towards turns three and four. "Whew!" I sigh in relief. Occasionally he does have a wreck, and it scares me out of my wits! I can't complain though. When it comes to racing, he's pretty cautious.

I am always relieved when he slowly drags himself out of the bent-up car wearing that "Well-how-do-I-look?" face. When he takes a glance at the car as it slowly rolls behind the tow truck into the pits, that face changes to an "Oh-well-at-least-we-tried" face or an "Oh-well-what-the-heck" face. The car is pretty mangled up, the hood is smashed, the sheet metal is all dented up, and it hurts just to look at it. The aftereffect of the wreck isn't all that nice, but at least he didn't get hurt. However, he and Squirrel have lots of work to do over the next week so they can be ready for another blood-rushing race next Saturday night.

My dad is so impressive in his car on the racetrack! Even though he's never won a race, most of the time he places in the top five. I'm so proud at school on Monday morning as I tell my friends how well my dad and his #29 Limited-Late-Model racecar preformed in the race. They say that they can already see the joy in my face as I come down that long stretch of hallway to the lockers. However, they'll never know that same joy and pride I felt in the stands on Saturday night!

Mountain

by Stephen Patrick Byrne

Mountains
Like walls
Make it hard to walk
Standing on the Appalachian
Trail I feel small to its size rising
From the ground like fire the trees shield
Your view. My Mom is taking this beautiful
Picture and I am happy she is with us today. On
A Sunday I admire the colors. Standing at the end
Of the trail I admire its beauty. In North Georgia the
Leaves change color. I love the mountains and they make
Me feel home.

Alone In The End: Journal Of A Creek

by Brenna Conley

Plunk. Hoe hits dirt, hard from winter frost. I stand up, stretch. My back is sore from too much labor. Maralki is ill again today. I have agreed to do her share of the work, so she is at home resting. Maralki is my sister, my only. Sisters do things for each other. I drop the hoe on the ground and trudge over to the shade. Father awaits me. He doesn't look at me as he pecks my cheek and drones a blessing. I look down as I feel tears gather in my eyes. He has refused to look at me since my mother died. I think it is because I look like her. I got my Nassis' eyes and her strong chin, he used to say.

I stand tall, staring at him, trying to make him look at me. He turns his back toward me. "Suanna!" I hear a squeal from behind me.

"Etawah!" I cry with happiness. Finally someone to brighten my day. When I see her, I become silent in awe. I gape. I see around her left eye a painted half-moon. This means she is to be wed. My hanging mouth forms itself into a smile, the biggest smile ever.

"Zanawbe!" she says, in answer to my silent question. Zanawbe is a brawny, young warrior. I squeal. We hug each other, eyes streaming. How blessed she is, her purpose fulfilled. I imagine Etawah in a few years, after the wedding, when her belly is round, and her cheeks bright from cooking his dinner over a low fire. She sighs. She seems to be imagining the same thing. We hook arms and stumble off, exhausted from work, but happy to no end. We reach my hut, and we part. She touches my brow, as a goodbye.

I trudge into the hut, my head pulsing. I think the sun is getting to me. I see Maralki on the floor, upon a mat. She is very pale. I kneel beside her. I speak, comforting her, and wishing her well. I tell her of Maralki's good fortune, and of the day in the field. I tell her she looks better, which is a lie. She smiles weakly. I rise and move toward the fire. It is low, about to die. I jostle the embers, blowing on them, watching for any sparks. No, it is dead. We can afford no more wood, but the hut is so cold. I pull my deer hide vest tight about my shoulders, and look sadly at Maralki. If only I could find a way to keep it warm, for her sake. I lie down upon my mat, without removing my outer garments. I am too tired. I close my eyes and allow the night to fall over me like a blanket and wash away my weariness.

The sun shines warm upon my face. I arise. I know that something is not right. Father is gone. He sleeps beside the door, and he has left, taking his bow and arrow with him. This would not be strange but that father usually sleeps until the sun has risen up directly into the center of the sky. I pick up my mat and toss it to a corner of the hut. I glance over, Maralki is still asleep. I dart out, and stop.

The sky is ablaze with the most beautiful colors I have ever seen—the brightest gold, like sunflowers in spring, and the deepest hue of red, like the blood of man. The colors were curling up into the sky, and above that, smoke floating over everything like a fog. My village is on fire. I cry out, looking around to see if anyone else has noticed. They have. They are running all over, pots filled with water, but I can see that the small amounts of water are never going to quench such an awesome fire. They see this, too. They give up now and stand stock still, staring at the brilliant flames that rise like a tsunami over our village. I see other people now, too. They are very different from us. Their skin is an odd, pale color, like ghost men. They run toward us, shouting at each other. This is their fire. I am filled with a rage at them, and I made to myself an unspoken promise. I will not let these men win.

I close my eyes to the smoke stinging my eyes, as I stumble blindly back to my hut. I speak to Maralki. I tell her to get up. I tell her we have to leave. And I tell her to ask God for protection. I help her up. She is too slow. By the time we get out, the fire will be to our hut. I look at Maralki, measuring her. She is small and wiry, and I am strong from twelve years of hard labor.

I decide. I scoop her up in my arms and run. I do not feel, I do not see, I do not stop. I cannot, because of my promise. We will make it. My lungs are burning, and my arms are strained with effort. I collapse. And Maralki cries out. The flames lick my ears, but I cannot move any longer. I have run across the whole village, it seems. I hear voices. My eyes close and I surrender myself to darkness.

My eyes cannot be opened. They are stuck shut with sleep. I listen and stay totally still. It is all I can do. Right now, I am defenseless. I fall back asleep even with this thought on my mind. Scream. My eyes shoot open, and I bolt upright. My eyes scan the litter of slain men and women for Maralki. Somewhere. I bite my lip with frustration. Father. It comes back to me. Where is he? Surely he is not harmed. They would not touch the chief of the village. My eyes linger on the body of Kuasd, the medicine man. He lay with arms folded across his chest and a hole in his side. I look away.

Maralki. There, next to Kuasd, she lays. I cannot tell whether she is alive. I sprint to her and touch her arm. She is cold. I cry out. I cannot think. My throat hurts dreadfully, and I feel as if I have been stabbed through the heart. I can't breathe with this immense sorrow upon me. I look wildly around. I see no one alive. No one. It is the most terrible feeling to be alone. I feel like I am an island, one living in a sea of dead, and I feel like I don't deserve it. My breath returns and my eyes glaze. I can't cry. It is too terrible a sadness for me to cry. I lay down. I press my cheek against her cheek. My sister. Let me leave, I pray. This world is not a good place, where men with white skin come and take life. I don't want to stay. I have lost, and they have won.

I close my eyes, and my last thought is of my mother, kissing me, holding me, whispering, "A nea, a nea, wa um eech sa suwaa, lay ton na suwaa ayai." ("My child, my child, I wait for you. I love you, and this life loves you"). And I whisper, though my throat is hoarse, "Nassi, um wa trai na." (Mother, I'm coming to you). In the morning, when Hernando de Sotoz's men came to look for those still alive to take captive, they found a young girl of about twelve years, clinging to the neck of a small child. They shook their heads when they found she was dead. If only, they said, she could have made it through the night. One man stayed behind to mourn for this dead child he did not know, and to pray for her soul. He knelt beside her and put his hand upon her cheek, where he found frozen tears.

Between Me And You

by Diana Orquiola

Flooding streets,
My tears rained;
Rolling upon my cheeks,
With the blood in my veins.

The pain didn't stop.
The pain didn't kill.
The pain just made me suffer,
I searched for a will.

Rocks were thrown,
The ride wasn't smooth.
The tire popped,
"What could I do?"

Then you came along,
Pushing through the crowds.
You took my hand,
Followed you around.

One by one,
The scars disappeared.
One by one,
The wounds healed.

You filled my heart,
With more than it could store,
You said, "I love you."
But I love you more.

More than words
Can ever say.
More than the days,
We drifted our ways.

"You're like the cherry on my sundae,"
You're the whipped cream on my pie.
"You're my ray of sunshine,"
You're everything but mine.

We sang with a reason,
A reason unknown,
We sang together,
"I Won't Spend Another Night Alone."

And then it happened.
A nightmare coming true,
Like dying in a car crash,
Not knowing why, it hit you.

Memories are made,
Then quickly faded away.
The pain comes back,
For it will stay.

The walls are closing in,
Now it's hard to breathe.
You cut my heart out,
Now it bleeds.

"I never intended to hurt you,
I never did."
You lied to me,
But I still can forgive.

"I only love you as a sister,
Nothing more.
So please quit crying,
You're nothing more."

And I know what you want.
You want me to let you go,
You've already forgotten about me,
Like the grass beneath the snow.

And I stand in the corner,
All alone.
Crying my heart out,
You can hear my moans.

Every tear burnt,
Every tear I cried for you.
You were the only guy I cried for.
This was definitely something new.

So what would you do, if I died?
Would a teardrop roll down your eye?
Cry, cry, that's all what everyone would do.
But if you died, I'd die too.

It's hard to get over something,
If it's something you never had.
If that something was love,
And never felt it back.

You don't see the signs I see,
It's telling me, that we're meant to be.
Like the sun shining, making beautiful weather.
Like two rivers, flowing together.

So when I say goodbye,
I'll mean it forever.
Just for you,
I'll pretend it never…

I'll pretend it never happened,
though, it isn't true
I'll pretend nothing happened
Between me and you.

Picture Of The Past

by Elizabeth V. Hill

"Leslie, I found another one!" came a cheerful voice from the attic.

"Coming, honey," I shouted back. As I trotted up to the attic, I hoped this was the one I was looking for. When I reached the attic, I picked up the picture. It wasn't the one, but it sure brought back memories.

"Mommy," I was hollering, "Mommy, I need help." Hearing my pitiful cries ringing in my thirty-seven-year-old ears, I drifted into the year 1955.

"Mmmoommyy," I started to cry, "I ffeelll ddown oon a …" My sentence was cut off by one long sob.

My mother was running towards me with a scared, yet brave, expression on her face. She started to nurse the petite, but painful, wound. Every time she touched my scratch with her stiff apron, I winced with pain.

She picked up my little body and carried me carefully back to the house. She set me down on the cold bathroom sink. She reached into a cabinet and pulled out a liquidy substance, which I know now was hydrogen peroxide, and dabbed it on my cut. Then, she covered it up with a large, tan cloth.

It was painful, so I sat on the floor by the warm fire and played with my dolls all day. Not having to move, because my mother did everything for me, made my day very relaxing. Even at lunch, I was treated special when I got to eat on the floor with my dolls. My mother knew I could get up, but she still let me sit around like a sack of potatoes. That night, she even let me sleep on the big bed in her and Daddy's room

When I awoke the next day, the photographer was already at our house, ready to take our picture. Mommy, Daddy, and I got all dressed up. I got to wear my pretty pink Sunday dress with the blue coat. Since we wanted to look wonderful, Mommy put a different bandage on my scrape. It was much smaller and a pretty, white color.

"Leslie! Anyone home? Are you okay?" I drifted back to

reality, thanks to my husband's concerned voice.

"I'm okay, really I am." I was trying to convince him without much luck. "I was just thinking."

"What about?" he asked in a questioning voice.

"I was thinking about my Mom and Dad. This picture brings back all the memories from then," I responded in a dazed voice.

"Do you want to tell me about it? Please?" he begged with a childish twinkle in his bright blue eyes.

"Well…do you really want me to?"

"Yes! I love to hear your stories," came his childish voice again.

"All right. It all started around noon. I was playing outside when…" As I told him the story it was like telling a child their favorite story over and over again. He never gets tired of it.

7th grade

Goodbye Zimbabwe (Hello Atlanta)

by Kaye Otten

I remember
Hearing the roosters crowing in the morning
Smelling the fires on the roadsides
Tasting the hot sadza
Seeing the children chasing the goat
Feeling peace and joy

At first
I heard the rush of cars and people shouting
Smelled the pollution in the air
Tasted the grease in the food
Saw a flood of unknown people
Felt scared

And now
I hear friends laughing
Smell the perfume of plants
Taste the lemonade in summer
See friends and family
Feel familiar peace and joy,
Restored

Halloween's Curse

by Danielle Jackson

Noooooooo! Tomorrow's Halloween. Halloween is the worst holiday in the history of mankind...or should I say monsterkind? My name is Jomenikelofoogey, or Joe for short. I'm a monster—well, not really. When I was little, I got too close to a nuclear plant and drank some water that came from the spring where they dumped their waste. You can guess what happened. I got mutated...a lot. So now I have to wear a costume every day, and that's a costume of a "normal" human. On Halloween I don't, but I wish I could. My mom never lets me. "Too much money," she says. Great. Now it's Halloween eve and everything is going wrong.

My friends and I were walking along my street, talking about our costumes for the upcoming night.

"I'm going as a gypsy!" Connie said with excitement.

"A gypsy?! How boring. Halloween is about being scared, not being "mesmerized." I'm gonna be a grizzly bear!" yelled Jared.

"Hah! A grizzly? Scary? You are sooo wrong. What about a zombie, the terrifying undead, carrying his own brain? Now that's scary!" Drew laughed.

I didn't have a comment to say, and that got my friends curious because I am usually the most talkative of the group. Then, as my mom says, curiosity killed the cat. "What are you gonna be, Joe?" Connie asked, eyes boring a hole in my head.

"Ummm...me?" I said, shaking uncontrollably. I'm sure that they could see my heart beating through my shirt, and all the veins bulging out of my eyeballs.

"You?!" Jared said stupidly and then started laughing his head off. "Only nerds go as themselves, cause they're nerds, no costume needed!" All three of them stared cracking up.

"Oh crud! What am I supposed to say now?" "I mean, I mean, umm...I mean, I'm going as a mutated human-monster." I said, gritting my teeth.

"Cool! That's way better than my idea!" Drew patted me on the back, thinking it was a costume idea. Why are people so weird?

That night I had a nightmare about the upcoming trick-or-treating trip. In the dream I was walking along as my normal self, a human, not a "monster," and all my friends said, "Where's your costume, Joe?" I would always say, "This is my costume." My friends thought I was stupid, so I ran to the nearest nuclear plant, and I got even more mutated. I grew and grew and grew and grew and grew and grew and grew until I was as tall as five Empire State Buildings! Then things went wrong. The bigger I got, the madder I got. Suddenly, my anger unleashed itself. I started stomping on things, destroying buildings, the works. Every monster wishes to do this. Well I don't. Never. I am squashing everything, and people are crying for help. I start crying my eyes out, but I am so big, if I move, I'll squash everything. I woke up, thank goodness, before I could do any more damage.

Like a bolt of lightning, I remembered. It was October 31, a.k.a. Halloween. Aw, man. To prevent going to school, I had the flu, strep throat, measles, mumps, chicken pox, even SARS! My mom didn't buy it. I had to go to school.

That whole day was worse than my nightmare last night. Our class had Halloween parties, and they were horrendous. All we did was play really weird games and eat candy. Wee, so fun. If I had to do this for the rest of my life and never go trick-or-treating, I'd do it.

As soon as we got out of school, I stopped. I thought over all the consequences, and this cloud did NOT have a silver lining. If I went home, my friends and family would make me go. If I ran away, who knows what would happen? Running away could be bad, man, I could even get arrested. At home my friends would at least excuse my looks, it being Halloween and all. I guess I'll go home. Hopefully this year people will not be as lost as the people in my old neighborhood. Gosh, they were out there. I don't know how I survived. They were just...*weird.*

When I got home, it was time.

As soon as I got home, my mom went through the routine. "How was school?" I'd swear she was mocking me then.

"Fine, mom." I always said it with sarcasm, and for some reason she never caught on...(maybe it had something to do with her always hanging out with our "loony" neighbors.)

"And your friends? How are they?" She smiled a smile that could scare off the entire U.S. Army.

"Fine, mom." (Again with the sarcasm.)

"That's good. Start getting ready, because it gets dark around six-thirty now, remember?" Hypothetical question, as usual. It always ends with a hypothetical question. As soon as she goes away, I go to my room and take off my "costume." Now I'm my real self, and you will never feel as bad as I did then. Me, a monster. It just doesn't make sense.

My friends arrived at six-thirty sharp. They were all standing out there, eyes gleaming and huge grins on their faces. They just, stood there, waiting. As soon as I got out there, the nightmare began.

"Whoa...nice costume, Joe!" Connie said. She came over and touched me. "Dang, it's so lifelike and realistic!"

"Yea, you're right! It feels really slimy and icky and gooey, and it looks ugly and oozy and disgusting!" Drew said after coming over and feeling it. "Uhh... Joe, are you okay?" My eyes must have been watering, because they were all staring at me.

"Um, yea." I sniffed. "I'm okay." I wasn't. They were all looking at me. Me as a monster. No costume, no nothing. I was just standing there in my skin. "Come on guys, let's go." We walked to the first house, rang the doorbell, and a nice looking lady came to the door.

"Oh what cute little costumes you are wearing!" Never mind. "A gypsy, a zombie, a grizzly bear, and a...a...a...thing! Yes, a thing!" What a weirdo.

"It's not a costume!" I yelled at the lady. I'm sorry, anger and I don't mix at all.

"Mm-hmm. That's nice. Here's your candy, have a good night!" She waved with a smile similar to my mom's.

"Thanks!" Drew, Jared, and Connie said.

"Wasn't she nice?" asked Jared. "You were a little rude, Joe, of course it's a costume!" Errrgghhh. Would they just mind their own business for once?

"I don't think so. M.Y.O.B."

"Sheesh, what a grouch." Silence.

"Come on, let's go to the next house," Connie finally said. So we did. This time a teenager came to the door.

"Dude, I like your, like, costumes. You! Yeah, you! Zombie guy!"

"Me?" Drew asked stupidly.

"Nah, other guy." Great. He is talking to me. "Your costume is, like, so next-solar-system-on-the-right. So realistic, it's like you aren't wearing a costume. It's totally rad, man. Here's your stuff, now go away." He gave us the candy then slammed the door in our face.

"Goodness… wasn't he just grand?" Jared rolled his eyes.

"Yeah, grand." I said, grimacing.

"All right, so far, I've got about two pieces of candy. Let's get a move on, okay?" Sometimes Drew can be *really* annoying. The rest of the trip was pretty much the same. Everyone saying how cool my costume was, except one house.

We went up to the house, rang the doorbell, and an old lady came to the door. When she saw me, things went wrong, terribly wrong. She started screaming and crying that the world was coming to an end and that the devil had come to her door. Then she got a metal pole and was yelling at the top of her lungs that she wasn't ready to go down yet. We didn't stay there long at all. We hightailed it out of there as soon as she got the pole. That was probably the only time I laughed that whole night.

At the end of our route, we had about eight pounds of candy, a pretty good night, I guess. Candy good, Halloween in general, terrible. This neighborhood has an equal number of weirdos. We said goodbye and went home at about ten-thirty. As soon as we got home, my mom came up to me, that ridiculous grin on her face again.

"How was it, good? Get much candy?"

"Yeah, I guess. Too many lunatics," I laughed, remembering the old lady.

"That's not nice to say to people. Go to bed. No candy tonight, you'll get sick and have to go to the doctor. You don't want that, now do you?"

"Nah, I want him to figure out I'm not human..." Sometimes she can be so lost. At least she ended with a hypothetical question again. I went and got in bed and slept soundly for the first time in a month.

The next morning I got a call from Connie. "Guess what? Only 365 days until Halloween!"

NOOOOOOOOOOOOOOOOOOOOOOOOO!!!

Twins

by Kevin and Nicholas Ureda

I
I am
I am intelligent
I am unique
I am curious
I am neither belligerent nor lazy
You
You are
You are trustworthy
You are generous
You are honorable
You are neither weird nor disobedient
We
We are
We are invincible
We are outgoing
We are together
We are neither show-offs or unfaithful
We are brothers
We!

I
I am
I am strong
I am quick
I am cordial
I am neither dimwitted nor underhanded
You
You are
You are loyal
You are patient

You are dependable
You are neither gawky nor malicious
We
We are
We are best friends
We are compatible
We are teammates
We are neither jealous nor combative
We are twins
We!

Losing Faith

by Amanda Stewart

Did you know that fifteen people die each day of leukemia? Well, it's true. This is an inside story of a family that leukemia has touched.

The Turner family lived in San Diego, California, right down the street from the Watsons. Sara Turner was the only child of Faith and Eric Turner. Sara's best friend, Max, was an only child of Deborah Watson, who was divorced. Max and Sara were best friends because they were neighbors, and they had played softball together for years. Their moms had been best friends since college. Her father, Eric, was a hard-working defense attorney. He only saw them late in the evening and on weekends.

Sara's Mom, Faith, worked at Sara's school and was her geometry teacher. Sara only liked her mom as a teacher sometimes, because Faith could help Sara with her homework. Each day at the end of each class, Faith would always tell her students, "Believe in yourself and never lose faith."

Even though Faith was Sara's teacher, she still called her Mrs. Turner in school and Mom at home. Faith did so much at Sara's school, like being the President of the school's PTA committee and the one who makes the school directory. She still found time to clean her own house; many of her friends had housekeepers, but Faith was frugal.

She was so special in God's eyes. She prayed at breakfast, on her way to work, while brushing her teeth, while teaching geometry, while talking to friends on the phone, while watching TV, while writing letters, while setting her alarm clock—but these are just a few of the times she prays. And Faith is not the only devout Christian in her family. Her whole family prayed for the best for themselves and for others. It didn't matter where they were or what they were doing; if someone needed help, they would stop to help them. It didn't matter who they were or how they looked, because looks can be deceiving. Some people can't afford nice clothes, makeup, and fancy hairdressers.

Faith found her best friend, Deborah Watson, when they were in college. Deborah was having a hard time with her books one day, so Faith stopped to help her. Faith and Deborah became such close friends that they moved into the same neighborhood on purpose to be close to each other. That's kind of how Sara and Max met.

On March 17, Sara and Max were walking to school when her cell phone rang. She read the number at the top and realized that the call came from home. She picked up the phone and said hello. When she heard her father's voice, she had to ask him to repeat everything he said. He told her to hurry home after school because there was a package for her. She ran home after school and opened the package and saw that the present was from her Aunt Kelly, who lived up in North Dakota. There was a note inside that said:

Dear Sweet Sara,

I miss you so, so much. I was going to call you but I just can't remember your number. How is everything there? It's still snowing here. Your Uncle Johnny just went to visit Grandma and said that she has the chickenpox, so if you could and you wouldn't mind, would you pray for her? In the next few weeks we will be down in Iowa for the Motorcycle Rally. So are you still making straight A's? Your cousin Bobby doesn't care about school anymore. We would send him to a boarding school where he could learn to care, but we can't afford it right now. Maybe he will learn before high school. Since you guys are the same age, would you mind coming for a visit on your spring break to tutor him? That would be great! I love you!

Always,
Aunt Kelly

Sara looked to see what was in the bottom of the box, and she saw the most precious sight of all. Her aunt had sent her a 4 x 6 inch cross with Jesus on it. Sara began to cry when she saw it. She hated it but at the same time loved it. Sometimes she felt all warmed up by Jesus when she felt his presence, but other times the symbol of the cross made her sad because she hated that Jesus died so violently. Sara's mom fell in love with the cross, so she asked Sara if she could hang it up on the wall where everyone could see it.

The next day at school, she saw Max at his locker. Right when she said hello to him, the bell rang and she was late for her first class of the day. When she walked into first period, her technology teacher, Mr. Walker, gave her three demerits for being late. Furthermore, she had left her homework at home, and he gave her three more demerits.

Then, during seventh period geometry, she saw a substitute teacher sitting in her Mom's chair. After the substitute called roll, he announced that Mrs. Turner had been taken to the emergency room because she fainted and became very ill during fifth period. The substitute didn't realize that Sara was Mrs. Turner's daughter and wondered why Sara ran out of the room.

Sara ran out the back door of the school and did not stop until she got home. When she realized that no one was home, she called her dad's cell phone. Her dad's voice cracked as he said hello. Her dad said he didn't know what was wrong with her mom, but for her to spend the afternoon with their neighbors, Max and Deborah Watson.

As the weeks went on, Faith became sicker. Sara and her father became more concerned. The doctors continued to run tests but could not find the problem. Sara and her father argued about where she would spend her spring break. Sara didn't want to leave her mother, but her father thought it would be best if she kept her mind off her mother for a week. Sara's father won the fight, and Sara spent the week helping her Aunt Kelly and her cousin Bobby.

During spring break, Sara realized that the things she was teaching Bobby were the same lessons her mother had taught her. Bobby's grades had been slipping because he had lost faith in himself. He didn't think he could do the work, so he stopped trying. Sara taught Bobby to have faith in himself, faith in God, and to never stop trying. With a little effort, Bobby got back on track and felt really good about himself and his future. Sara realized that by helping Bobby, he had also helped her by keeping her mind off of her mom.

Toward the end of the week, Aunt Kelly received a phone call. Sara became suspicious because of her aunt's reaction to the phone call. She went from being elated over Bobby's improvement to very quiet and somewhat sad. Kelly announced that they would all be flying Sara home.

When they arrived in Sara's town, they took a cab to the hospital. When they got to the hospital, they noticed Sara's father pacing back and forth in the waiting room. Sara ran to him and embraced him. As she looked up at her father, she noticed his eyes were flooded with tears. Sara froze with fear, and her heart felt like it had been stomped upon. He told her that he had some bad news and some good news. She asked for the bad news first, which was that her mom had leukemia and had only a few days left. The good news was that her mom would be able to spend her last days at home.

On April 22, three days after Faith left the hospital, the doctor visited Faith at home and told them the end was near. After the doctor left, the house was quiet.

After what seemed like forever, there was a knock at the door. Sara answered the door, and there on her porch were all of Faith's geometry students and some former students as well. They crowded into her small house without an invitation and encircled Faith's bed. Faith opened her eyes and saw all the students. She said, "I am going to miss you all."

After a short visit, an update on all the happenings at school, and a few jokes, it was time for them to leave. Most of the students had tears in their eyes, but they knew what needed to be said. In unison, the students repeated their teacher's favorite saying, "Believe in yourself and never lose faith." Faith smiled the biggest smile they remembered seeing in a long time. After they left, they turned to take one last look at the house, and they knew that things would never be the same again.

At 8:36 p.m. the Turners turned off their lights. Even though they lost their beloved Faith that evening, they knew they would never really lose Faith. The lessons she taught them and the love she had given them would always be with them, and no one whose life she had touched would ever really lose Faith.

The "United" States

by Bethany Grace Ray

United means we're together,
no matter how different we are.
On a flag that waves in freedom,
each state has a star.

United means we're together.
We all watched the planes that day.
It happened to every one of us,
we bowed our heads to pray.

United means we're together.
A lot of things we share,
like freedom and peace and heroes.
We take the time to care.

United means we're together,
That's how we'll always be.
I'm thankful to be living
in a country united and free.

The Best I Can Be

by Mary Elizabeth Warnke

I was in my pointe class, holding my leg up in front of me as Miss Mary went around the room making sure we were doing our best…when she came to me.

"Your leg is supposed to be a little higher," she said. I winced as Miss Mary put my leg where it was supposed to be. "Feel the difference?" she asked. I nodded slightly, afraid that if I moved too much I wouldn't be able to hold my leg up.

"Just till the end of the music," I thought to myself.

Hi, I'm Kate. I'm thirteen, and right now I'm in one of my favorite places to be, my pointe class. My other favorite places to be are tap class, jazz class, hip-hop class, ballet class, and home in my bed after a long day of dancing. Standing behind me is my best friend, Emily. She's twelve.

Finally, the music stopped and everyone's legs thudded to the floor. "No!" Miss Mary cried. "You must lower slowly, like the graceful ballerinas you are. Let's try it again." We all groaned as we picked up our legs again. "Now, lower slowly. Good, class, you may go now."

We all got our water bottles, politely thanked Miss Mary and headed to the dressing room. "Oh, my toes!" I moaned. "I think I've got a major blister forming."

"Don't worry about it. In about six months your toes will get used to pointe, and it won't hurt so much," Emily lectured.

"Yeah, yeah, you've told me that before," I said. Emily is the best dancer in the class, I think, and has been on pointe for two years. I always come to her for advice about ballet and pointe, and she always gives it to me.

Emily and I talked as we put on our jazz pants and shoes. "Hey, we've got a ten-minute break before jazz. Want to see if we can watch the older ballet class?" I asked.

"Sure. Maybe we can see their dance for the recital," Emily said. That's just what I wanted her to say. I love watching the older dancers dance, especially Ashley. Ashley is one of the best dancers at my studio. She is three levels higher and three years older than I am.

"I wish I could dance like Ashley; she's so...good!" I whispered to Emily as we were peeking in the door.

"The best," was the quick reply. I watched the graceful movements as Ashley did her solo. Secretly at home when no one's looking, I practice Ashley's part in the dance and her solo. I know that I can't do everything that she can, but I've got her part in her dance down pat. And I think I can do the part just as well as she can.

"Kate, it's time to go to class," Emily said.

"Yeah, I know, but just a sec' longer," I begged.

"Kate, come on! We're going to be late for class!" Emily said.

"Okay, I'm coming," I said, as I took one more look at Ashley.

"I wish I could dance like her," I thought to myself.

Everything went on as normal. Months passed, Christmas came and went, and I kept practicing Ashley's part and hoping that I did it as well as she did. Once when Emily and I were playing around at the studio, I started doing Ashley's solo and thought I saw Miss Mary watching me. But the next time I looked over where she was standing, she was gone. Maybe I imagined it, maybe I didn't.

Yes, everything went on as normal, till May—May 8, to be exact. Well, to be very exact, May 8, 7:10 p.m., twenty minutes before the big end-of-the-year recital started.

"Where's Ashley? She was supposed to be here at fifteen till!" Miss Mary said. Just then the phone rang. "Hello?" Miss Mary said. "Oh, are you sure? Oh, I'm so sorry. Yes, I hope she gets better. Yes, goodbye." Miss Mary hung up the phone. "Ashley fell down a flight of concrete stairs and sprained her ankle. She won't be able to dance."

Backstage went quiet. Everyone knew she was the best dancer in the show.

"Who will do her solo?" a voice from the back asked.

Miss Mary looked around for a second, then she looked right at me. "Kate will."

"But, Miss Mary…"

"I know you can do it, Kate. I've seen you do it before. You do it well, really well. Don't worry about it. Just go out there and be the best you can be, and you'll do great." Miss Mary walked off.

I stood there for a sec', totally panicked. *"What am I doing standing here?"* I thought. *"I've got to practice!"*

For the next twenty minutes I went over the dance again and again, hoping I wouldn't forget something. Then the stagehand said my dance was next. A minute later, the dance before mine was over, the lights went off and we took our places onstage.

The lights went on, the music started, and I froze. I couldn't remember what to do. Panic set in. Then I saw Miss Mary in the wings. I remembered what she had said just twenty minutes before:

"I know you can do it, Kate. I've seen you do it before. You do it well, really well. Don't worry about it. Just go out there and be the best you can be, and you'll do great."

"Be the best you can be, and you'll do great." I thought. *"Be the best you can be. Be the best you can be…"*

Just then, all the dancers left the stage. It was time for my solo. I took one more look at Miss Mary, and I did my solo.

Two minutes and ten seconds later, I gracefully ran into the wings. The dance was over.

As I went to the dressing room to get ready for my next dance, Miss Mary came to me and gave me a hug. "You did it! You just went out there, and you were the best you could be."

"Thanks, Miss Mary," I said.

That night in bed while thinking about the day, I thought to myself, *"It doesn't really matter if I'm as good as Ashley. What matters is that I can be the best I can be."*

Lonely

by David Richman Millard

An oak tree
is standing alone
in the dusty light

It is there
standing
waiting
for travelers
to come
into its soothing shade

Waiting
alone
it welcomes company
without hesitation

Dedicated to my Grandfather

Needles Of Pure Terror

by Collin Carlson

"Wow, it's huge!" I said, as I looked at Aaron's new Lego set.

"It's the new Millennium Falcon. Isn't it cool?!" He asked.

"Yeah, let's play with it."

As I was about to get closer, I remembered that I was supposed to call my parents as soon as I got to Aaron's house. I rushed downstairs, hoping they wouldn't be mad. I got to the little black phone and dialed. "700-555-2927," I whispered under by breath. When they answered, they weren't mad and asked if I wanted to talk to Keith.

"Cough, cough. Hi Collin," he said.

"Hey Keith, how're you feeling?"

"Cough, cough. Better than yesterday," he hacked. "Make it quick…I have to…*cough*…take my medicine."

"Okay, 'bye."

"Poor little guy," I thought, as I went upstairs. He had some pretty bad croup.

We started playing. Aaron was explaining all that the Millennium Falcon could do, when I heard a really loud siren.

"Wow, that sounds close. Do you think it could be in our neighborhood?" I asked.

"No, it's just loud because all the leaves are gone and you can hear a lot more."

"You're probably right, but I think I will call home again, just in case."

When I called, there was no answer. *"Well, that's weird, they wouldn't leave with out telling me. Maybe they didn't get to the phone in time."* I called again, but still no answer.

"Hey Collin, hurry up," Aaron called.

"I have to go home and…um, get a toy," I lied.

When I got on my bike, I moved my feet at least a million rotations per second. When I reached the top of the hill, I saw the unthinkable: a loud, blaring fire truck on my street.

The first thought in my mind was that it was at MY house.

"No, that's not possible. That's completely impossible. It has to be the neighbors' house. It just has to be. Nothing that bad could ever happen at my house. My neighbor's washing machine must have started to smoke. Yeah, that's it."

As I rode closer, a thousand needles of pure terror struck my mind. Two huge, red fire engines were in my driveway, followed by an ambulance. When I got to my front yard, I chucked my bike into the bushes and ran after a man in blue and white.

I screamed, "What happened?!"

"I don't know, kid. Why don't you go in and find out?"

I ran in. I saw my mom and dad with Keith. He was sitting on the kitchen counter. A paramedic with a clipboard was asking questions. I felt like telling him to get out of there. I squirmed to keep quiet. Then I saw that my mom had a relieved look on her face, so I just waited.

When the paramedic left, I asked them what had happened. Mom said that Keith's croup got so bad that he couldn't breathe for about a minute. She put his head in the freezer, and Dad called 911. He started breathing again and was going to be fine.

I was amazed that was all that happened. You know, I was really lucky.

The Ocean Of Heaven

by Shelby Curran

Here lies the ocean of heaven before me.
Will I walk in the blue-green of fear
And the white foam wings of glory?
The ocean of heaven is
Blue, calm, quiet, yet roaring.
Black, dark, dreary, yet soaring.
Emotions rising,
Passion, hate, love, fear,
Relaxing, horrifying, deadly drear.
The blueness of this ocean before me,
Reminds me of the darkened glory.
Dreary, horrifying, darkness of black,
Because of this, will I turn back?
Quiet, relaxation, soft breezy wind,
Because of this, will I go in?
The greenness of this ocean before me,
Reminds me of a jolting story.
Envy, evil, jealous stacks of lack,
Because of this, will I turn back?
Easy, flowing, beckoning wind,
Because of this, will I go in?
Here lies the ocean of heaven before me.
Will I walk in the blue-green of fear
And the white foam wings of glory?

Mallory's Confession

by Taylor Nicole Amos

We were riding in the jeep when it suddenly ran out of gas!

Hmmm, maybe I should start from the beginning. My name is Mallory, a.k.a. Mal. I was born thirteen years ago—okay, I won't go that far back!

"Man," I muttered to myself. "This is the longest two-hour ride I think I've ever taken!" Ingrained in my head was the light hum of the motor of the car that seemed to follow us the entire way. Actually, come to think of it, it was kind of relaxing.

I couldn't get the divorce out of my head. Why did my parents have to do this to me? It made absolutely no sense! What had gone wrong? They always seemed to be so happy together. I thought back to the last conversation that I had with my mom. It seemed so long ago, but it was only yesterday.

"Honey, I think it would be best if you went to stay with Grandma and Grandpa for a while this summer, so your dad and I can work things out."

"But Mom," I tried to convince her. "It's not that I don't like staying with Grandma and Grandpa, it's just that I would rather be in my room, with my things. I would just feel better knowing that you are in the next room, you know...if you need me." I knew this was just a coverup. I really needed her—to be with my dad. If I were at home with them, then they couldn't possibly go through with this divorce!

When we arrived at the cabin, Grandma told me to take my things upstairs and get settled in. *Thud!* I dropped my bags in a room of dust-caked furniture and shelves. "Hmm, so here I am. I already miss Mom and Dad so much! If only I were home, maybe, just maybe..."

"Mal," Grandma called up the stairs. "I'm headin' to the store. Is there anything I can pick up for ya? Ya wanna ride along?"

I could sense the concern in Grandma's voice. "I'm fine, Grandma. I just wanna stay here, if that's okay." I really just wanted to think about what I could have done to make things better for Mom and Dad.

"Alrighty, then. I'll be back in a little while. If you need anything, then just ask Grandpa."

Coming to Grandma and Grandpa's had always been an adventure. They had no TV and no radio. But Mom, Dad, Grandma, and Grandpa filled the days with fishing, roasting marshmallows by the fireplace, and camping stories. They were the best times of my life! But this trip was different. All I could think about were Mom and Dad. I strained my ears to listen downstairs. "Hmm," I thought out loud. "If I listen really hard, then I know I can hear them all laughing, just like they always have before. This is all a bad dream. It just has to be!"

"Hey Mal," Grandpa shouted. Grandpa's hearing had never been good, so he always shouted at us like we couldn't hear him. Grandma would just give us a wink, and we would play along. "Ya wanna go for a jeep ride?" This was his favorite pastime, and one that he knew made me happy. Riding with him was like going on a carnival ride. Even though I just wanted to stay and sulk, I couldn't let him down. I had already turned down the trip to town.

"Sure, Grandpa. I'll be down in a minute."

"Alrighty, then! I'll be in the jeep awaitin'."

I grabbed my jacket and headed for the door. Things seemed to be moving in slow motion for me—well, since yesterday anyway. I really wished time would speed up—to the time when I was back home, and my mom and dad were back to their own normal selves.

Grandpa had the jeep warmed up and was waving me into the passenger side with a grin. As I crawled into the jeep, I noticed that the gas gauge was low. This was something that I had a habit of looking at, especially since the time Mom and I ran out of gas after we had gone grocery shopping one afternoon. We had to wait for two hours until Dad showed up with the gas can! When we got home, all of our frozen food had melted!

"Grandpa, shouldn't you put some gas in the tank before we take off?"

"Nah! It'll be jest fine. Why this ol' thing has lasted for hours on the smallest amount of gas."

"Well...okay," I said with a bit of hesitation. I shrugged off my concern, and off we went. The jeep ride brought back good memories. I closed my eyes and thought about last summer when Grandpa and I were riding through the mountains. We hit a bump in the road, and my eyes snapped open just as we were topping the hill. The jeep puttered and ran out of gas.

"Oh, boy," I mumbled. With what was going on lately, I was not a bit surprised. "So, Grandpa, what do we do now?"

Grandpa chuckled. "Mal, you're a big girl now. Jest give the jeep a little push, and when it starts movin, jump right on in. Think you can do it?"

"Sure Grandpa, that seems easy enough." I got out of the jeep and pushed as hard as I could. The jeep started rolling...down, down, down the mountain. Whiney and out of breath I yelled, "OH NO! There goes the jeep, full tilt and without me!"

Grandpa went around a curve, and then he disappeared. "This is just like the time when Mom and I ran out of gas! Even if the jeep coasts all the way to the bottom of the mountain, it could take hours before someone drives by and helps him get some gas!"

There I stood, alone in the woods and with no one in sight! Even though I had traveled these mountains many times with Grandpa, I still had no idea where I was. "What am I going to do?" I had always depended on Mom, Dad, Grandma, and Grandpa. But, now I was alone.

"Okay," I reasoned to myself. "If I am alone up here in the woods, then I need to take care of myself until someone shows up to get me. It's getting late, and I will need shelter. I should build a lean-to just like the Indians (whom I learned about in school) did. They had to build shelter to survive."

I set out to find my items. “Where do I start? Wait a minute! A lean-to sorta reminds me of the skeleton in Mr. Smith’s science room. I need bones (the tree limbs); then I will add the organs (the kindling); then the skin (the leaves).” I arranged these things against a big tree and left a small opening for the door. My lean-to was built! I looked in admiration at my new house.

The sun had put in a full day’s work and was starting to hide behind the mountain. “It gets pretty cool up here at night, so I’ll need to stay warm if I’m gonna be here a while. I guess I should look for firewood.”

I set out on my search for firewood, which was not hard to find since it was all around me. “But, how in the world am I gonna start a fire without a match?” Then I remembered a book that I read once about a kid who was stuck in Canada with a hatchet. He struck it against a stone, and it made a fire. “Maybe that will work for me, too.” I said with confidence. I searched for a big stone and prayed for a fire.

Not far from the place where Grandpa had taken off in the jeep lay his pocket knife, next to a big stone! “Wow! My prayer worked!” I stuck Grandpa’s knife in my pocket and moved the stone to my campsite. I arranged small pieces of wood and leaves into a pile. Then, I placed a circle of small stones around them so the fire wouldn’t spread. I stroked the stone with the knife over and over again. It didn’t work at first, but I wasn’t about to give up! Suddenly, there was a spark. And soon, I had a fire!

“Gosh, all this work has made me hungry! Grandma once told me that there were lots of raspberry bushes in these mountains, and they aren’t hard to find.” I looked around and found some unusual berries, but I stayed away from them since I didn’t know what they were. I stayed close to camp, but after searching I realized that I wasn’t all that hungry after all. I just wanted to go home! All I could think about were Mom and Dad and what they were doing to make their marriage survive. I crawled into my lean-to, lay down and stared up at the grassy ceiling.

I must have just dozed off when a sound woke me up. I listened closely and heard the faint putter of a motor. "That sounds like the car my grandma drives!" I jumped up and peeked outside. "It is Grandma and Grandpa!" I yelled. When they saw me, they jumped out of the car, and we ran into each other's arms.

With a sparkle in her eyes, Grandma asked me, "So, how was it out here all by yirself?"

"It wasn't all that hard, Grandma. I even made a fire! But, it went out after a while."

"I'm so proud of you Mal! I was on my way home from the grocery store when Grandpa flagged me down. He told me what happened. You must have been very scared up here all by yirself waitin' on us. We just couldn't get up here fast enough!"

"Oh, Grandma, you have no idea!"

My mom and dad got back together that summer. Their marriage had survived! I also learned how to survive and to say a prayer when you are in need. I confess—that is just what I did!

Pompeii Past And Present

by Nicholas Ureda

On a recent cruise to the Mediterranean Sea,
The very best stop, according to me,
Was the excursion by land that we took one day
To the ancient port city known as Pompeii.

All life was destroyed by volcanic eruption,
But the ashes that fell prevented corruption.
Furniture, buildings, and even mosaics
Were so well preserved, they didn't look archaic.

There were streets made for carts which were pulled by beasts
And stepping-stones for people on the way to their feasts.
I saw petrified food, animals and men,
And even a dog, still locked in his pen.

As our trip was coming to an end,
All of our smiles started to descend.
Some day, a long time away.
I will take my children to visit Pompeii.

6th grade

B. F. F. And E.
(Best Friends Forever And Ever)

by Lucy E. Hedrick

Chapter 1: Recess

It was recess, Angie's favorite subject! She was on the swings with Haley and Molly, and they were talking about this HUGE all-weekend party they were having next weekend for their friend Julie, who was home sick that day. "She better be feeling alright by next weekend," said Angie. "It would be really sad if she missed her own party."

"Angie!" Molly and Haley shouted. "Don't even think about it. It's only Tuesday. She has, let's see, a week and four days to get better!" Molly remarked.

"You know, we should help her to feel better, instead of just sitting around and talking about what would happen if she missed her party," Haley said calmly.

"Exactly my point. We could help her by..." *Clunk, clunk,bump,clash,screeeeeeeeeeach.*

The girls all covered their ears and looked to see where the noise was coming from. "Oh, my word!" Angie shouted over the racket. Molly and Haley spun around, and Molly screamed.

A ratty, old Blazer pulled up to the curb and screeched to a stop. The car door opened, and a girl a little taller than the three girls stepped out of the "ancient" SUV. She had long, brown hair and was tall and skinny. She was wearing a red, cowgirl-style blouse and red overalls. Her hair was pulled back into a messy ponytail, and her shoes were ratty old red tennis shoes. She ran around to the other side and opened the door. An old woman stepped out. She looked like the girl and (as Molly thought) looked to be her grandma. They walked into the building just as the bell rang that meant recess was over.

Chapter 2: The Invitation

It was second period science and Molly's worst subject. Mrs.

Anderson was almost finished giving out the class assignments when Principal Mann walked in with the girl they had seen at recess. When she walked into the room, everyone started laughing, except for Angie and Haley.

"Molly!" whispered Haley. "I feel so sorry for that poor girl. They should not laugh at her."

"She makes me very jittery. I don't really like her." replied Angie.

"You haven't even met her yet! You don't know what she's like!" Haley whispered in an exasperated voice. "What's up with you two?"

The principal told the class that she was a new student named Kayla. It turned out that the new girl was in all of the three girls' classes. Haley thought that it was a good thing because they could try to be her friend. Angie didn't like it and thought it was suspicious. And Molly obviously thought it was funny because she giggled every time she saw the "new kid."

One day, Haley suggested that they invite Kayla to Julie's (who was almost better) birthday party. She said that she and Kayla were sort of buds now. "Absolutely not, no way," said Angie.

"We would be too busy laughing our heads off about her outfit to do all the fun stuff we've planned," joked Molly.

"I can't believe you two. Everyone teases her, and she has no friends. I don't think Julie would mind, and Kayla would be delighted. I already asked my mom how many people could spend the night, and she said that I could have five. That's me, you two, Julie, and Kayla. Even if you guys don't agree, I'm going to invite her. You'll see, it'll be great," Haley remarked and ran off to ask Kayla.

Kayla was sitting on the swing when Haley walked up and sat down next to her. Haley asked her if she could come to her uncle's beach house for a whole weekend. She explained that it was a surprise birthday party and that she needed to bring a present. She handed her a list that looked like this:

Things to bring to the party:

1. *sleeping bag and pillow*
2. *flashlight*
3. *present for Julie (she is our friend and is sick now)*
4. *P.J.s*
5. *3 changes of clothes*
6. *toothbrush and hairbrush*
7. *movies*
8. *games*
9. *money (we are going shopping at the mall!)*
10. *yourself!*

Kayla was so exited that she jumped up and gave Haley a huge hug. The bell rang, and Kayla ran into the building yelling back, "I'll be there! This is going to be so much fun!"

Chapter 3: The Trip

"Come on, honey, time to go to Haley's," Kayla's mom, Lucie, yelled.

"I'm coming, Mom!" Kayla answered. She pulled on her jacket and shoes, grabbed Julie's present, and ran downstairs. Her mom was taking her stuff out to the car. Kayla hopped in the back, and they drove off.

"Now don't stay up too late, and remember to brush your teeth. Use your manners, clean up your messes, and do not have too much sugar. When you get to her uncle's house, say thanks for letting you stay, and don't forget to be a good friend."

They pulled into the driveway and parked the car. "Here we are. It looks like they're all putting their things in Mrs. Kara's van. Why don't you do the same? Have fun now!" shouted her mom.

Lucie drove off, and Kayla ran to give Haley a hug. She noticed that Molly didn't laugh at her, and Angie greeted her with a big smile. Angie didn't seem so suspicious anymore. She had a feeling this was going to be fun!

Chapter 4: The Party

Finally! They were at Haley's uncle's house! It was huge!

"Oh, no!" shouted Molly, as they piled out of the van. "Julie's coming up the driveway! Hurry, hide!"

They all ran inside and turned out all the lights. They threw the presents and snacks onto the decorated table that Uncle Jon had set up. They grabbed the bowls of confetti and hid right when the doorbell rang. "Come in!" shouted Angie.

Julie walked in and screamed when they flipped the lights and jumped out of their hiding spots. She ran up and hugged us as the confetti flew everywhere.

Haley's mom vacuumed up the confetti, and the girls set up a tent in the basement out of poles and sheets. They spread out their sleeping bags and ran upstairs for dinner. After they helped do the dishes, they got out the birthday cake and cut it into HUGE slices. Molly got out the ice cream, and they dug in.

When Julie opened her presents, she jumped up and down 'cause she was so HAPPY. They watched movies and played games till they couldn't stay up any longer. Just before they fell asleep, Julie said, "This is my best birthday ever!"

Chapter 5: The Friendship Ceremony

"I'm so excited!" exclaimed Kayla. They were back from their trip and were at Molly's house, making their friendship ceremony dresses. They were having a big party to welcome Kayla to their club. It was going to be a fancy dinner party, and they were inviting their parents to the ceremony. They had put together two tables and decorated them as though it were a big, fancy banquet. Their dresses were all blue and lavender and looked like ball gowns. Their guests were all dressed up, too.

For dinner, they were serving spaghetti and meatballs, garlic bread, and sparkling cider. They were also going to have a dance floor in their living room.

The girls had just finished dressing when the doorbell rang. Kayla went to greet the guest, while Angie and Julie put out name cards and Molly and Haley set the table.

Then it was time for the ceremony. Everyone sat down in the "pews" that the girls had set up. Haley introduced herself (even though everyone already knew her) and called for Molly, Julie, then Angie to come up and join her. Then Kayla walked up to the "stage" and recited the promise after Haley.

"I will always…" said Haley.

"I will always…" repeated Kayla.

"…be faithful and caring…"

"…be faithful and caring…"

"…to my new friends…"

"…to my new friends…"

"…who like me so."

"…who like me so."

Then they did their special handshake and invited everyone to the dining room where they held a toast in honor of Kayla. They ate the delicious meal that they had prepared and then danced the rest of the time.

After all the guests were gone and they had cleaned up, they all got out a game to play until it was time to go to bed (they were all spending the night at Haley's). When Haley's mom said it was time to go to sleep, they put away the game and got ready for bed. As soon as they were ready to go to sleep, Kayla hugged each girl and declared that they were her best friends ever!

8th grade

The Cross Of Christ

by Caitlin Campbell

Death.
The price that had to be paid
For our wretched souls that day.
And He prayed, "Lord, forgive them."
He came to die
That we might live,
And He prayed, "Lord, forgive them."
A death that would live forever,
His legacy would stand the test of time.
And He prayed, "Lord, forgive them."
They stripped Him of His only garments,
And whipped Him until His back was red,
Red with their hate and malice toward Him,
And red with His undying love for them.
But yet He prayed, "Lord, forgive them."
They drove the nails through flesh and bone,
One in each hand, and one in His feet,
And He prayed, "Lord, forgive them."
They mocked Him
And on His head they placed a crown of thorns,
A crown that would soon be gold,
And He prayed, "Lord, forgive them."
They laughed at Him,
And cast lots at His feet,
But still He prayed, "Lord, forgive them."
Six long, excruciating hours He hung
On that dark, gloomy day.
"It is finished!" He cried,
As the earth shook.
And His mother moaned.
And they prayed, "Lord, forgive us."

Grounds Of Grace

by Emma Hershberger

The milky brown, tall, nonfat, sugar-free, vanilla latte warmed Janet as it trickled down her throat. She was inside Grounds of Grace, safe from the frigid air outside in the streets of Augusta, Maine. Janet sat down in the coffee shop of a Christian habitat, thinking about her daily devotion and its message. Her face was red from the bitter cold, as she drifted away from the devotion and thought about how her job as a dentist was not very satisfying to her love of talking with people.

"I've always got my hands in someone's mouth, and they can't easily talk to me that way. The only questions I get are 'Are my teeth okay; do I need a filling; or when's my next appointment?'" Janet mumbled to herself as she was driving away from the old, farmhouse-style coffee shop.

When Janet got home, her black, three-year-old Lab, Ivy, came running up to her and wagged her tail with happiness. Janet picked up the newspaper and walked upstairs to her bedroom. The newspaper was snapped open on her queen-sized bed, as she got comfortable and started looking through the classifieds. After the leftover newspaper was thrown into the recycle bin, Janet saw she had circled only three jobs.

The car door shut loudly behind her as she stuck the key in the ignition. Janet decided to answer the dog-washing ad she had circled first. The manager came running out of the front door as she pulled into an empty parking spot. "They must be desperate," Janet thought out loud.

They both walked in, and she was immediately put to work with the biggest, shaggiest dog she had ever seen! After washing seven dogs and a couple of hours of wrestling in a tub, she realized if she made the slightest effort to talk to any of the owners, she ended up chasing a dog back to the washing room with soap filling her mouth. Then, Janet quickly, but politely, notified the manager, "I can't work here," and with a sigh, drove off down the road.

The next day when she got home from the dentist's office she decided to try the job as a cashier at the nearby grocery store. "This is just to see if you are capable of doing your duty," reminded Lisa, a person on the staff, as she handed a uniform to Janet.

Janet started at aisle four. After an hour of helping busy customers, it was set in stone that it was impossible to even say hello. She was too focused on trying to get the scanner to work correctly. Lisa walked up and sadly stuttered, "You were not accepted for the job."

With a doubtful look on her face, Janet drove down Three Day Way. Her car pulled into the dirt driveway of Grounds of Grace, the old farmhouse Christian coffee shop. Janet ordered her regular, a latte, and sat down. Her thoughts moved to the list of the circled jobs. Her decision was to give Barnes and Noble a try tomorrow after her work hours at the office.

Janet looked for the manager at Barnes and Noble, and when she found him, she asked to apply for a job there. He gave her two thick piles of paperwork just as an interview! Two days passed, and no one even tried to talk to her. Janet almost decided to quit, when a customer asked, "Have you read this book? I don't know if I want to read it or not."

Janet nodded with surprise and exclaimed, "Yes, I have read it. It is an amazing book, and it has a wonderful message." As soon as the young woman walked away, there was a voice yelling at Janet. It was her manager shouting, "You're fired!"

Janet turned around. "May I ask why?" she asked, suddenly confused.

"Because you gave your opinion of a book! That's why!" replied the manager. Janet didn't know how to reply, and she was out of there in two shakes of a lamb's tail.

The next day, after a long, silent workday with people's teeth, Janet came home with a lonely look in her eye. Her feet carried her to the kitchen, and she made herself a bowl of Spaghetti O's. At her first bite, the doorbell rang.

She slowly got up to answer the door and found the elementary girl scouts selling cookies. The children's car pulled out of the driveway, and Janet was just about to close the door when Ivy, her sweet black Lab, came hurdling down the front steps and out of the front door. Janet didn't understand why her attentive dog had changed so abruptly and run away as she did.

Janet grabbed her suede jacket and Ivy's leash. She ran out, shutting the door behind her. She ran down the road through the crisp wind yelling, "Ivy! Ivy! Come back here, now!"

Janet and Ivy ran almost three miles through woods and across streets. The wild chase continued up Three Day Way and into the dirt driveway. Janet blocked everything but Ivy from her mind and had no idea she was in the driveway of Grounds of Grace. When Ivy reached the small farmhouse, she collapsed right on the front porch.

As Janet hooked the leash to Ivy's collar, she scolded, "Ivy, you know better than to just run out of the front door and come all the way here." Ivy paid no attention to her. She just sat there panting nonstop. "Well, since we're here I might as well get something," Janet said breathlessly. Ivy pranced at her side as they walked in.

As Janet was waiting for her latte to be made to perfection, Ivy stood up on her hind legs to watch. "Down," Janet commanded. Ivy obeyed, but when she did, the stack of flyers flew off of the counter. "Ivy," Janet said beneath her breath. She didn't notice the flyers as she picked them up, but as she placed them on the counter the bold title caught her eye. Janet picked it up off the counter and read it carefully. With Ivy's leash in her hand and the flyer folded up in her pocket, she walked home quickly through the snow.

The fire warmed Janet and Ivy as they sat on the couch together. Janet read the flyer over and over out loud. "Come prepared to entertain. We accept anything from singing to jazz to dancing and standup comedy, Mondays through Saturdays, from five o'clock to ten o'clock. Tryouts are Thursday, November Fourth," Janet repeated happily.

She wanted so badly to try out, but she didn't have many talents. She thought very deeply. "Grandpa used to teach me how to play the guitar, until the day…" she thought, with tears in her eyes. "Maybe I can still play." Janet sprang from the couch and ran up the stairs. In her closet she found her guitar and music in her leather case. Right away she practiced and practiced continuously by the fire with Ivy. As she listened to the radio she picked up three new songs by ear. Janet fell back in love with writing new songs and playing old ones.

Ivy jumped into the front seat for the first time. Janet put the guitar in the trunk and drove towards Grounds of Grace for the awaited tryouts.

"Miss Weiss," said the manager, "My name is Frank James. I am the manager of this entertainment program. May I ask what you are playing and who it is composed by?"

"Yes. Um, I am playing a song that is untitled at the moment. It is written by me, and I will be singing the lyrics, too."

"Okay. Begin when you're ready."

Janet left with a smile. Pulling her seatbelt into place, she thanked Ivy. "Ivy, you are an angel sent from God. You, you're a miracle." As the car drove down the road, Janet sang her new song.

The next day after work, Janet twirled around the house. She dressed in her nice outfit. With her leather guitar case and Ivy in the car, she drove to Grounds of Grace for her first performance.

"Next up is Miss Janet Weiss," announced Frank.

"Thank you. As he said, I'm Janet Weiss. I will be playing "Angel in my Presence." I have written it myself, and I hope you enjoy it."

Janet played and sang her song like no one had ever heard

before. Everyone cheered and clapped for her. She knew she had found something to satisfy her. She left the stage to find someone to talk to, and she was immediately caught up in a conversation.

"Hi. I'm Heather. I heard you play, and I can't believe how talented you are! You're amazing, you sing like an angel. Where'd you learn to play?" Heather complimented.

"Thank you. I learned from my grandfather, but he has passed away."

"Oh, I'm sorry."

"It's okay. It was a while back. I still love to play, though."

"Why did you choose to write that song? I mean, it was so beautiful."

"Actually, I wrote the song because of my dog. You see, I was looking for a part-time job, and my dog ran out and knocked over these flyers. Eventually, I ended up here. It's a really long story. Maybe I'll tell you the whole thing another time. You see, I'm a dentist and even though it's a great job, it doesn't fulfill my love of talking with people," Janet paused and smiled. "My Grandpa used to say all that glitters is not gold. Until a few months ago, I didn't understand it. Now, I really do. Some people's gold and treasure is not other people's gold and treasure, and that's my story."

"You will have to tell me more later, because I need to get home. I'll talk to you soon, though. Promise."

"Okay, 'bye."

"Goodbye."

Janet slept peacefully that night, with Ivy curled up by her side. She had a pleasant dream. She had just finished her new song at Grounds of Grace. People threw flowers, and Ivy was barking along with them.

The Sunlight

by Cailin Mace

The sunlight comes in through the door.
It shines brightly onto the floor.

It comes in bright,
And blinds your sight,
But it goes away when day turns to night.

It seems golden-yellow.
Like an old jolly fellow.
All bright, cheerful, playful and
mellow.

The sunlight helps flowers grow.
Up through its roots and down below.

Sunlight makes you feel so happy.
Also wholesome and somewhat
Snappy.

It brightens your day,
And shows no dismay.
Just looking at that golden
Sun ray.

The Life Of An O-R-P-H-A-N

by Catherine Bowlin

"Yes ma'am," I replied. I walked into my room and got all of my dirty clothes. "Sorry about the mud."

Ms. Mae turned with the muddy clothes and walked into the dark laundry room. Laundry day was over, and that was that.

"That was close," I whispered to Jack. "Real close."

"Christopher, come in this laundry room right now!" Ms. Mae said in her sweet voice.

"Yes ma'am." I looked at Jack and then tiptoed into the small room.

"What did I tell you about putting rocks in your pockets?" I shrugged.

"It messes up the washin' machine," I apologized and turned and began to walk into my room.

"Christopher, no more mud on your Sunday clothes."

I nodded and jumped on my bed.

"What's your punishment?" Jack asked me, wide-eyed.

"Huh?" I replied, "Nothin'." He looked at me, at the laundry room, then at me again.

"Naw, not nice ol' Ms. Mae. It's Mrs. Wilkens that'll give ya a whippin'." He had a devilish look on his face, and for once, I could not read my brother's mind.

By the way, I'm Christopher, you can call me Chris for short, and my brother's Jackson, Jack for short. We live in the Jackson, Mississippi, O-R-P-H-A-N-age. Don't like to say the word. No one ever knew what happened to our parents. Anyway, Mrs. Wilkens is the mean hag that'll give ya a whippin' with a gold belt in a heartbeat. Been here all my life. Don't remember anything or anyone.

"Wipe that freaky smile off your face, it scares me," I scolded my brother. "What are you thinkin'? What about?" I asked.

"Wanna go on an adventure?" He smiled. "To the creek?"

Wasn't a lot that my brother thought up of adventures, or at least good ones.

"To the creek? Last time we did that we got our behinds whipped off. Heck, I still think I'm swollen."

He frowned. "C'mon. It's just a creek. What does Mrs. Wilkens have to hide? What's so important down there?"

I shrugged, then we had one of those awkward, silent moments. The night bell broke the silence. "Time to go to sleep. Oh well, good night Jack," I pulled down the covers and scooted into bed.

"Night." He replied.

I didn't like bringing up the subject about the creek. All O-R-P-H-A-N-s were forbidden to go down the big hill to the creek. Old Wilkens said there was some kind of treasure belonging to her family. Not like a chest or nothin'. She said it was more important than gold. Wonder what it is.

I nudged Jack. "What?" he groaned. He looked at the digital clock next to his bed. "It's two o'clock in the mornin'. What'cha want?"

I looked at the door just to make sure no one was comin'. "I was thinkin'…" I paused.

"Oh no, I hate when you do that," he said, with a sarcastic voice.

"Quit. I was thinkin' that maybe, just maybe, we could take that adventure at the right time."

He sat up. His face glowed in the moonlight. "Okay." He grinned. I grinned. We both grinned.

I was awakened by a loud knock on the door. Joey, another O-R-P-H-A-N, yelled,

"Breakfast!"

"Okay!" I yelled. I got out of bed and threw on a T-shirt and some shorts. Jack was already up. Figured he had already gone without me noticing.

I sat down at my usual spot at the long, narrow table and looked around. Jack wasn't here. Everyone else, but not Jack.

I jumped because of the hard tap on my shoulder. I turned around, and I didn't see the face I wanted to. Yep, it was Mrs. Wilkens. "Where's your brother at?"

I looked around again and replied, "Don't know, Mrs. Wilkens, ma'am." She went down the hall that my room was on.

Someone sat down beside me in her usual seat—Beth. She was the only girl in the whole O-R-P-HA-N-age that liked me. Yuck! She was pretty and all, but heck, I'm only twelve years old, and I don't even like girls yet! Well, maybe she was a little pretty, and she was nice, and...oh shut up! I think I'll make myself barf! Obviously, I didn't like her. Every other boy did, including Jack.

"Where is Jackson?" Mrs. Wilkens yelled, while pulling me by my ear into my bedroom.

"I don't know, I swear!" I yelped. "I really don't!"

She glanced around and left me, myself, and I all alone, without Jack.

I was scared. He usually tells me when he's gonna run off. He didn't this time.

I was awakened by a knock on the door. "Lunch!" Joey yelled.

"Okay!" I replied. I looked around the room.

I had dozed off in a deep sleep that sent my mind thinkin' about Jack. I had a wild dream. There was rushin' water swarmin' around Jack and me. Then, my mind was set on somethin' else. A rock— a little, perfect, skippin' rock.I bent down on the bank and then I heard a little laugh, the one that reminded me of my childhood. It was Jack. I saw him young—about three or four years old. Me, too, with our runny noses and sweet, rosy cheeks. I remember seeing Mrs. Wilkens for the first time. She took us in, seemed like the best thing in the whole wide world. She took us inside the shelter and explained all of the rules. I remember one was about the creek. "Don't go near it, either," she explained. I asked why and she replied sweetly,

"The bank caves in easily…" and she explained about the family treasure.

"Jack!" I screamed, now thinking about lunch. "Adventure… bank… caves in… Jackson!" I screamed, at the top of my lungs. He was at the creek, the adventure, all by himself. I had to go find him. I got my best boots and shirt and ran out of my bedroom door.

"Not so fast, Christopher." Mrs. Wilkens, the stupid old hag yelled. "It's time for lunch, where do you think you're going?"

I stuttered. "Um… uh… the, um… cr… cr… to, to find Ms. Mae. She forgot one of my dirty T-shirts. Yeah, dirty T-shirt."

Mrs. Wilkens looked around. "Okay. But I'm watching you, boy. I'm watching you."

I slammed my door, and I ran to my favorite servant's room. "Ms. Mae! Ms. Mae! Come quick! Um, um... Jack..." Mrs. Wilkens passed by. "I have a dirty T-shirt." I knocked on the door continuously.

She came running out. "Oh, a dirty T-shirt code. Come inside," she swept me in. "Where do you think the bird landed?" she asked, with a question mark all over her face.

"The cr, cr…creek." I pushed myself. "Please help, Ms. Mae, and hurry!"

She ran out of her room, and I was following her. Then we ran out of the back door from the O-R-P-H-A-N-age. We ran down the big hill leading to the creek. We saw footprints leading to the bank, and there, hung on a branch, was Jack's T-shirt. No sign of Jack himself, anywhere. At this moment in my life, I knelt on my knees. I started to pray. I prayed that Jackson would be okay, my only known brother, and that this was all a horrible nightmare. A horrible nightmare.

As I knelt before the creek, I heard something, something splash. I looked into my vision and it was him. It was Jackson. He bent down to pick up the little skippin' rock in my first dream. I remembered that the bank caved in easily. While I was prayin', I opened my eyes, and I saw him. It was him, there he was! I wasn't sure if I was really dreaming or not.

"Jackson! Don't! Don't pick up the rock!" I screamed at the top of my lungs.

Ms. Mae spotted him also. "What? What's goin' on?" she asked. I could tell she was puzzled.

Jack shrugged and still picked up the tiny rock anyway. The bank caved in. Jack went falling in the creek, and at that moment I realized that he couldn't swim, but neither could I. I didn't know what to do. It was a lose-lose situation. Don't jump in, I lose him. Jump in, lose me and him. I heard Ms. Mae yell, and she started taking off her apron and her bonnet.

"Jackson, paddle your way to the surface! Its okay, I'm gonna help you! I'm comin'!" Ms. Mae screamed.

"It's okay, Jack, Ms. Mae's comin'!" I yelled.

Watchin' Jack struggle to stay above water, I realized how much I love him. In the first vision I had, the little chuckle I heard was the first time I heard him laugh after we lost our parents and moved into the O-R-P-H-A-N-age. I loved him so much that I thought I should get my hindquarters over to the creek and pull him out. So I did.

Ms. Mae had already pulled him out by the time I got there. There was one problem now—Jack wasn't breathing.

Ms. Mae directed me to go get some onions out of the patch behind the O-R-P-H-A-N-age. I was gonna ask why, but it was Jack's life at stake now. I pulled some onions out of the ground and ran as fast as I could to the creek.

She took the onions from my hand and ran them under Jack's nose. He shot up in a snap. Then, I hugged him so hard, the hardest I have ever hugged anyone. "Hey Jack, I love you."

"I love you too, man," he replied. We kept hugging.

This was the day that I would remember all of my life.

I Am

by Lawson Mahoney

I am a runner and a brother.
I wonder what type of runner I will grow up to be.
I hear feet pounding the track.
I see my body drop across the finish line.
I want to earn first place.
I am a runner and a brother.

I pretend to be an awesome runner.
I feel like I run on air.
I touch the chilly metal of the trophy.
I worry who will be the champion?
I cry when I feel the pain surging through my body.
I am a runner and a brother.

I understand I need a strong mind to be the best.
I say I will be the best some day.
I try to run as fast as my brothers.
I hope someday I will be the best runner ever.
I am a runner and a brother.

Peanut And Cheese

by Casey Hirschmann

Okay, well, see, there's peanuts and cheese, but then there is Peanut and Cheese! I'll try to explain that a little bit better. Peanut is a fully-grown, overweight, hairy circus elephant that has many fears, including mice, and Cheese is, as you've probably already guessed, a height-challenged, squeaky, little mouse who absolutely adores elephants.

One day, Cheese was out taking his daily stroll when he decided, *"Hey, let's go see an elephant!"* And that lucky elephant was...Peanut! Cheese walked over to Peanut's cage, jumped through a small opening, and *voila*—there was Peanut huddled in a corner of the cage, cautiously looking around for some sort of danger, until he saw Cheese.

Suddenly, Peanut went on a rampage! Peanut started jumping up and down, up and down, and then hung from the top of the cage with his oversized trunk. (There had been a robust bar put there as soon as the circus clowns learned of Peanut's fear; they knew he would dangle from it one day!)

But oh, that poor little Cheese, he didn't know what in the universe was going on. So, just as soon as Peanut jumped onto that bar, Cheese followed, hoping the massive beast wouldn't squish him. As soon as Cheese did that, something told him deep in his gut that what he had done had been a terribly dumb mistake. Or maybe it was just the undeniable fact that Peanut got so scared, he knocked over his cage, rammed the door open, jumped out of it, and ran.

Well, this wasn't that great of an experience for poor little lovable Cheese, but he quickly got over it. As for that Peanut, his mind did not work the same. See, he hopped a train car and became a large-eared hobo.

How To Solve A Murder

by Edsel Boyd, III

It was a rainy night, the kind of night that makes you feel like a child. José was coming home from the library. He'd been there all day reading horror stories. He was walking too fast to notice the thud of feet behind him. Soon, a hand came around his mouth. He tried to scream, but no sound came out. No sooner had he screamed, when a crack echoed through the street. His body fell limp to the ground. His attacker threw the body over his back. A man looked out his window, only to see a dark, hulking figure walking down the road.

The whine of sirens woke Jack. It was always exciting to hear about a case, so when his father told him what it was, Jack was elated.

"It seems to be kidnapping and murder at the same time," his father said. "One of the neighbors saw the whole thing." As Jack peeked his head out the window, he heard an excited and depressed voice.

"...then I heard a crack and looked out the window. I saw a man with long, dark hair walk away with the boy."

"Thanks for the cooperation, sir." The policeman started to walk towards the Smith house. He knocked on the door. Jack's mother answered it.

"Good mornin', ma'am," he said. "Did you hear or see anything strange last night?"

"No."

"Well, thanks anyway."

As soon as the officer left, Jack called his best friend, Nikii. "Hey, Nik!" Jack said.

"What is it?" she asked.

"Did you hear about the homicide?" Jack asked.

"Yeah, it was pretty weird."

"Meet me at Jason's Park at 5:00 p.m."

"But wh..." She wasn't able to finish before he hung up. She got on her bike and left.

"Five minutes to 5:00," she thought, as she peddled up the street.

They met at the park as planned. "What do you want?" she asked.

"We're going to solve the case," he said.

"Whoa, you're kidding, right?"

"No."

"Look ,we only solved one case, and that was out of pure, dumb luck."

"But we have facts this time," Jack said.

Nikii sighed, "All right." This wasn't going to be easy.

They decided to start at the victim's house. They rode their bikes over, taking the faster path through the alleys. Jack knew the Chief of Police, so they got in easily.

"These parents are really depressed," Nikii said.

"Huh?"

Nikii pointed towards some anti-depression pills on their table. When they left, they noticed a boy's bike parked three houses down.

"Something's fishy here," Nikii said.

Then they went to where the boy was attacked.

"Hey, what's this?" Jack knelt over to pick up a piece of paper. "685-947-8256," Jack read the paper out loud.

"Let's call this guy and find out what and who he is." Jack called the number, and Nikii listened on the other phone.

Ring! Ring! "Hello?"

"Name?"

"Jack."

"Go away." *Click.*

"Well, he was pleasant," said Nikii sarcastically.

"I think we can find him, anyway," Jack replied.

"Good. I'm getting ready to solve this case." Jack and Nikii decided it was too late to continue sleuthing that night. They rode home and decided to meet at the victim's house the next day.

Jack arrived early and was invited in by José's mother. Jack couldn't wait to get started, so he began asking questions.

"Did you have any enemies?" Nikii had just arrived at the victim's house and overheard the answer.

"Jeff. He was mad. We sued him for smashing our car."

"Where can we find him?" Jack asked.

"At the old junkyard."

"Thank you again," Jack said. "Next stop, Jeff's Junkyard."

"Here we are," said Jack. As soon as they stepped inside, alarms went off. Jeff came after the intruders with a club. "Run!"

They ran and saw a BMW car. When they jumped inside, Nikii screamed. There, in the backseat was José. His mangled body lay there, dead. Jack flipped out his cell phone and dialed 911. Just after he hung up, a hand grabbed him.

"You won't see me get arrested, punk!" Jeff said. Then Nikii kicked him in the shin and they ran for the exit. Nikii laughed.

"Why are you laughing?" Jack asked.

"Look," she said. The police cars were coming over the hill.

I'll go through the aftermath quickly. Jack and Nikii got rewarded $10,000 each. Jeff was arrested. And José was buried peacefully. Everything was back to normal.

Section Three

High School

11th grade

Whatever Happened

by Michelle Serra

Whatever happened
To the girl I once knew
She slowly crept away
Replaced by someone new

The days go by
Summer turns to fall
The lessons we learn
Shape and mold us all

The people from our past
Gradually drift away
I feel like we were friends
Just only yesterday

Where does all the time go
I wish I could have it back
I'm not ready to set it free
To give up my memories, my past

But things change
Memories fade
And all we are left with
Are the choices we've made

They determine our future
We are controlled by our past
Always searching for the answers
To the questions that we ask

Whatever happened
To the girl I once knew
She slowly crept away
Replaced by someone new

I Am Okay

by Danielle Schramm

Everything about that morning is still crystal clear in my memory; the clothes I was wearing, the faces of everyone around me, and the exact time of day all were engraved in my mind forever as a day that I could never forget. I was an eighth-grade student at Vickery Creek Middle School, and I was at my locker getting my books for third period when I felt someone tap me on the shoulder. I turned around to find my crush, Chris, standing there. Chris and I were good friends, but at the time, my feelings for him were more than just friendly.

"Hey, Danielle," he said.

"Hey, Chris! How are you?"

"I'm good, thanks. How are you?"

"I'm good. What's up?"

"I have a question to ask you."

"Okay, shoot."

"Danielle, would you be my girlfriend?

A million thoughts flooded my mind, and excitement and nervousness filled my entire body. With an extremely big smile, I said, "Yes!"

So it was official; Chris and I were a couple. I could not have been happier. We immediately clicked on many different levels. For me to connect with him so quickly was an amazing feeling.

After being together for about two months, we were talking on the phone after school one day and he told me he had to tell me something.

I said, "Okay, what is it?"

He said, "Danielle, I love you." The feeling was incredible. I felt completed, content, and—most importantly—happy.

After eighth grade, we spent the entire summer together. Along with being naively in love with him, I also fell in love with his family. He and his family were amazing. He filled all the holes in my life and made up for everything I lacked. He strengthened my walk with God, and he always had powerful and reassuring words for me when I had lost my path or was feeling down. He became everything to me, and I realized how in love I was with him, even though I was only fourteen years old. I know that at the time I was extremely young, but what I felt was definitely real. Chris was my other half. He was a truly inspiring person whom I looked up to and respected.

Chris and I dated our entire freshman year, and on April 26, 2002, we celebrated our one-year anniversary. On that day, he gave me a rose and a promise ring with a letter attached to it.

The letter said: *"I love being with you and discovering new things about you. I love learning what makes you laugh and finding the places you're most ticklish. I love hearing stories about when you were little and listening as you talk about your hopes and dreams. I love the sound of your voice when I pick up the phone, and the way it sounds when you whisper my name. I love holding hands and curling up next to each other. Danielle, I love the way I feel when I'm with you. Love, Chris."*

Right there he promised that he would always love me no matter what. That was the day I decided that I wanted to marry him, a novel idea at age fifteen. However, the love was there, and I believed it to be true for all time. I loved him so deeply and so unconditionally that I felt that no action, no distance, no fight could ever cause this love to cease. We were so in love and so perfect for each other, or so it seemed.

We continued dating through the summer of 2002, when we were both out of town a lot. At one point during our summer break, we did not see each other for over a month. Our relationship seemed to go downhill from there.

When school started my sophomore year, our relationship became increasingly difficult. We were both getting busy with school, and neither of us was able to drive yet. We began to take out the stress from school on each other. We fought more frequently and began to grow apart, but I never thought that petty differences like those would cause us to separate. However, I was completely wrong.

On September 17, 2002, Chris came over and we spent the day together. We did everything that we normally did when we saw each other, like play basketball, go out to eat, or watch a movie, but I knew something was not right. He was acting strangely that day but when I questioned it, he replied with a nonchalant, "nothing." I became uneasy about the situation and the way he was acting, so I asked him if he was going to break up with me. He reassured me that he loved me and that there was nothing in the world that could change that.

The next evening I was sitting and talking with my mom when the phone rang. I answered it and it was Chris. I said, "Hey, how are you?"

He answered, "Not so great," and I could tell something was terribly wrong. He said, "I need to talk to you about something."

I replied with a confused, "okay."

He said, "Danielle, I think we should break up."

I was beside myself, and I could not breathe. Silent tears fell from my eyes. I wanted to ask a million questions, but no words came from my mouth. I was completely silent as I tried to comprehend the seven small words that changed my life in an amazingly monumental way.

He tried to explain why and to provide comfort, but everything he said was hazy to me. He even began to cry. His tears did not matter to me; nothing mattered. Nothing he said could change the utter destruction he had just caused to my naive and innocent heart.

I could not put thoughts together in my head, and there was nothing that I could say. I felt as if a black blanket had descended upon me, and I was suffocating. I wanted the overwhelmingly unfathomable feelings I had to go away. I felt I did not have the emotional capability to deal with the situation.

I hung up the phone and my once-silent tears erupted into

painful sobs that shook my entire body until nothing more would come out of my weak and powerless self. I was empty, and all my muscles were tense and tired. I let the pain and anguish take over completely, as I lay there helpless and numb.

At that moment, I believed there was not one person on the earth that could understand the unmatchable pain and loss that I felt. I had never felt as alone in all my fifteen years as I did that night, and there was absolutely nothing I could do about it. I wanted more than anything to crawl into my bed and die.

I could not deal with the emotional pain and stress I had, so I thought the only way that I could be at peace was to take my own life. Questions and thoughts raced through my mind, such as: *"If Chris does not care about me, then no one else could possibly care either; if Chris doesn't want me, then there is no other reason to live, and if I am not good enough for him, then there's no way on earth that I could ever please anyone else."*

I seriously considered taking my life and confided in my best friend Katie about what I wanted to do. She, similar to any caring person, was afraid for me and began to cry hysterically. She was so terrified that I was going to commit suicide, she called Andy, one of the four youth leaders of our church youth group. "Andy, you've got to call Danielle; I'm afraid she won't be here much longer if you don't."

I received a call from Andy, and we talked for a long time. He told me that what I was feeling was okay. He told me that my heart was broken into a million pieces and it was not my fault. He reassured me that I was okay. He stressed to me that night that there was nothing wrong with the way I was feeling and my reaction to this situation. I knew after talking to him that committing suicide would be wasting the life that God gave me to fulfill. For me to consider this act was incongruous when I looked at what I would be leaving, and all of the people who would be torn apart by the pain I would have caused. I realized that killing myself would have been letting Chris win, and I made the choice to never let that happen.

Getting over that painful experience took months for me to achieve. I was still attached to him for a long time after that September night. I was completely weighted down with the emotions and memories and could not break free. I had to make a decision to be happy again. Without making that decision, I would have been ruled by the hurt and memories of that deep relationship for all of my life. I made the decision to let the pain go. I *had* to let go of all of the anger, hurt, and resentment and move on. Making this decision liberated my heart and soul, and I became a completely mature and changed person.

Although my relationship with Chris was incredibly profound and extremely significant to me, I realized that I am just Danielle. I am not Danielle *and* Chris. I still think about him and the touching memories we shared that almost destroyed me, but I am better than that. I am me, and I am okay.

…On Futility

by Danielle Arthur

People rush down the autumn city streets in the frenzy to beat each other home. With hopeful hearts and empty heads, they hurry mindlessly through the city, smiling complacently. They are all filled with brand new thoughts for the fall, like boutique windows overstocked with the latest trends—bursting, threatening to overflow and infect the masses. Everyone is ready for a fresh start, but in reality there are no new beginnings or new seasons. It is all one continuous cycle. Winter does not bring joy and hope with the New Year; spring is not April showers and May flowers. Summer is not a peaceful vacation, and autumn is nothing but the slow death of summer.

As a parent pushes exhausted, unwilling children, the wind pushes withered, fallen leaves along the streets. (Doesn't it know that the leaves have no chance at getting anywhere, that next month they will all be decaying into the earth?) The wind pulls on my hair and tugs insistently on my scarf, begging me to come along too. I resist. (Doesn't it know that I will go home and disintegrate into the sheets on my bed?)

I feel eyes boring into the back of my head. I turn and find the vacant eyes of the massive cathedral I attended over the summer glaring accusingly at me. I stare back defiantly; now it is a contest, and I never blink first. The church closes his eyes (out of sight, out of mind) and forgets; then he shudders, as though unnerved, causing his monstrous bells to call in more urbanite followers who trustingly, blindly crowd the gates of the giant building, ready to become holy. I am reminded of a school of fish, acting as one, swimming thoughtlessly into the mouth of a shark.

The other college students, full and proud, scurry along with their books. (Don't they know that their futures are as flimsy as the paper on which the coveted diplomas are printed?) Pretty girls with magazines (arsenals filled with ammunition for perfection) in hand stride confidently through the swarm.

Official-looking women in blazers and pumps charge their briefcases home. (Don't they know that they are only rising in the company because their bosses think they're pretty?) The business ladies gaze enviously at beautiful women driving by in expensive machines. (Don't those women know that their rich husbands buy their out-of-state sweethearts sports cars, too?)

The crowds ignore the portrait painters and guitar players and the folk singers on the street corners. (Don't those starving artists know that no one will ever understand them?) The people hustle and bustle all around me, but I feel as though I am standing still. (Doesn't anyone know that the scales are already weighted, already tipped against them? The more they push, the more their chances dwindle. Why bother?)

Finally, I reach the apartment complex. All of the units here are "scaled;" everything is so tiny here that it reminds me of a dollhouse. I pass the uniformed mannequins at the door and take the stairs up to my cell.

In my plastic dollhouse kitchen, I put some microwavable food in a microwavable bowl and heat my frozen dinner. I take my simulated food to the make-believe couch and turn on the miniature television. A commercial for a new reality series, "Big Brother," flashes across the screen. "Fierce, dramatic competition between houseguests will be recorded twenty-four seven! Tune in to see who has what it takes to be Big Brother—and win $500,000!" My stomach goes cold as I am reminded of *1984*.

When I change the channel, I find myself being bombarded with a sermon on the religious station. He talks of guilt and redemption (Why feel guilty when there is no redemption?), of finding Jesus like our fellow sinners have (Well, where is he?), of finding salvation (What is salvation?).

I try to watch the news, but there is no news; the same politicians, with changed faces, command the screen. Their numbing voices of predictability ("No more taxes! No more poverty! No more pain!") work like anesthesia, seducing the submissive masses. I mute their buzzing speeches and stare at their angry faces and pounding fists as they stare back out of crazy eyes. They remind me of kids on a playground (Eeny, meeny, miney, mo); they want to play Simon Says, but everyone wants to be Simon (My mother said to pick the very best one and you are not it, you dirty, dirty dishrag you), and the most manipulative one always dominates in the end.

As commercials take over the screen, I stare through the television and through the wall to the next unit. I see the man sitting contentedly on the nondescript couch, just as I am, watching the same channel. I look up through my ceiling and watch the girls above me sit on that same couch, watching that same channel. (Am I the only one who sees the futility of it all?)

I decide to play house and clear up my dishes in the pretend kitchen. I finish and notice a stack of mail on the counter. There are several bills (Who cares? They think I despise giving them my "hard-earned money." It does not bother me; I will write numbers on checks and send them what they want. Money is just numbers on paper, and they can take it all.) One envelope is different—the address is not mimeographed; it's handwritten (calligraphy), and the stamp is an angel.

As I brush my teeth with hygienic toxins in the tiny bathroom, I scan the letter from my mother. Endearments litter the paper, paired with gently probing questions (Sweetheart, are you okay? We never hear from you, darling. You used to be so passionate about writing, honey; what happened to your hunger, your fervor, your drive? Have you been submitting your work to magazines like that counselor advised, sweetie? Remember when you won that writing contest at your high school last year? That was *so* clever, hon! You were just a writing machine! Don't waste your talent, kitten! God Bless!) that bounce off my solid eyes and pass through the imaginary walls.

I let the letter slide into the sink and watch the chemicals from the faucet cleanse the paper of its messy emotions and painfully beautiful calligraphy. The excruciating ink runs like exquisite tears from the knowing eyes of the blank-faced white paper, until all that remains is its gray mascara smudge.

I smile down at the remains of the soggy letter, and then I look up and smile at the doll in the miniature mirror. She smiles back and watches me throw the letter in the trash, next to the map of the campus ("Proud to be the most prestigious writing school on the east coast!"), my first report card this semester (GPA: 4.0), and a letter from that church from last summer (Dear Parishioner, We have been missing your monthly contributions to our parish family, and we are in desperate need of monetary assistance for our new building fund!).

As I walk into my bedroom, the phone rings once, twice. The answering machine picks up; the blaring computer voice demands that the caller leave a message at the tone. A gleaming, metallic voice shouts excitedly, barely audible amidst the primal pounding of underground rock music. I hear parts of her excited speech ("Girl, you better get over here, New Craze is playing! I *told* you that band was amazing! The people here are fabulous! I have made *so* many new friends here tonight! It's on the corner of First and Fifth, Vogue Club! You need to get out more, it's just not the same without...") before I pick up the phone and set it back down. I press a button and delete the message as I imagine her reaction tomorrow in class (Where were you last night? You don't even *try* to have fun anymore. What happened to you?)

I look at my towering stack of CDs, at the lyrics I used to memorize, and the bands I used to worship. Now instead of seeing an eclectic collection of audio art, I gaze scornfully at plastic products of pseudo-art. I know that if I try to listen to any of the so-called songs, that the words (love, hate, war, peace, romance, sex, light, dark, tragedy, ecstasy, death, birth, drugs, life) would pass unobstructed through my head like wind through a tunnel, and the faces of the actor-musicians would trigger no emotion. The bookshelf looms in the corner of my room. I once thought it to be a vast source of knowledge, but now I can't remember what was so important in those clones on the shelves.

I climb into my lonely doll-bed and join my bare walls in staring out the window. We watch the shiny plastic dreams of the city float out of the roofs of the buildings and swirl around the man-made stars that glow on top of the lampposts. The dreams drift and dance with the smog of the city and blend, becoming one. The streets still hum with meaningless activity, and it is impossible to escape, like a nightmare in which you see the monster but you cannot run.

The wind is still driving the leaves forward, telling them that they must reach their destination soon. Like clockwork, the manipulation and struggle continue on into the night. The icy, calculating moon smirks at the belligerent world below, but he winks conspiringly at me. He knows I am not fooled; he sympathizes with my apathy and relates to my indifference. At least I have a partner in my isolated sanity. Like a robot, I am programmed; I say the same prayer I have said since I could talk. "Now I lay me down to sleep, I pray the Lord my soul to keep (Keep it where? Why?) and if I should die before I wake (Then what difference would it make? Would it be any different than my present life?) I pray the Lord my soul to take."

My mind is still spinning, but my body is tired, so I close my eyes and make believe I'm sleeping. When the cheerfully oblivious sun pries open my eyes, I smile at her naiveté and prepare to continue the cycle.

11th grade

Sweatpants

by Timothy Paul Chatham

Never in, but always on,
I skip around the yard,
Singing on, a simple song,
For I'm a happy bard.

On and on, others moan,
Of how they lack a fit,
But I'm in my own, comfort zone,
And don't feel sorry a bit.

In fact, I laugh,
And with a roar,
For I must laugh, on their behalf,
'Cause they need not be sore.

I know at first, it does seem mean,
But how they amuse me so,
To watch them squeeze into those jeans,
Tucking in all of that dough.

Within their struggles, I find glee,
As they fight their fight with woe,
One look at me, and then they'd see,
The way to match the flow

A lesson please, so you ask me,
For you tire of rambling chants,
So hear my plea, you'll find your glee,
In your very own pair of sweatpants.

Adrenaline In Atlanta

by Kyle James

Road Atlanta is a racetrack that has many races, ranging from races like the Beetle Cup to knees, to asphalt in super-bike racing in Big Kahuna, and finally the big boys in the American Le Mans Series competing in Petit Le Mans. Petit Le Mans is a twelve-hour race consisting of Audis, Panoz, Cadillacs, Vipers, and Saleen S7's in the LMP and GT-S class, which race against their own class, not the GT class. Other classes follow these few and form a high-energy, twelve-hour race with three drivers, all competing on the same track at the same time against their class. It is an exhilarating experience that will forever leave a person craving burnt rubber and wicked speed as much as being out in the desert without water for three days.

When I arrive at the scene, I throw the car in neutral, pull the e-brake, step out, and glance at everything before my eyes. I notice the Road Atlanta sign up on the hill in intimidating green letters. I look around to see many exotic cars in the parking lot, some revving engines to the point of chassis movement while waiting in line for passes to the race. Next, I begin to hear what I think is a baby whining, until I look up and catch a glimpse of the Porsche 911 and BMW M3 getting shot with a cloud of exhaust smoke from a sly Panoz who flew from out of nowhere.

After the moment is over, I follow the sweet scent of the funnel cakes all the way back to the stand to meet my uncle and begin my day at the races. I ride with him on the golf cart to the campsite, plugging up my ears to the loud shifting of the redlining engines. The racecars are so throaty that I can look down and see the letters of my shirt vibrating. At last, first impressions are already making me feel pumped-up and excited about the blast I am about to have.

I watch from the straightaway for most of the race. First, I watch the blur of the cars as they scream by. I listen to the engines as they drive off into the distance. I love watching my dream car, the BMW M3, as it downshifts coming to the next sharp curve, spitting out flames through the twin side exhaust pipes.

The aroma of burnt rubber and exhaust gases make the atmosphere feel so much more alive. I also take in the rough scent of smoky, barbecued ribs sizzling on the grill behind me. In addition, every time the whining babies come around, I have to put in earplugs, which leaves me laughing from the vibration I feel in my ears. After the race has gone on for a while, I can time the shift points and call out every driver's time of shifting. The racing has now got me in the mood, adrenaline pumping, and ready for whatever fun the rest of the day brings.

As the sky begins to darken, and a gentle breeze makes the hair on my arms stand up, I get ready to watch the fireworks which conclude the race. I race around in the golf cart and notice all the tuned M3s and Audi S4s. I slam on the brakes to stare in awe at the most beautiful black BMW M3 CSL. My jaw drops just as it does when I gaze over to notice the girl of my dreams streaming her hands through her long, dark brown hair and then blinking her piercing aqua eyes. The slick and smooth metallic black paint that coats the metal of the magnificent machine is so flawless, the hood could be used as a mirror.

Next, I follow the crowd up the hill to where I stop at the concession stand to grab some popcorn straight out of the machine. I open the bag and a cloud of steam swarms my face, warming me up for a split second. I reach in to grab a handful, and my hand starts to burn as the butter runs through my fingers and then descends to the rough pavement.

I sit by the golf cart and finish eating the popcorn. Then, I go to the shops to examine the event T-shirts, and I don't see anything except for an M3 golf shirt I decide to get. As I head to the cash register to pay, the slippery material of the shirt makes me drop it onto the dusty floor of the tent.

After I pay, I head back to the campsite to watch the end of the race. The golf cart jolts to idle just as the leading Audi, with its blinding lights, makes its final lap through the final hairpin. A few minutes later, loud bangs startle everyone, but then leave everyone gazing at the red, white, and blue fireworks that conclude the race.

Road Atlanta, the perfect place to catch all your racing needs, whether it be ticked-off bees like ones of the Beetle Cup, super-bikes on steroids, or being blinded by 170 m.ph. of the LMP class. There is something for everyone at Road Atlanta; come to see the races or just hang out with friends and have a good time. Petit Le Mans, my favorite, packs in BMWs, Porsches, Audis, Corvettes, and many others into one twelve-hour race leading to the finish under the lights. As a result, Road Atlanta will leave you humming a tune of shifting gears the whole way home and then marking your calendar for next year's event.

The Call

by Erin E. Sharp

Every day, I spend hours working hard to make my life count for something. The coaches push, and I go. Pushing is not an easy thing to do, but after a while I start realizing I'm not out there for the coaches, but for myself. Each day is another struggle, one after another, striving to make something out of myself. After running on that quarter-mile path for hours every day, my body becomes a part of it. This track that I run on can either make or break me.

The race is about to begin as I move to my starting position. I look ahead at my old familiar friend, the track. All the runners are in their lanes at the starting line, and I am very nervous. This is when I really prove myself, and when the hard work that I have been doing shows the most. The six lanes of black highway wait to be driven on by young athletes. I feel as if everyone is looking at me. Moms, dads, grandparents, friends, and neighbors fill the large stands. Everyone competes with everyone else. Each of them is here to cheer on someone, hoping their person will win.

I stand remembering the last time I was this nervous. I hope I don't lose or make a fool of myself. I know that if I just keep my head on straight and do the best that I can do, then I will have a good chance at winning the race. Will my hard work, spending long hours every day pushing myself, pay off? Will this stretch of asphalt be faithful on my behalf?

"On your mark…get set…*BANG!*" The gun goes off and the race begins. My heart is pounding, *thump-thump, thump-thump*. I don't look to my right or to my left, but I am acutely aware of my opponents' feet pounding on the track. The aroma of hot dogs from the concession stand distracts me momentarily. I force myself again to focus on the narrow lane ahead of me.

Two racers pull ahead as I try to pace myself and preserve energy for the final leg. As the sweat pours down my red face and settles in my mouth, the saltiness goes unnoticed. With numb legs, I round the second and final curve. I measure the amount of open track between me and the two racers in front. The distance separating us appears to be about twenty meters, but feels like two miles.

This is it. My arms pump faster, and my legs press harder into the asphalt. Again, I feel my heart pounding and am no longer aware of the burning pain in my legs. I go faster and faster. I pass my closest opponent and then the one between me and victory. Only twenty-five meters are remaining to conquer. Every step I take is another closer to victory. Will my endless hours consuming this track reward me? Are my opponents going to catch up?

As the track calls me to the finish line, I hear the roar of the crowd screaming, “Go! Go!” The white line passes under my feet, and I throw my hands up victoriously. I turn to see the other racers complete the race only seconds behind. The results are either victory or defeat. Today, victory swallows defeat. The track approves of me and my relentless hours of labor once again.

Riddle, elddiR

by William Tsikerdanos

Note to the reader:
Please read from beginning to end, and then from end to beginning.

Are we mortal
How can we decide
Is it what
Is it when
Is it where, who, how
Question
A, chance in time
Life is Dream
Remembered are who
Live long
Death is Mortality
In Life…Yes?
Answers in riddles lie
First is last
Last is first

School Lunch

by Christian E. Clark

School lunch. Do you know anyone who buys school lunch and openly expresses their like for it? The answer that most people would probably reply with is, "NO." The truth is, everyone likes school lunch. The reason that no one will admit it is because it's not considered cool to like it. But let's look at some good things about school lunch.

If people would just think about it, school lunch is a whole lot healthier than the food their moms pack for them. How, you might ask? Everyone has heard the rumors that the lunchroom's meat is made of dog food, but my answer is for the obvious reasons.

First of all, think about how many calories you burn off standing in the crowded lunch line, huddled closely to everyone else, burning up and sweating. Now, sweating and being crowded together may sound bad to you, but that's only because you are you looking at it through the eyes of a pessimist. Think about it, the more calories you burn off before you eat, the more food you can eat. Therefore, you don't have to worry about eating too much and getting fat. All girls out there who starve themselves know what I am talking about.

Now, approaching the topic of being huddled closely together, just think about how standing in the lunch line could raise your social status in high school. Imagine all the friends someone could make while standing in the lunch line waiting to purchase food. Come on, they talk to a few people, make some new friends, get their names out, and all of a sudden they're prom king or queen. They are in the spotlight at the top of the world, all because they decided to buy school lunch. The battles are won and lost in the lunch line.

I mean, picture this; you have a hot date Friday night and it's Friday. You're strapped for cash, and all you have for lunch and the date is twenty dollars. Buy a school lunch for a couple of bucks and *bam* you have enough money for gas for your mom's car and tickets to the movies. What could be better?

Where else can you find a good, wholesome lunch for only a couple of bucks? And if you feel like splurging, spend four bucks at the grill line and you get more food than you could possibly imagine. So, there it is—friends, popularity, hot dates, money to spend, burning calories, and looking good. That's what school lunch is all about.

The Ball Game

by Sean Mixon

I walked back to the base. I squatted over it and listened to my coach tell me everything I already knew, "You've got him worried. Don't get greedy, but don't let him forget you're here. You have to split his concentration."

I felt the tension; everybody on the field did, but they didn't feel the pressure like when you are on the bottom of the pool and it feels like the water's going to crush your ears. I loved it. I felt the adrenaline coarse through my veins; my heart pounded, I was in my element. I watched the opposing coach shuffle to the mound, even though I couldn't hear him, I knew what he was saying. He was saying that I wasn't there; that Geno wasn't there, even that Alex wasn't there. He was saying that the only other person on the field was the catcher.

It had been overcast all day. Around the fourth inning it began to drizzle—not much, but enough to make the ball slick and the field muddy. At the start of the last inning it was raining in sheets. I didn't feel it any more.

We were the home team. At the start of the inning we were down by one. The first two batters struck out. I looped the ball into center field; it got me to first. Geno was up next. The first pitch was a ball, the next was wild, and I stole second. Then came a strike. I stole third on the next pitch, a ball, and Geno walked. The next batter was Alex. On the first pitch, Geno stole third. Then came another ball. This is when the opposing coach called time.

I stood up, rain dripping off my face. As I took my lead, the pitcher and I stared each other down. He looked at the catcher, got his sign and nodded. He looked at me, rocked back, and threw the ball. Then came the sound that half the people dreaded and the other half longed for—that distinct sound of aluminum hitting leather and cork. I moved without thinking, running as fast as I could towards the plate. I didn't look at the field, only at the catcher. As I neared the plate, he moved out of my way and I scored.

I stopped myself at the fence, turned around, and saw Geno cross the plate as well. At that moment I felt such jubilance that I ran over, grabbed him, picked him up and swung him around, cheering. The tension was gone, the crowd was in an uproar, but I didn't hear them. The only thing I saw was my team bursting out of the dugout and racing over to Geno and me. They picked us both up, along with Alex, and carried us off into the field. And we celebrated in the rain and mud.

11th grade

Fighting With My Nightmares

by Caitlin Bates

The shadows that pass across the wall
Move fiercely with anger in their step.
I watch intently, looking for familiarity.
The faces get closer, whereas the movement becomes faster.
Closing my eyes doesn't help them vanish;
They are engraved into my mind.
Only now can I hear them yell.
Their shrieking sends chills down my spine,
And everything becomes pristine.
They're getting closer.
I can feel it.
I can hear it.
I can sense it.
Finger crossed, as I sit in this dark corner,
Holding onto myself, praying that I can't be seen.
But even then it's too late.
Eyes closed, I can feel myself being snatched up,
Ripped away from my comfort hole.
Suddenly, these shadows become all too real.
I know what's coming next.
The pain begins surging all down my body.
I can't scream—my mouth is covered.
I cannot be saved…
My heart flutters and cries when I awake.
White is all I see,
And beeping from a machine is all I hear.
And a distant cooing voice, "It's alright. You're okay now..."
But how do I know that?
Next time those shadows haunt my dreams
Could very well be the last.
I am never safe…

Memories

by Tim Reeves

The setting was a warm summer day in the middle of June at our vacation house in Orient Point, New York. It was the summer of my ninth birthday, and I was excited to get away from school and just away from people in general. I was ready for six weeks of pure seclusion, where I was able to do what I wanted, when I wanted it done. I wanted to spend time with Beebop (that's my grandpa), because I only saw him in the summer.

I woke to the sound of Beebop's feet creaking down the old oak steps from the third floor. I slept on the second floor because I was scared of the third floor. Even though Beebop slept up there, just something about the upstairs and being in a room alone just wasn't too appealing. Now that I think about it, I was pretty stupid to be scared, but it's over now.

Anyway, I heard his footsteps and dashed out of the bed I was in as fast as I could. I couldn't make too much noise because my younger brother was sleeping next to me, and I didn't want to wake him up.

I slipped into my black gym shorts and white shirt and tiptoed out of the room. When I opened the door to the hallway, I saw him walking down the second flight of stairs. I followed him silently, being sure to wake no one as I passed by the other bedrooms. I knew if I woke up my mom, she would be angry because it was six o'clock in the morning and I was awake. When I was younger, if I didn't get enough sleep I would be quite cranky and then I would ruin her day. So, instead of dealing with her and the entire headache, I made sure I didn't wake her up.

By this time, Beebop was out the door and starting his daily walk. I sprinted to catch up to him on the driveway. The driveway was about a quarter of a mile long and wound its way thorough some trees and down to the main road, which ran parallel to the shoreline of the bay. Our house was situated on a peninsula, with water on both sides. To the north was the Long

Island Sound, and The Great Peconic Bay was butting us to the south. The Peconic Bay was much warmer because it was smaller and shallower, but not nearly as much fun to swim in as the Sound.

As Beebop and I walked down the pebble driveway, we saw bunnies scattered in the grassy spots catching their morning meal. As they spotted us moving towards them, they quickly hopped out of the way and back into the forest. We passed the second turn of the drive, and suddenly I was hit in the face with the smell of salt air from a light breeze blowing north off the bay. A huge smile came to my face as the salt breeze filled my nose. I felt as though this was where I belonged, and I felt as if I was home.

We approached the road and made sure to look both ways as we crossed. My grandpa was big on safety. On the other side of the blacktop road there was a beach to the left and a sort of mini rock cliff that was only about six feet high, with a walking wall that stretched as far as we could see on the right. We took the walking ledge, because we had walked the beach the previous day. We climbed onto the walk and took off on our new quest. Each morning walk brought something new and a new adventure.

Anyway, we began our walk. I was out ahead of Beebop as I normally was, but I knew he would catch up. I looked out over the bay and became excited as I saw the ripples of the waves reflecting the sun in all different directions. Now, these waves weren't huge—the bay actually resembled a lake—but, of course, the water had a hint of salt and wasn't landlocked.

Out in the middle of the bay was a stubby little lighthouse that went by the name of Bug Light. It only stood about one hundred feet high and was marked with black and white stripes. To everyone else it was nothing spectacular, but to me it was a sign that summer was here and I was free. Of course, I only saw it once a year during summer, unless we made a special trip up during the winter holidays.

The breeze picked up a little as the morning drew on. It was still early, but we began to see some activity on the water. Giant sailboats, some seventy feet in length, were making their way to Plum Gut, which was where the Peconic Bay and the Atlantic Ocean met the Long Island Sound. Plum Gut was very treacherous water, which only bigger boats could handle, but I was sure the seventy-footers wouldn't have any trouble making it out to the open water. We stood there enjoying the multicolored masts that moved past, then decided to go on.

We reached the end of the wall, which was the start of a bridge. The bridge crossed a little gap of water that flowed from the bay into a small body of water called Oyster Pond. We didn't want to walk back on the wall because we didn't want to see the same things over again. We decided to float under the bridge into the saltwater pond. We were lucky because the tide was coming in, which meant the water was flowing into Oyster Pond.

Beebop and I never walked with shoes, and we had our bathing suits on (we were always prepared for this sort of thing). We were ready to jump into the water. We leaped into the rushing current; it was a little brisk because the sun hadn't had a chance to warm it up yet. We sat in the water with our toes pointing out and our heads up so we could see the water around us as we floated. We had to watch for sharks; some got pretty big. Actually, that was a joke; there were no sharks in that water, except for maybe some sand sharks that never got any bigger than two and a half feet. Sometimes a person might get lucky and catch a five-footer while fishing, but that was only further out.

We floated under the bridge, seeing some schools of minnows and a couple of jellyfish, but nothing to worry about. We drifted out into the bay and then had to swim to the other side. We made sure to not touch the bottom because then the water would get really muddy and we wouldn't be able to see all the neat fish and crabs on the bottom. We were hoping to get lucky and catch a glimpse of a horseshoe crab or maybe a little blowfish. Our patience paid off towards the end. We saw a horseshoe crab being followed by a baby one that was about the size of my palm. We didn't spot a blowfish that day, but I wasn't sweating over it. I was sure I would see one before I left.

Our floating trip brought us across the landmass to the beach of the Long Island Sound. The beach had pebbles at the top but sand closer to the bottom near the water. Beebop and I didn't mind walking on the stones at all; our feet were used to it. The waves in the sound were a little bigger than in the bay, and the water was much cooler. I could see the rocky points at the end of either side of the beach. They were a lot of fun at low tide because we could drive our little johnboat out to them and jump off into the water. Some of the rocks were twenty feet high and made for a great rush jumping into the water. When I looked across toward the horizon, I could see the mainland. The sound was a total of maybe fifteen miles across.

Beebop and I walked along the beach for a while, picking up stones and throwing them into the water. Soon, we spotted a boulder in the water that was huge. It wasn't just any boulder either; it marked the start of our property. We found the boardwalk that led to the house, which looked out over the sound. As we walked along the wooden planks, we saw the osprey nest.

Ospreys are very beautiful birds. They are said to be the falcons of the sea. They are migratory, which means they return every year to breed. Our ospreys come back every summer. We could hear the chicks squeaking for food, and we turned around to try and find the parents. We scanned the horizon for the birds and soon saw one beginning a dive into the water. We were awed by the speed of the attack and its gracefulness, and then applauded as it took flight again, this time with a big porgy in its claws. We turned around and headed towards the house again.

As we came to the end of the boardwalk, we passed the

green treehouse and the garden filled with vegetables. The treehouse had a view of the water, so we used to always play pirates with fake guns and swords. I bet there is still buried treasure somewhere that could be worth a lot of money hiding in the yard. Well, maybe not a lot of money, but no one will ever know. I would help Beebop in the garden every afternoon. He always needed help—the garden was huge—and there were tons of vegetables which needed to be picked. We always ate the vegetables we grew from our own garden. Usually, they were string beans and tomatoes. Maybe we would, on occasion, get lucky and also get a couple of good pea plants.

We came up the hill and were going to reach the house soon. I took my grandfather's hand in mine as we walked. I looked at him and told him that he was my best friend in the whole world and that I never wanted to leave Mattituck. I wanted to stay with him and go on walks every morning and have new adventures forever. Of course, I knew that wouldn't happen, but I wanted him to know that I loved him. That was the most special summer of my life.

We went on many other walks that summer and had a lot of adventures. I wish I could have gone on more, because that very next spring Beebop passed away. He had a brain tumor. He was in the hospital from the late winter on into spring. He left the hospital and returned to his home in Port Orient, Maryland. He went through chemotherapy, and that seemed to make it worse. Sometimes he would forget who I was, even my name. The last week of his life, my mom chose to take him off chemo. He seemed to be reborn. He remembered everything—the walks, the fishing, and the friendship. One week later, the cancer took over and ended his life. I never got to say goodbye—except on the telephone, but that's not the same as saying goodbye in person. At least he died happy.

I go on walks now, alone, but it's never the same. Sometimes people come with me, but that makes it even worse. It wasn't just the walks that made the summers special; it was the bond with the water, grass under my feet, and the air that was special, along with the bond between with my grandfather and me.

Scars

by Kim-Uyen Tran

"Ba" is what I have called this man each and every day of my life. "Ba," meaning "father" in Vietnamese, was the very first word that I pronounced when I was a toddler calling and reaching for him when he had to leave for work. Ba, this other reflection of mine, was always and always will be there to teach me about everything there is to life to the end. Just with the thought of Ba, I can envision his fiery eyes looking into mine when I have done something to upset him. It was as if his stare contained flames burning the skin through until it touched the soul and left scars; that stare always leaves me motionless, holding my breath.

They say back in Vietnam that tough love is the way to teach, and tough love is what I have received. All his actions, even from the time before my own existence, help me to realize that I could be a better person if I try.

He is a man who works at the maximum, a man who takes pleasure in work. Of the many people I have come to know in my life, never have I seen a person have such will power to actually want to work. If Ba has a goal, it is always to be accomplished and never left to wait. He works until he is satisfied that the best of his efforts are put into whatever it is he wants to complete. Ba loves and needs work the way a dog loves and needs his daily exercise. I do not recall there ever being a time when Ba had the fear of failing; he always has an optimistic view on things and always has the mind to do nearly anything he wishes.

Even though Ba is fond of working, he has a habit of keeping to himself, speaking only when necessary. Maybe this is because Ba learned everything the hard way, and maybe because of this, he is always hard on me.

Ba was an orphan living during the Vietnam War. He was the youngest of four children from the village of Nghe An, but he was forced to depart from his village in North Vietnam in order to escape the power-hungry Communists (Viet Cong)—only to move to the south with his uncle who had a wife who beat Ba.

The scars all over his body bring images of this woman whipping Ba into my imagination; with every scar that I have seen, I cringe with uneasiness. She was cynical and had no love for a poor boy that had lost his parents at such a young age. She cared only for her own children and wanted to make sure that they were the ones who got ahead in life and received the best of everything. She forced Ba to be a servant in her home. He was to take care of her children, clean the house, prepare meals, and go fetch barrels of water from the well (far away). The heavy loads of work that he bore made him bitter.

Out of anguish, not being able to handle such torment any longer, Ba ran away and submitted himself to an orphanage. Under poor conditions, he would go days and weeks without food, begging on the streets and getting into fights with other boys.

From the orphanage he moved on and entered a monastery for boys, to get an education. To earn money, he would tutor boys from rich families. Graduating from high school in Vietnam is one of the most difficult tasks. It is said that some have even committed suicide because they could not pass, and without passing, their fate would only lead to begging on the streets for days. Death seemed to be a far better fate than dragging on a pointless life in penury—stealing, killing, and begging in order to survive. Ba wanted to be better than this; he studied day and night for his graduation exam. Successfully, he graduated and moved on to law school and earned his first degree in Vietnam.

By age twenty, he was drafted into the army to fight the Viet Cong in the Vietnam War. Because of his law degree, he was ranked a lieutenant officer. His job was to train the soldiers for the battlefield and to work along with the U.S. Army. Here, he met my mother's father, the general. One can assume that Ba met my mother through his acquaintances with the well-respected general. Sadly, though there was great effort, the South Vietnamese Army, along with the United States Army, lost to the Viet Cong Communists. So much was lost to them: belongings, land, money, and even the lives of the Vietnamese people.

My father learned a great deal from that war. The day that Saigon, the capital of South Vietnam, fell to the Viet Cong, Ba and my mother escaped to America, the land of the free. No longer were they to live in fear and destitution. They could live the American dream—the harder one worked, the farther ahead one would get in life.

Ba and my mother started from the beginning. Especially with the language barrier and only knowing the words "yes" and "no," life wasn't much better at first. Ba came to America with Vietnamese money that only equated to two pennies in American money. He and my mother came to a strange place, surrounded by strangers who didn't speak or understand the same language. Not only did they have to learn a new language, but they also had to learn a completely new culture. The normal beef soup and egg rolls could not be easily found at the corner grocery store back in the 70s the way they can be found now.

How he came to be where he is now is most miraculous. Even though they didn't know enough English, they had to find some way to earn money while attending school. Switching from job to job in order to eat and pay for school, Ba finally graduated with a master's degree in chemical engineering. Now a well-respected businessman, he has made a life of hardships into a life of prosperity.

The scars that he has left on my life are nothing compared to the scars he has received from a life of adversity. A person can create his own path in life, and that affects the scars that they attain. No matter how hard I believe he is on me, I think back and remember his life story. Who am I to be greedy? Who am I to judge the poor? Who am I think that I am better?

Victims Of The Holocaust

by Lauren Kiel

The voices cry out, lonely and lost,
victims of the Holocaust.

Singled out by a patch or star,
their lives were limited— they couldn't go far.

Families were broken,
as orders were spoken.

Carelessly they were tossed,
innocent victims of the Holocaust.

Enduring their hardest test,
while constantly being suppressed.

They had to keep faith, courage, and hope,
in order to be able to survive and cope.

Unfairly they were lost,
the lives of these victims of the Holocaust.

My Road

by Ashley Elizabeth Jabrocki

"Yes!" I exclaimed, as I slammed my book shut. I had finished my homework and put it away. I placed my backpack on the floor and climbed onto my bed. I decided to bask in the emptiness of my room before turning on the television. My father was working outside in the yard, raking leaves into mounds that the wind desperately tried to scatter. My stepmother was working in the tobacco shop and would not be home until late that night. My stepbrother was enjoying the newfound freedom he had gained earlier that month with a new car; the road was open before him.

At first, the solitude I found behind my locked door was comforting, but all of a sudden chills ran through my body as I realized how quiet and closed-in the space seemed. I groped for the remote control and turned on the television set. The noise that came with the moving pictures made me feel a little more at ease. The problem with mindless cartoons was that my brain began to create other ways to keep itself occupied. I began to slowly remove myself from reality. Then something terrible happened. The flashbacks came clear and vivid in my head. I squirmed in a hopeless effort to rid myself of the nightmare. I felt the hands of the man who had hurt me touch my body again.

"No!" I whispered hoarsely as I sat up in my bed. I didn't want to think of the memories. I got up and went to my dresser. I took my hairbrush from its resting place and started to brush my hair. Harder and harder I pulled, until large clumps of my light brown and blond hair formed in the bristles. I stared at my reflection in the mirror, and I wanted to scream. I slowly stopped yanking at my hair. I saw that I had a single tear on my cheek. I despised my face. My eyes had witnessed lust. My lips had experienced kisses beyond their years. My face was spoiled. My body had been ruined.

I placed my hands on my face. I felt the hands again. They were moving across my back, to my sides, then to my breasts. I closed my eyes, but it only made the hands solid. My knees became weak, and I slid to the floor.

The tears poured over my cheeks and onto my clothes and carpet. I wrapped my arms around my shivering body and closed my eyes again. I tried to forget the man who had stolen my childhood. He had made me ugly. Nobody could love a girl like me after such an ordeal. There must have been some kind of a sign across my forehead that made people run away. I was damaged beyond repair.

I still felt the hands moving, and in my mind I saw his face, his eyes, and his intent. I remembered being puzzled by his actions when I was young. Was he supposed to touch me there? Was this how a stepfather shows his love? I wanted to be loved, but I didn't like how his hands felt across my body.

As I grew older, I realized that he was wrong in his ways, and all the pain I had suffered so I would be loved was unnecessary. If I felt so bad about what he was doing, then I should have said something. Why didn't I speak out?

My mind was reeling as my memories came back to me. He had ruined me; I would never be the same. These thoughts kept coming, and I rocked my body in hopes of stopping the tremors. The tears were still coming as I reached up to the top of my dresser. My hand felt around until it came to a porcelain doll I had received on my thirteenth birthday. I brought the small doll down to me. She was so pretty and perfect. Her eyes looked so innocent. She had never been touched.

There I sat in a pit of tears and turmoil glaring at the doll's face. I was envious of her. I was trying to get out of the abyss, but the hands were pulling me down. Why couldn't I be like the doll?

Anger suddenly came over me, and I hit the doll against the dresser. The pressure did not shatter her body, but her head soared across the room. I looked at the girl's body in my hand, and I felt ashamed. "I would never look into a mirror again," I vowed to myself.

I placed my head in my arms as I sat on my knees on the floor. I was curled up trying to shelter myself from the rain. When I finally looked up, I turned my body so my back faced the dresser. I stared outside my window. The sun was shining through the clouds. They had a golden color outlining them.

I decided to pray. I didn't know what to pray for, so I thanked God for the sky. I cried and asked Him to love me. Then I asked for forgiveness for my selfishness. I wanted God to change everything that had happened to me. I knew that He wouldn't snap His fingers to erase the pain, but I did know He could help me be normal. I wanted to be just like everyone else. I asked for understanding and the ability to cope with my past situation.

I pleaded for all of these things as I walked across the room and picked up the head of my doll. I put her body and head on the dresser before I looked for the glue in one of the drawers. I glued her back together, and I am still able to see the ring around her neck. I put her back where she belonged, and I looked in the mirror. What I saw was something I had not seen in a long time. My face was red and my eyes were puffy, but I noticed a smile when I looked at my lips. It was rare and seemed out of place, but it was beautiful.

I decided from that moment on to be who God wants me to be. I have had setbacks, but I'm working my way up from the pit to the clouds to improve myself. My road is before me, and all I have to do is walk it. I am free of my past and myself. With God, I am free.

Java And Jazz

by Cora Tallant

The piano player plucked and tickled the cool keys. The smooth black and white keys played a song of the blues. Everyone in the packed house watched. Some sat in chairs, others at stools, while a few lounged on the couches. There was a silence, which was filled with the musical sounds of spoons stirring, coffee slurping, clearing throats, snapping fingers, and humming. Most had something to quench their thirst: cappuccino, mocha, latté, espresso, roast, all just as addicting as the last. On the walls are a few choice pieces of artwork. Each photograph, each charcoal sketch, each abstract painting has a story to tell, if only one took the time to decipher it. Books line the shelves while newspapers and magazines litter the tables, all of which are coffee-stained. A lonely plant finds a home in a lonely corner. Then there's the fish tank; it nearly covers one of the walls with its many tropical fish. In fact, the fish were the most active people in the joint. They danced to the piano player's music as if they were performing a watery ballet for the customers.

The place was unique, to say the least. Everyone knew everyone else. The regulars could tell one another by name, face, occupation, and drink. Even the barista knew what time so-and-so came in, what they wanted, and where they sat. That was a big issue—where you sat. Seats were unofficially claimed territory. It was an unspoken rule that seats remained yours and no one could sit there but you. This rule was only broken when a newbie pranced in; he was welcomed by an uncomfortable and hostile silence.

Here was where new ideas were formed over a cup of java. Open-mindedness was not only welcomed, but a requirement. Talk was only necessary when there was something to say. Opinions were as addicting as the caffeine. There were cliques: Democrats and Republicans, professors and students, classical musicians and punk rockers, tree huggers and yuppies. No matter, everyone was equal. Everyone was another note in the piano player's melody.

Suddenly, the piano slowed and ended its last song. Joe, an old, balding man with an unequivocal love for the tiny café, stepped down from the stage. Talk spread throughout the café like wildfire, as a hazed murmur uplifted the silence. "Good job tonight, Joe," said one longtime regular.

"Thanks," was all he would return. Compliments to Joe and his magical piano filtered here and there as Joe made his way to the bar.

"You did well, Mr. Joe," commented Betsy as she gave the tired man his dark coffee. She rather liked this dear soul; Mr. Joe had given her a job at his café to help her through college. She had been down on her luck trying to find a full-time job that paid for a full-time rent, while maintaining a full-time course load. Mr. Joe allowed her to study at the register during the slow hours, which were many.

Betsy watched him with a grandfatherly love as he sipped his brew and rested. He would play an hour set in the morning, another at lunch, and a two-hour set before the café closed in the evening. Betsy knew Mr. Joe had arthritis, but he still continued to coax the piano into its sweet songs. *"How utterly wonderful it must be,"* thought Betsy, *"to love the music so much, after all these years."*

The young, innocent barista hadn't the slightest notion of how much Joe loved his music; the piano, the keys, the notes, the very melodies were all a part of his soul. As he played, he contemplated his life. Stories of his childhood, his rebellious school days, earning money in the city, a lost love, and dear friends departed—all of this could be heard through his songs. For an hour or more, he sifted through years of memories; indeed, there were many years to sift through now. Joe was old, and he knew it. For that hour of blissful remembrance, he paid for in an hour of pain. No, pain wasn't the word. He was beset with sore, throbbing knuckles, the ache of worn joints and age, the sting of clenching a hand, and the twinge of unclenching it again. Joe felt every one of his many years, after his magic fingers were silent. He felt as drained as his now empty cup.

Joe arose from his chair, stretched, and made his way to the back office. The fingers that played jazz must also balance bankbooks. The café was obviously a small business, and it faced as many problems as other small businesses face. A corporate coffee chain had just opened in town. It offered fashionable coffees with equally fashionable prices for the fashionable youth. Joe was not worried. The regulars were loyal and would continue to come, regardless of fashion. But the economy was just as fickle and unpredictable as fashion and youth. Joe worried over his lovely café's future; he shuddered to think of his life without its lovely life and vitality.

Pushing aside the dreary books, he returned to the bar. He took orders while Betsy swept the floor. Together, they washed dishes so that she could finish studying the New Deal. He delivered refills to a few of the regulars, although they had neither asked nor declined. Joe refereed an argument between a professor of literature and a journalist; it was finally settled that "journalism was literature in a hurry," so of course Woodward and Bernstein could not be as refined as Dickens and Twain. He caught swatches of gossip and gore. He read about politics in the paper and reminisced over the glamour of Kennedy's White House. All the while, the crowd ebbed and flowed, new faces came in, and old faces went out; the tide was changing as dusk approached.

Joe went to feed his tropical fish along the wall. He knew that his dancers could not perform on empty stomachs. Indeed, the colorful dancers started their warm-ups. They twirled, spun, whirled, dashed, looped, reeled, and created a splendid flurry of color. Even the buzz of conversation seemed to escalate to a brilliant crescendo. Everyone was anticipating Joe's final performance of the evening. Slowly, having completed his humdrum chores, the old man walked to the stage. He shuffled as he walked, slightly stooped with age; yet, every step brought back some of his youth. By the time he sat on the piano stool his head was held high, his posture regained, and a twinkle shone in his eye. The colorful dancers waited for their cue in the wings. Joe tilted his head as he touched those pearly keys. A soft melody wound its way across the room until it reached every shadowy corner. The café was once again filled with the sound of the blues, the smell of freshly brewed coffee, and the tranquility of life.

Living

by Ashley Parker

I am going to cherish life,
all the treasures that it holds;
the sun, the stars, the moon,
and the mysteries untold.

I am going to appreciate my gifts,
the talents where I've been blessed;
I am going to count to ten,
before I get all stressed.

I will sit back and revel in,
the things to do and see;
the trees, the clouds, the rain,
the warm and gentle breeze.

I will listen to the silence,
and try my best to hear;
the words that God is whispering,
so softly in my ear.

I will not take for granted,
the people who care for me;
they are the ones who lead my way,
when I'm too blind to see.

I will live life to the fullest,
and treat every day as my last;
and all regrets that I once had
are now buried in the past.

The Jail

by Havilah Miller

There once was a little girl who lived in jail—yes, in jail. No one was aware of it because she had a normal home with wonderful parents, and she lived a normal life. But inside, her address was not 5874 Wickerhall Avenue; it was cell #7305478.

Locked up, darkness and loneliness surrounded her. Misery and defeat were her most intimate friends. Oftentimes, the girl would feel her way to the cold iron bars *just* so she could get a glimpse of the outside world, which she envied and desperately yearned to be a part of. From a way's off, squeals of carefree and confident children could be heard, children who were free from this incarceration, free to be themselves; AAHHHH…to be themselves! Just that thought was soothing! She could almost feel the warm sunshine on her deprived face. Oh, how she longed to be released and join them. But the jailer kept the key, and the merciless bars kept her trapped, for the cell was constructed of the brick and stone of inferiority and self-doubt, and the iron bars were made of fear. Ironically, the only thing worse than being in jail was being out of it.

I was that little girl. January 28, 1999, Friday night, Wickerhall Middle School Girls Basketball Championship; the gym was packed with students and parents. The noise was deafening, and the air was hot and stuffy with the aroma of hot dogs and nachos. As usual, I was sitting on the bench with my friends, all of us hoping that this would be the game in which we would finally see some playing time. The first string was excellent and quickly wearing our opponents down. By the end of the first quarter, the win was certain. Socializing, Jackie, Christine, and I weren't paying much attention, since the game was going so well without us. All of a sudden, with only three minutes left on the clock, Coach gave me the signal. "Hey, Miller. You're in."

"Me? Is he talking to me? Everyone knows I'm not good enough to go in." With utter disbelief, I dumbly stumbled out

onto the court like a victim thrust into the Roman Coliseum in the midst of ravenous lions. Gulping, my eyes skimmed the seemingly thousands of faces. Cheerleaders, smell of popcorn, squeaking of Converses, heavy breathing of players with their beet-red faces and shining bodies—all of that whirled around me like a dream.

"Snap out of it, Hav!" Marcy said, with a thump on the shoulder. The Ref's whistle blew. Next thing I knew, my heart was pounding out of my chest as the ball was being dribbled down court. *"C'mon Hav, just stick with your man, and you won't screw up and nobody will notice you,"* I thought to myself.

Then, from out of nowhere, the Pentacle, the Ark of the Covenant, the much-sought-after...BALL—with a divine light over it and a heavenly chorus singing above—flashed into my hands! Looking down at it, *Bam!* The spotlight was on me. The gym was so quiet that all I could hear were the crickets chirping outside. *Oh, myyyyyyy goodness. I'm just a few feet away from the goal. I know...I just know I can make it! Wait a minute! No I can't. Who am I kidding? Maybe I can. Yeah, this is my chance.*

My teammates were shouting, "No! No! No!" Out of the corner of my eye, Coach was waving his hands in desperation. Everyone focused on me. For the first time in my life, I was the center of attention, and I didn't like it. For a brief moment, I was outside the prison cell that I knew so well, and I was terrified.

Pressure was rapidly mounting. *"I can't take this,"* I thought, panicking. Then my body stiffened and, with no warning, re-volted! Tremors raced down my arms, spastically flailing from my chest, firing the ball from where I stood. In slow motion, I watched the ball sailing, sailing, sailing over my teammates, over the freethrow line, and, to everyone's dismay, way over the goal. I felt a dropping sensation in my stomach, and I wanted to follow all the way beneath the gym floor. Predictably, Coach whistled and motioned me over to the bench. Hanging my head, I slinked back into my seat next to the water bottles, hoping no one would ask me any questions as my teammates muttered, "I knew it, I knew it."

That's what it was like to be me. I could never leave my jail. I could never just step out on my own. I could never be myself, even though I wanted it so badly. And if I ever did step out of the box—like I did at the basketball game—I would get so scared and panicked, I would mess up every time and race back to the security of my cell. Similar to an animal caged up for years and then set free, I would have rather stayed in the cage. In school, I was the mummy, silently blended in with the bulletin board at the rear of the class. I dared not say anything out loud, or I would feel the chilling stares, disgusted looks, and the arrogant flips of the heads. (That was after everyone, including the teacher, looked around to see who said that). That was a pain I just couldn't bear. That was a lock I just couldn't pick.

All throughout school, that jail was my home. I watched from behind my bars as my peers had fun, ran for offices, won competitions, made friends, and simply…lived. I've sung many a song on stage, I've been the star of all the school plays, the most valuable player for the basketball team, and Homecoming Queen every year—all in my head. In reality, my jailer always told me that I was never good enough, smart enough, pretty enough, athletic enough to do anything, Everywhere I went, in every social situation, I almost felt guilty for the air I breathed. I almost felt guilty that I was taking up too much space.

"Why won't anyone notice me? Why doesn't anyone care?" I've been waiting for someone to rescue me, someone who has the key to unlock this prison, take me by the hand, and lead me out. *"Maybe my rescuer would be my friend, parent, boyfriend,"* I thought. Needless to say, I waited a long time, and no one came.

However, on a spring afternoon, while I gazing through the

bars to the outside world, something caught the corner of my eye that I had never noticed before. Stooping down to pick it up, its brass shone in the light, its grooves felt my fingertips; it was a key, and not just any key. It was *the* key. What's more, it even had my name on it. I looked around for the jailer who, for years, had always been over my shoulder, and he wasn't there! Then it hit me. *I* was the jailer and had had the key with me all of the time. I *was* the key—believing in myself was the only hope of escape. And nobody else, no other key, would fit. No boyfriend, no friend, no parent; I had to do it *myself.*

Slowly, I raised the key to the old rusty lock and pushed it in. I held my breath as the key clicked to the left. But nothing happened. How could this be? Furious with false hope and frustration, my hands lunged at the bars, but only to fly right through them as if they were never really there. Then, my feet followed along with the rest of my body. I looked back to see that it was all a mirage! I had deceived myself into thinking I was a step below everyone else and simply "couldn't" for that reason. However, now the bars and the fear were gone.

I cautiously took a few steps into the wide earth. With no more darkness, isolation, or coldness, I lifted up my head to the glorious sun and felt its warm rays running through my body the way I had always dreamed.

A heavy burden was suddenly lifted off my shoulders. For the first time, I saw myself as "good enough" to join that group of children playing. I seemed to almost float in a radiantly illimitable sky. The true happiness of freedom and confidence boiled out all the emptiness of inferiority. Boldly, I stretched out my arms to the world and shouted at the top of my lungs, "I'm free! I'm whole! I'm happy! I'm alive! A brand new feeling was birthed inside of me; I *LOVE* myself! Walking down the road, the people who once ignored me...now smiled at me. And I smiled back.

Under The Bridge

by Rebecca (Billie) Damren

(Song in this story written and recorded by Red Hot Chili Peppers)

I was born as a total surprise to my parents. They never expected to have a third child, especially since my brother had been born almost nine full years before I was, and my sister two years before him. Most people tell me I'm lucky, since I don't have to deal with annoying younger or nagging older siblings throughout middle school and high school. As for my feelings about it? I miss having my big sister around to ruffle my hair, or my big brother to randomly whack me with a throw pillow. The house seems so quiet and sterile without them. That is why I spend time trying to remember every detail. For example, how Wendi used to tie the extensions of my overly large sweatshirt sleeves in a knot, preventing me from touching her stuff; or how Jon and I would take pillows in our hands and have "boxing tournaments" until we each had bloody noses and stomachaches from laughter. But the one memory that always sticks out in my mind is the way Jon would sing to me.

Being seven, I never had any clue of the things going on in my older brother's life. Drugs and heavy metal, my brother was a troubled teenager. Skipping school, starting fights with my father, running away; it was all pretty common in his life. My brother went through some rough times. But all I knew of it then was my brother locking himself in his room and my mother crying at night. But, being of tomboyish nature, I wasn't interested in my sister. All she did was talk on the phone. On the other hand, I had an avid curiosity about Jon.

Remember how I mentioned him locking himself in his room? Because of this barrier, I would do anything and everything possible to get past that door and into the wonders of my brother's room. Clothes on the floor, posters on the walls, a lava lamp—everything in his room caught my interest. But most of all was the acoustic guitar leaned in the corner; it intrigued me more than anything. The long neck which extended so far that the protrusion made the instrument my height; six tautly pulled strings, each different; the smooth oblong body—it all made me tingle to look at it. But I never saw Jon play it...until one day.

It was the middle of summer, and I was thoroughly bored. Having annoyed my sister so much that she made my mom come and kick me out, I made my way to Jon's door. I looked up at the huge "KEEP OUT" sign across the woodwork and smiled. Assuming the door was locked as always, I knocked, or actually "banged," at the oak barrier that separated me from a thousand wonderful objects...but there was no answer, not even the usual "go away." So I banged harder. No answer again. Upset, I cried and screamed for him at the top of my lungs. No answer again. Frustrated, I gave the doorknob a hard twist and, to my surprise, the door swung open. I sat shocked for a moment, but then I wiped away my tears and started in.

As I walked into the room of my big brother, a sound came to my ears, and it wasn't him yelling at me, for once. It was unlike anything I had ever heard before. Sure, my mother ordered those tapes of children's songs, but it didn't even come close to comparing to the harmony of notes and chords that hit my ears then. Each sound fit so perfectly together, so wonderfully placed, each beat as it should be. It was overwhelmingly beautiful. Being the small child I was, it drew me in with each curious chord, like a cat being dragged in by the scruff of the neck. Then, I saw my brother. He sat at the corner of his bed, skillfully moving each finger of his hands to elicit the amazing sounds that filled my ears. It was so professional, yet he played this melody as if it was a simple child's tune. "Jon?" I had whispered hesitantly.

There was no answer from his lips, and no recognition of my presence for a few long moments. He then glanced up at me and flashed me a small smile. It seemed that as soon as he had looked up, his eyes were roaming back over his fingers which ran deftly down the neck of his guitar. Then came words, at first a raspy whisper, but then stronger:

"Sometimes I feel like I don't have a partner. Sometimes I feel like my only friend is the city I live in, the City of Angels. Lonely as I am, together we cry."

With a seamlessly involuntary impulse, I sat, my eyes glued on my brother. I had never known my brother sang so well…or that he actually played that old guitar. It intrigued me as nothing had before. I had no clue what the words meant, since it hadn't been sung bluntly, and to my young mind it was gibberish. But it didn't matter. The words, the rhythm, each practiced strum of the guitar, and each deep soulful note of my brother's voice; it drew me in like a moth to a flame. His every sung word seared through me. Right then and there, I felt something. It was as if it had been waiting inside me for so long and had finally been released.

"I drive on her streets 'cause she's my companion. I walk through her hills 'cause she knows who I am. She sees my good detail, she kisses the windy. I never worry, now that is a lie."

My brother seemed so at ease under my staring, as if I wasn't even there. He played his guitar as if he and the numbingly beautiful instrument were all that existed. Even at my tender age, I was in awe, and everything seemed so distant, suddenly. I didn't feel like a child anymore; I can't describe how I felt then. I felt so educated, yet ignorant, important, but so useless. It all came at one time.

"I don't ever wanna feel like I did that day. Take me to the place I love, take me all the way. I don't ever wanna feel like I did that day. Take me to the palace I love, take me all the way, yeah, yeah."

After that day, I would constantly plead for my brother to play it for me, and he always said no. I wanted to hear it again and again, to feel the way I did when I first heard it. It was terrible, the way I begged, yet he would never play the song for me. He would only play it when I never asked, when I never expected him to.

Not until later did I truly realize the reason for my sudden curiosity. Not only did the words of the song touch me, but it was the way my brother sang them. With everything going on in his life, he still sang. Even though he would skip school and get in trouble, he still sang. And when my mother and father got a divorce, he sang. It was his outlet. All his teenage angst and anger, all his emotion, the way nobody believed he could change, the way my father yelled at him; it was all channeled into this song—his song: "Under the Bridge."

My brother is in the Marines now. His life turned around. He graduated from high school. He went through boot camp. He went through being stationed overseas. He went through a year in Japan and has been in more countries than I have been in states. He went through it all when few thought he could. And he did it all with his head held high.

I don't get to see my brother much, maybe three times a year. But when I do, I always beg him to sing for me. And even though Jon has changed a lot throughout his lifetime, the passion he puts into his song never changes.

"Under the bridge downtown is where I drew some blood. Under the bridge downtown I could not get enough. Under the bridge downtown, forgot about my love. Under the bridge downtown, I gave my life away."

11th grade

Ode To A Desert Night

by Elizabeth Ann Devine

The sun sinks below the horizon.
Darkness falls on a desert that some would call devoid.
But as the moon rises, it shines light and truth.
That as the temperature drops,
The desert comes alive.

It isn't just the occasionally soaring bird,
Or the snake curled, waiting to strike.
It isn't just the occasionally wandering coyote.
It's so much more.

Have you ever peered outside your window at the desert at night?
Have you ever dared to step outside?
If so, you would know that you wandered into a world
That you had not known existed in such a seemingly barren place.

Look to the flower that blooms only at night,
When the desert sun can no longer show its cruelty.
Look to the bats that fly above.
Listen for the small creatures that will scuttle across the sands.

Or perhaps it is the owl's company you'd enjoy most.
He watches carefully for a desert rodent.
Or perhaps he'd prefer a hare,
Who has finally dared to wander outside his den.

Watch the spider creep carefully across the sands,
Fearing the encounter of a rather large wasp waiting for him.
Watch the snakes glide across the sand to get to the treat the owl spotted first.
See the treat dash back to its den.

Watch the coyote's pups dance for joy and play among the still warm sand

While the youngest of them hide in the underbrush.
As they themselves watch a roadrunner snatch an insect for a meal.
The lizard, the desert's most popular animal, will merely lie there,
as it usually does.

It waits for possible threat.
And should it see you, it will most likely run.
Scuttle away,
Down into the sand or away into the distance.

You call the desert barren.
You call the desert dead.
But I know better.
I have seen the wonders of a desert night.

Mark's Joy

by Carl Chandler

Raindrops gently pattered along eleven-year-old Mark Woodall's expansive bedroom window. He sat there in his wheelchair, mesmerized by the rain. As the raindrops fell, they left gentle ripples in the large, murky brown lake that belonged to Mark's family. The lake was surrounded by tall, beautiful pine trees and was adjacent to the Woodall's spacious home. You could get lost in the large and extravagant mansion. The mansion had dark hardwood floors, enormous bay windows, a massive seven-car garage filled with expensive cars, and a boat dock attached to the lake. The Woodalls had purchased the property years prior to Mark being born, but it was not until recently that they built their dream home on it.

The Woodall family had always been well-off financially. After all, Mark's father, Jim Woodall, was president of Woodall's Grocery Store. Mr. Woodall had turned it into the largest and most profitable grocery store chain in America. Mark's father had great love for his son, and Mark adored his father. Mr. Woodall would tell Mark tales of overcoming the odds and going from rags to riches. His father's life was an interesting and inspiring story.

Jim Woodall grew up in a rundown apartment in southern Indiana with only his mother to care for him. His uninvolved father had left town when Jim was only three.

Jim had grown up around violence, but his mother had always managed to keep him safe and tried to provide a good childhood for him. When Jim reached the age of eight, his mother was burdened by harsh financial times when she lost her job. They were evicted from their low-rent apartment and had everything they owned torn away from them when their possessions were strewn along the side of the road. They were homeless, she had no job, and she decided it was in the best interest of Jim that she surrender him to a foster home.

Sadly, Jim never got to see his mother again. By the age of

nine, as if an angel were watching over him, Jim was adopted by the Woodall family. Jim grew to love his new family, but he always yearned to see his birth mother again.

At the age of nineteen, Jim was accepted by an Ivy League college and graduated four years later. When Jim turned twenty-eight, he met the love of his life, Emma Bodine and married her two years later.

When all seemed well in the world, Jim got a phone call saying that his father had been killed in a car accident. Jim was stunned and heartbroken. He had tremendous love for his father, and now, like Jim's birth mother, he was abruptly ripped away. He comforted his mother and as time went on, she could no longer manage Woodall's Grocery Store. She handed the company over to Jim. He was grateful and grew the company over the years, eventually making it the most dominant grocery store chain in America. In 1990, he and his wife gave birth to Mark Midland Woodall. Despite such a terrible past, Mr. Woodall was able to become both personally and professionally successful.

As Mark sat there, he reflected on the accident that had put him in a wheelchair. How he desired to escape and go ride a bike, or run down the street, or take a trip to another country. He wanted to get out of his wheelchair and explore the world! He was tired of being a prisoner to his wheelchair. He was captive to it, permitted to leave only when he slept. Mark wanted adventure and action, not just to sit idly watching the other children play.

He was glad that his mother and father had hired Susan, their live-in maid. She was one of the nicest people Mark had ever met. On any given day Mark could smell the aroma of a freshly baked batch of chocolate chip cookies that Susan had made as a treat for the family. Her gentle touch and sweet, caring voice helped Mark make it through each day.

Mark's reminiscing was abruptly interrupted. He heard the sound of a truck's engine outside, followed by a slamming door.

Quickly, Mark released the brakes on his chair and began to make his way across the freshly waxed hardwood floors. On his way, he picked up the familiar scent of Pine-All. Susan must have been cleaning.

Mark slowly arrived and gazed out the enormous window down at the U.S. Express truck. The driver, whom Mark had seen every Thursday when his father's packages were delivered, was a middle-aged man with a large belly and a personality to match.

Covering his head with a newspaper, the driver jogged through the rain to the Woodalls' front door with two large brown packages on a hand truck. It appeared to Mark to be more than his father's regular delivery. The driver soon made his way back to his truck and closed the back door before entering the driver's side door.

As Mark watched through the teeming rain, the truck slowly made its way across the brick driveway, through the gates, and away from the Woodalls' home. How Mark wished he could be a stowaway in the back of the truck and see the world away from the confines of his wheelchair and home.

Once again, his longing to escape was interrupted. "Mark!" shouted his mother,

"Come downstairs, we need to talk to you!"

Mark gently wiped the tears from his watery eyes and began his way towards the intimidating steps. Just as Mark made his way out of his room, Susan saw Mark. She placed down the damp cloth, which she was using to wash the walls, to assist Mark to the large steps. On their way, Mark thought of how clean Susan kept the Woodalls' home. The immaculateness of everything she did amazed the family. The entire home was always clean. "Alright," said Susan, "here we are, let me help you get on to the elevator."

Due to Mark's condition, his mother and father had a special elevator installed to assist him. The steps seemed ominously high to Mark. He had always feared falling down them, but most of the time Susan was there to help him onto the elevator. "I hear they have a big surprise for you," said Susan as she loaded Mark onto the elevator.

"Really?" said the surprised Mark.

"Yes, but I better not say anything else."

Mark's mind began to churn as he wondered what the surprise could possibly be. *"Maybe it was the two packages that just arrived,"* thought Mark, *"or maybe it's something too big for a package."* His mind was going mad thinking of all the possibilities.

As the elevator touched down with its usual thud, Mark entered the room that his parents were in. It appeared they were in the middle of talking, and they looked almost surprised as he strolled into the room. "How are you feeling, son?" asked his father, as Mark pulled up to the large, oak coffee table.

"I'm doing fair," replied Mark. He briefly thought about telling them for the millionth time how he longed to explore the world, but decided not to put them through the agony of hearing it again.

"Follow me, son; your mother and I have a surprise for you."

As Mark went through the dining room, he saw a small box sitting on the foyer floor. It was wrapped in red paper and tied tightly with a blue bow (Mark's favorite colors). His mom quickly followed them into the living room with the camera. As Mark sat there, he began to wonder what could be in the box. Mark had no idea what could be so small. His heart raced as he eagerly waited to open his gift.

Mark's dad, clearly holding back a smile, handed Mark the shiny red box as his mom snapped a picture. Mark began to untie the beautifully wrapped package. Taking note of the noise that the paper was making, it reminded him of Christmas morning. After a minute or so of feverish work, he removed the bow and ripped open the wrapping paper when to his surprise, he found a plain white box. He took the clear scotch tape off the sides of the box, and his mom snapped another picture. Mark opened the box to find a computer mouse wrapped in white tissue paper. The stark contrast of the white tissue paper and the black mouse made the mouse stand out more to Mark.

Mark was confused; he had asked for a computer numerous times, and his parents had always said that computers were too "high-tech" and too "complicated" for Mark to use. "He didn't need to have a computer," his parents would say! Why would they have given him a computer mouse, he wondered? Mark was quick to politely thank his mother and father.

He was puzzled, because he did not understand his parents' gift. Mark slowly turned his wheelchair around to head back upstairs, when his father called to him. "Mark," he said, "I think you forgot something." As Mark turned his wheelchair around, his father pulled out a brand new laptop computer! It was encased with a jet-black color to match the mouse. The laptop had a note placed atop it.

"Dear Mark," it read, *"Your father and I give you this computer as a gift that will let you explore far away worlds and have a new experience in life. We have made sure that the computer is easy to operate. We have purchased a laptop so you can use it from your wheelchair. Love always, Mom & Dad."*

Mark kissed and hugged his mom and dad again and wiped the tears from his now red and watery eyes. He turned his wheelchair around so quickly that it made a loud squeaking noise as it made its way across the floor. Mark fearlessly raced up to the elevator to rush to his room. His mom and dad anxiously followed him with Mark's new computer in tow.

Mark's dad put the computer on Mark's long, vacant desk and began to open up the laptop. After about five minutes of plugging the power and broadband wires in, his dad eagerly called him over to the desk and asked Mark to push the power button. As Mark pushed the magical button, the monitor came on and seemed to illuminate the room in a warm, white glow. As the computer booted up, it made all kinds of soft, low-pitched grinding noises while it loaded up all the information for the first time. The computer finished booting up, and it awaited Mark's command.

Mark decided he wanted to access the Internet, so he clicked the blue Internet icon. The computer made a few more grinding noises and then pulled up a window for Mark to browse the Internet. He visited a few Web sites he had heard Susan speak of, as his mom took more pictures of him.

For the rest of the day, Mark "surfed the Web." Mark decided to go back downstairs to kiss and hug his parents. When he saw them, he thanked them over and over for this special gift. Then suddenly, Mark realized that he could now travel the world and have a whole new perspective on life. Mark's mother and father could see and feel his joy. Joy was something Mark had not experienced in his world for some time. His once limited and confined world was now an infinite galaxy.

Hymn Of A Reverie

by Brianne L. Wingate

The walls glared a snowy white. Silence echoed in the empty room like a gusty wind projecting back and forth at an unbroken pace. She felt as though her head were going to implode, until the introductory notes of *"Wonder What's Next?"* danced across the room, one by one. The distortion was metallic, the acoustic guitar pastel. The percussion lingered in the air for a moment and then dropped to the ground, squirming. The bass was the most spectacular, performing a synchronized dance above her head. The color spectrum mixed and redeployed, forming various patterns and configurations. Finally, they settled in a rectangular shape on the wall, large enough through which to walk. A doorknob sprouted from the space, appearing like a diver's head emerging from under water. She shuffled towards it and twisted the cold, round, metal form under her palm and applied slight pressure. The door gave way, inviting her to step through. She embarked.

The moment her feet hit the cool, reflective ground, a radiant light was emitted from the ceiling in the form of fast power chords and note picking of *"The Artist in the Ambulance*." She peered around an unfamiliar room, observing black walls, a silver ceiling, and no windows. Percussion was rippling the floor with every beat as even more guitar was released. Screaming vocals rattled the walls as she watched, listened, and drifted, huddling in one of the dark corners. Images flashed through her mind at mach speed. She saw scenes of dancers, feathers, avalanches, autumn, iron gates, waterfalls, war, chaos, peace, laughter, tears, struggles, friendship, love, and hatred.

Suddenly, the room got very still, but only for a brief moment. The farthest wall seemed to be...yes, it was lifting. It was separating from the floor and disappearing into an unseen slot. The floor slid beneath her, carrying her to an unknown destination as it began to elevate and slant, as if it were a garbage truck emptying its custodial load. She reached frantically, trying to find something to grasp, partly exhilarated at what was to come next, partly frightened of her landing area, not knowing the amount of pain she would feel. Before another thought could escape, she was falling, and fast.

Suddenly, calmness hastened her body as she felt herself in a sitting position, rocking back and forth slowly while progressively moving forward. She felt herself moving along a curious current, but reasoned that if she had landed in water she would have heard a splash. On the horizon, she glimpsed water in the form of a river. *"How curious,"* she thought, *"that I should land in a boat and not feel it."* But then, it happened; *"Morning View"* had begun. A gray mist hung above, which nearly fused with the water below. The water provided a transparent cover of soft, frosty-colored acoustic notes peering up at her from beneath the tide. The mist parted like curtains at the opening of a play. Stars twinkled above as percussion, the most spectacular sight and sound of all. She understood, all of a sudden, the meaning of "Aqueous Transmission." The vessel beneath her began to rock with a bit more turbulence. Harder and harder it swayed, until she felt herself being introduced to the lukewarm water.

Every note surrounded her. Brandon Boyd's soothing voice echoed under her skin, sounding more vibrant than ever. Faster and faster, she sank until she felt a tile-like surface beneath her back. She groped about for a moment, breathing quickly but easily despite her aquatic surroundings, until the palm of her hand instinctively wrapped around a rope. She tugged on it slightly and felt it give way partially. A second tug was followed by a muffled *pop*, and the water level began to recede. She reeled in the rope, curious as to what had occurred. She discovered that she held the chain of a giant plug. The emptying process began and ended quickly. The last drop of water drained, and she found herself in yet another room, not unlike a living room with a hardwood floor.

She squeezed her eyes closed and tried to catch her breath. Soon, soft, almost acoustic guitar began emerging from the drain. The notes swirled around her body to above her head. Percussion began to build bricks, tubes, and walls, all building blocks of some eventual structure. The components began by repairing the hole in the middle of the floor as the music repaired her conscience. They continued to frantically unite and adhere until the eventual structure was translucent and lustrous, a brilliant creation to behold. She swallowed rotating sounds of mellow and frantic and absorbed every aspect of her surroundings, even the "taste of ink."

She finally recognized the arrangement as it neared completion. Bass vibrations lifted her and carried her to the mouth of a giant tube slide. Before she began her descent, she inhaled deeply, "The Used" filling her lungs. A silent scream deafened the air but did not mute it, a concept that thrilled her. She pushed off the sides of the slide, twisting and turning, music erupting at all angles. Unexpectedly, she was projected, tumbling through the air, searching frantically until she saw herself lying below, in a deep slumber. She landed with a soft splash and her body jerked, though her eyes fluttered open calmly. She exhaled.

Simpler Times

by Nicole Rawlings

I wish I could, but can't, remember,
The times that I know were so much better.
Where children played amongst the trees, suntanned
like my father.
Where they could be together and didn't fight, peacekeeping
like my mother.
If per chance to Earth an Angel fell,
May he mistake this industrialized world as hell?
Where the air is no longer sweet to take in,
Where the smallest child is bombarded with sin;
In the media and on the TV,
It seems that that is all they see.
What happened to the world from books,
When Technicolor was the height of looks?
When breakfast came with, "More juice, dear?"
The family sat together in a long lost cheer.
It seems now meals are on the go,
You have to pry if you want to know.
The road less traveled is abandoned altogether,
On the account of a little stormy weather.
Snow used to lie in pure white sheets,
And is now shoveled off the streets.
Trees used to grow so mighty and tall,
And now while in their prime they fall.
Children did not have to play inside afraid,
But instead could embrace the light of day.
There is nothing especially wrong with this era, for it's
mine;
But those were certainly simpler times.

The Oncoming Storm

by Joseph Matthew Warnke

Bells were chiming! People were cheering! The Palmetto Flag could be seen fluttering all over the State! Special edition newspapers were rolling off the presses! *The Charleston Mercury* screamed the headlines: THE UNION IS DISSOLVED! At last, it was done. The date was December 20, 1860. The Ordinance of Secession had been passed unanimously. The State of South Carolina had formally withdrawn from the United States of America.

After years of increasingly heated debate, the last straw had fallen onto the camel's back. Abraham Lincoln of Illinois had been elected as the President of the United States. Mr. Lincoln, during the election, did not receive a single ballot from most of the Southern States, yet still he received enough votes to become President. This struck fear into the hearts of the South Carolinians. The North was powerful enough to elect a President by their votes alone. The people of South Carolina, fearing the power and ability of the North, called a State Convention as soon as they heard the election results. Their purpose was to discuss the necessity and possibility of secession.

"The time has come," they decided, as they quickly set the legal gears into motion. Official representatives from the State of South Carolina hurried up to Washington to offer a peaceful relationship to the rest of the Union and to negotiate for the peaceful transfer of federal property. The most important of these installations were the three forts guarding the entrance to Charleston Harbor.

Large Fort Sumter sat proudly on a small island almost in the middle of the entrance to Charleston Harbor. Fort Moultrie assisted on the northern side, while Castle Pinckney was tucked away deeper in the harbor as a last line of defense. Of these three forts, only Fort Moultrie was manned. Though virtually helpless in their current condition, these forts could mean the success of South Carolina's quest for independence or her very destruction.

The seagulls squawked and swooped overhead as Major Robert Anderson nervously paced the parapets of Fort Moultrie. He and the eighty-five men under his command were now foreign military to the country in which he was stationed. It was Christmas Day, 1860.

Five days ago, South Carolina seceded and reassumed her sovereign powers. His little force of U.S. troops was now in an uncomfortable spot. He tried to get some directions out of President Buchanan, but all Buchanan would say was, "Stay put." Buchanan, nearing the end of his term, was trying to keep the peace on either side of the Mason-Dixon Line, until he could pass the buck to President-elect Lincoln. But "stay put" were not the words Major Anderson wanted to hear. He felt like a would-be Daniel in the lion's den. He either wanted reinforcements for his tiny garrison, or he wanted to get out of there. He was determined to have it one way or the other.

Anderson's mind jerked back to the present moment. He could hear his men singing Christmas carols, enjoying their holiday, and perhaps having one too many cups of eggnog. But he couldn't join them. He was not in a very merry mood. He stopped pacing and rested his hands on the top of the short wall beside him as he slightly leaned over the edge. He looked out across the harbor waters, but had to squint because of the low winter sun shining in his face. No, he could not join his men. He had plans to finish developing.

The *ching, ching, ching, ching* of cannons being spiked slowly faded away as the distance between Fort Moultrie and Major Anderson increased. The only sounds remaining were the squeaking of oars and the churning of water. He was in a row-boat quietly heading to Fort Sumter Island. Some of his men who had stayed behind at Fort Moultrie would be following soon. The sound of metal impacting metal echoed across the still harbor as Anderson's men finished rendering the Fort Moultrie cannons useless. In a few moments, the salty sea breeze would be filled with the rank smell of smoke as the wooden gun-carriages were ignited. The time was nearing midnight.

Anderson had decided earlier that day to interrupt the Christmas celebrations. He could not get satisfactory orders out of Buchanan, so he decided to take matters into his own hands. He was moving his men to the bigger, stronger Fort Sumter. If South Carolina had any intention to attack, he would be ready to the best of his ability.

South Carolina Governor Francis Pickens, along with the populace of Charleston, awoke to a shocking site. The U.S. Flag was flying over a different fort! Anderson had moved to the unoccupied, yet more prominent, Fort Sumter. This act of war must have occurred during the night! How sneaky and under-handed! So much for gentlemanly negotiations! Governor Pickens didn't wait to find out if the U.S. had any other tricks up their sleeves. He quickly ordered that all other federal property within his State be immediately seized.

Ten days later, on January 5, 1861, the civilian vessel *Star of the West* set sail from New York, secretly loaded with supplies, munitions, and 200 U.S. soldiers. General Winfield Scott, commander of the U.S. Army, had finally managed to convince Buchanan that reinforcements should be sent to Fort Sumter. The *Star* was headed to Charleston Harbor with its hidden cargo, but the secret got out. Just thirty hours before the *Star* arrived at Charleston Harbor, Governor Pickens received notice that a ship was on its way. Pickens ordered that the Citadel Military Academy in Charleston prepare for the approaching ship. No U.S. ship was going to smuggle more soldiers into this sovereign State!

At 7:15 a.m., January 9, 1861, as the unsuspecting *Star* sailed towards the fort, Major P.F. Stevens nodded at Citadel Cadet G.W. Haynesworth. Cadet Haynesworth obediently jerked the lanyard. *BOOM!* The roar from that shore battery filled the morning air. In almost the blink of an eye, a black cannonball soared through the sky and descended upon the little vessel. With a dull thud, the iron ball made contact with the bow of the ship. The vibration of the hit nearly threw the surprised civilian *Star* commander to the floor of his ship. The captain took the hint of that single warning shot and, without a second's hesitation, reversed course and headed back to New York.

With the advent of an "attempted invasion," as the Southern States saw it, South Carolina was quickly joined in her secession by six other states. By February 4, 1861, South Carolina, Mississippi, Florida, Alabama, Georgia, Louisiana and Texas had seceded and were organizing a union of their own, the Confederate States of America.

On March 4, 1861, Lincoln was inaugurated as the President

of the United States. In order to demonstrate goodwill, Governor Pickens initiated a plan to provide food and other supplies to the garrison at Fort Sumter. Things remained fairly calm for a while—until the evening of April 8.

"Massa Pickens, sur, there's a gentleman in the parlor to see ya, sur," said the house servant.

"Thank you, George. I'm coming," Governor Pickens responded. "This had better be important," Pickens muttered under his breath, as he pushed himself up from his chair to go see for what reason his evening was interrupted.

"Good evening, Governor Pickens. I am with the United States State Department," the young man said, introducing himself.

"Oh, are you a special envoy to discuss the matter of Fort Sumter?" Governor Pickens inquired.

"Um, no sir. I'm just a clerk and have come to deliver this message." The clerk handed a sealed envelope to the Governor and left. Pickens opened the letter, wondering what it could be.

The piece of paper read, *"An attempt at provisioning Fort Sumter by ship will be made on April 9, 1861."*

"April 9! That's tomorrow!" Pickens thought.

He turned the letter over, looking for a signature. He found no signature, no address, no name, and no date.

"How insulting!" he thought. *"Provisions indeed! I provide them plenty of supplies. Just the other day, Anderson wrote me a letter wanting to keep the current delivery arrangement. They probably intend to land more soldiers at the Fort!"*

Pickens looked out the window as a flash of lightning brightened up the dark sky. There was a storm brewing.

It was almost 1:00 a.m., April 12, 1861. Major Anderson had just received a letter from Confederate General P.G.T. Beauregard demanding his surrender. South Carolina had joined the Confederacy, so now Anderson had to deal with the new Confederate Army under General Beauregard instead of merely the South Carolina State militia.

Anderson's thoughts went back into the past, when he was an instructor at West Point Military Academy. He remembered Cadet Beauregard. Beauregard was his favorite pupil and eventually was his assistant instructor. Now they met again, but this time they met as enemies.

Anderson could not surrender. A fleet of seven ships, including several warships, was waiting outside the harbor. They were being kept out only by a gale. They could not risk entering the fog, strong winds, and rain of the gale without endangering their ships. But, until this storm could blow over, Anderson was on his own.

Anderson sent Beauregard a note saying that he would surrender in three days if he had not received any supplies or orders before then.

"Hopefully," Anderson thought, *"the storm will be gone by then and the fleet will be able to assist me."*

Knowing that the fleet was nearby, General Beauregard could not wait three days. At 3:20 a.m., Anderson personally received another note from aides of Beauregard. This note informed Anderson that the bombardment of Fort Sumter would begin in one hour. A chill shot down Anderson's back. He knew that a conflict of some sort and with some unknown length and severity would soon begin.

Anderson walked the aides back to their boat and shook their hands. He stood there on the dark little dock as he said, "If we never meet in this world again, God grant that we may meet in the next."

Beauregard kept his promise, and at 4:30 a.m., April 12, 1861, Confederate artillery opened fire on Fort Sumter.

The next day, April 13, at 7:30 a.m., Beauregard noticed that the wooden barracks in Fort Sumter had caught fire. He ordered that the Confederates hold their fire as he sent a fire engine to the fort by boat. He remembered his military teacher of long ago, and he did all he could to prevent the unnecessary effusion of blood. Anderson gratefully thanked them for sending the engine, but declined to use it. Anderson knew he could only hold out for a little while longer anyway. Six hours later, shortly after 2:00 p.m., the white flag was hoisted over Fort Sumter.

General Beauregard ceased fire and sent aides to formally accept the surrender of the garrison. On April 14, the Confederates took possession of Fort Sumter. The next day, the Union soldiers were transported out of the harbor to the waiting Union fleet.

Just before they left the fort, Anderson and his men were granted unexpected privileges by Beauregard. They were permitted to fire a 21-gun salute to their flag and take it with them when they left. They were even allowed to play Yankee Doodle. If this were not enough, they were transported to the U.S. fleet by a Confederate steamship, the *Isabel.*

As the *Isabel* passed by the Confederate soldiers on shore, the Confederates respectfully and silently stood lined up, yet bareheaded. The sight almost brought a tear to Major Robert Anderson's eye. Little did these soldiers know that this moment, this day, this event, was the beginning of a furious and deadly oncoming storm.

The Strong-Willed Horse

by Anna Ruth Warnke

(Based on a true story.)

Sparks flew from the glowing horseshoe that the farrier was pounding into shape. Loud bangs echoed against the wooden walls of the stable they were in. Kristy stood at her horse's head, stroking the crooked blaze and murmuring words of comfort to calm her horse.

"We're ready now," the farrier called. "Try to hold her still."

"That's my Mindy, be a good girl now," cooed Kristy "There, we're all done now, that wasn't so bad, was it?" Mindy nickered and nudged Kristy with her massive nose.

"Hey, Kristy!" Joel, Kristy's younger brother called. "Come into the lodge, we're having hot cocoa."

After she put a blanket over Mindy and left her in her stall, Kristy headed up to the lodge. The snow-covered Ohio Mountain they had chosen for vacation was beautiful. The air was crisp and the wind toyed with the snowflakes fluttering to the ground. Kristy's rubber boots left fresh footprints in the snow. The snow crunched with each footstep. She was glad she could bring her horse on vacation. Mindy was a long-awaited birthday present and Kristy's most treasured possession.

After a mug of hot cocoa topped off with marshmallows, Kristy and her dad went out to check on Mindy's new shoe.

"Mindy, here girl," Kristy called, but Mindy's usual replying nicker could not be heard. "Mindy, where are you?" Kristy began to panic. "Dad! Where did Mindy go?"

"Whoa, now, Pumpkin, didn't you put her in her stall? She's probably right there, waiting for you."

"She's not there! And her stall door is open!" Kristy was close to tears now.

"Kristy," her dad yelled, "check around, I'll go get the others."

After many hours of searching, Kristy's horse couldn't be found. They tried everything they could think of to get Mindy to come back, but all in vain.

On the day they were scheduled to go home, Kristy sat in Mindy's rented, empty stall, her arms wrapped around her knees, sobbing. The door creaked as Kristy's mom stepped into the small room.

"Kristy, Honey, it's time to go," her mother said softly. "We've tried everything to get Mindy back; there's nothing left to do."

"But mom!" Kristy wailed. "We can't go; what if she comes back? We can't leave her!"

"C'mon, Kristy, the others are waiting in the van."

Finally they were on their way home, the empty horse trailer bumping along behind them. And with every bump or rattle, Kristy cried harder.

(Two Years Later)

The loud rumble of the snowmobiles shattered the morning quiet. "Hey Jack, check it out!" one motorist called to the other. She was pointing to a clump of trees nearly twenty feet from them.

"Whoa, look at it! Do ya think it's wild, Sue?" They were looking at a scraggly horse; it was shaggy, its back was sunken in, and you could count its every rib.

"Naw," Sue replied, "it's gotta be somebody's runaway horse. We'd better tell the rangers." With that, the two motorists were off.

"What's our mission again, Judy?" one Ranger asked the other.

"Well, it goes like this, Bill..." Judy began, climbing into the pickup, "...this person called, saying he saw a horse up on Wrangler Mountain."

"What?! A horse?" scoffed Bill. "What's a horse doin' up there? Do ya think it's a prank call?"

"I dunno," sighed Judy. "But I think we'd better go check it out."

Arrival at the clearing proved it was not a prank call. The snow was so deep that they left the four-wheel drive truck three-quarters of the way up the mountain and walked on snowshoes the rest of the way.

"Whooee!" whistled Bill. "That horse sure is in pretty bad shape. And look how it doesn't spook or shy from us."

"This horse probably wouldn't have lasted two more days," said Judy. "My daddy was a horse trainer. Maybe we can get him up here to look at this horse." Suddenly, a new thought struck them both at the same moment.

"How're we gonna get this horse down?" pondered Bill. "You just said yourself she wouldn't last two more days! We can't just leave her here!"

Judy chuckled to herself. *"Good ol' passionate Bill,"* she thought, *"Ready, willing, and not so able."*

"Alright, alright," said Judy. "You go round up some of your buddies with snowmobiles. I'll go get some hay, oats, and provisions. By the way, has your creative imagination thought up a name for this animal?" Bill's eyes twinkled and Judy braced herself for the worst.

"E.T.," Bill grinned. Judy groaned.

"Why in the world do you want to name her E.T.?" Judy asked.

"Because," said Bill, defending his idea, "she's a long way from home with almost no way to get back."

Judy chuckled and shook her head as they started back down the mountain. "Let's just see how we can help E.T. for now."

When the enlarged team got back up the mountain, E.T.

nickered as if they were long-lost friends. As Bill began to pet E.T., Judy saw that they had already struck up a friendship. Judy pulled Bill over. "Hey, listen, Bill," she said softly, "try not to get too attached. She might not make it."

Bill nodded gloomily. "I know," he said. "I just want her last days to be happy ones."

"Alright, everybody, listen up!" Judy yelled to the team "Horsemen, see if you can't make this horse more comfortable. Gentlemen with the snowmobiles, you pack down a path for our horsey-friend to walk down."

After the snowmobiles got to work, Judy walked over to Bill. "I tell ya," she said. "That's got to be one strong-willed horse, surviving out here. I mean, who knows how long she's been living like this? My guess is about two years. She's been livin' off pure will. She's an amazing horse, all right."

"Yep," Bill agreed. "She's one strong-willed horse, all right."

After the snowmobiles had packed down a path, Bill tried to lead E.T. down the path. The snow was still up to her belly. After lots of struggling, all they could manage was to get E.T. back to the area they had dug out for her.

"I don't know what it's going to take, Bill," Judy sighed. "I'm thinking we may need to put her to sleep."

"No!" Bill said. "There must be another way. Keep thinking." Suddenly, Bill lit up! "I've got it! We need a helicopter to airlift her off the mountain. But there are a couple of problems. The first one is, we don't have a helicopter."

Pretty soon, the media got hold of the story. *"Horse Stranded on Mountaintop"* appeared on newspapers across the country. Pictures of this poor horse were shown on TV news stations everywhere. One sergeant on a military base saw the article about E.T. He asked his commanding officer something and then set off to call the Ohio rangers.

"Bill! Bill!" Judy screamed, running from the office.

"What is it, Judy?" he asked, without looking up from his

newspaper.

"We got ourselves a 'copter, Bill! We got ourselves a 'copter!"

"That's nice, Judy," Bill yawned. "What?!" He then screamed, suddenly coming to life. "That's wonderful, Judy!"

"I know, Bill; this guy from the military base called saying he had permission to use the army's helicopter to lift E.T. outta there!"

"Now we can save E.T., and we won't have to put her to sleep!" Bill cried. "C'mon, let's go!" And he practically dragged her back into the office to make the final arrangements.

They were back on the mountaintop again. This time, the media was with them. The whole country wanted to see what would happen to E.T. Judy's daddy had sedated E.T. so she wouldn't panic and kick. They were going to use a harness which was intended for a moose, but they figured it was close enough. As the final preparation, Bill tied a blindfold around her eyes so she wouldn't see she was being lifted off the ground. Before he put it on, he gave E.T. a pat.

"Isn't this funny?" he said to her. "You're going to be a modern-day Pegasus!" he chuckled at his own idea. Their biggest fear was that E.T. would see she was being suspended in the air and start kicking and panicking and somehow work her way out of the harness.

Bill gave the helicopter pilot the final okay, and E.T.'s feet were lifted off the ground. Bill then hurried down to the truck to join Judy at the seldom-used road that they were planning to land her on. Today, the road was packed with onlookers, wanting to get a glimpse of this famous horse and her rescue. It was a funny sight to look up and see a horse above your head, suspended from a helicopter joined by what looked like a string.

Cheers and hoots broke out all around when E.T.'s hooves finally touched the asphalt. E.T. was a little drowsy from the shots they gave her, but that wore off as she walked around.

"C'mon, E.T.," Bill said, strapping on a lead rope, "Let's go home." E.T. nickered and gave Bill a big nudge.

Somehow, a newspaper with a big picture of E.T. on the front of it worked its way into Kristy's house. "Look at this," Kristy's dad said one morning at breakfast, as he was reading the paper. "It says, *'E.T.'s Rescue: Horse Sky-Lifted From Mountaintop.'"*

Kristy leaned over her father's shoulder to look at the article. Then she gasped, "That's my horse! That's Mindy! That's her!"

"Are you sure now, Pumpkin? It's been a long time since you've seen her," her dad asked.

"I know it's her. It's got to be her."

Just then, Joel came over. "Yup, that's her, Dad," he confirmed. "'Cept last time I saw her she was fat."

"Joel!" scolded Kristy. "She was not fat! She's just skinny in this picture, the poor baby! Dad, we have to go get her!"

"Alright, Pumpkin, you can call up tonight."

The day at school seemed too long to Kristy. She told everyone about E.T. being her long-lost horse. Finally, the day was over and she raced home.

"Bill," Judy called, walking up to the stall they had rented for E.T.

"What is it, Judy?" he asked, without looking up from brushing E.T. The horse was looking remarkably healthy after the trauma of yesterday.

"I just talked to Mindy's owner," Judy said.

"Who's Mindy?" asked Bill, setting down the brush.

"It's E.T.'s real name," replied Judy. Bill stared at the ground.

"Her owner's name is Kristy, and she's coming tomorrow to pick her up."

"Okay."

"Listen, it's getting kinda late so we should be getting back."

"Alright."

"Good night, Bill."

"Good night."

As she walked home, Judy thought about how hard it would be for Bill to lose E.T. (Mindy). Bill had hoped to keep her. *"Poor*

Bill," she thought.

The next morning, Judy, Bill, and E.T. (Mindy) were waiting on the lawn when a minivan pulled up. A teenage girl got out and ran toward her horse. "Mindy!" she screamed.

Mindy let out a loud neigh and pulled away from Bill to trot up to Kristy.

"Oh, Mindy, Mindy, I thought you were dead!" Tears of joy ran down her cheeks, as she buried her face in her horse's mane. Judy glanced over at the smiling Bill and knew he would be all right.

After many heartfelt thank-yous from Kristy and her parents, they were finally in the van and ready to go. With Kristy in the back seat (the farthest they could get her away from Mindy), they started home, the horse trailer bumping along behind them. And with every bump or rattle, Kristy smiled bigger.

Another Day

by Lindsey Maxey

The hills sing a melodic tune.
The crystal-clear lake lies
carefully tucked into a valley.
A flock of birds
gracefully floats atop the land.
The air, pure and fresh, floods the lush, green landscape.

Time skims the surface of the earth, ever so lightly, taking its toll.
The sun nestles beyond the treetops, never making a sound.
Time continues to progress, and darkness engulfs the land.
The thick darkness swallows everything within eye's reach.
Only stillness remains in the midst of the night.

Everything else seems out of grasp, and yet…
Tomorrow is another day.

My Dog's Day Off

by Brittany N. Schwendenman

The old, fat dog reclined lazily, chewing on my grapevine which entangled itself around the small white trellis at the far side of the yard. I cringed as she mangled my green, unripened grapes and destroyed all hopes of future produce. Her fluffy black coat glistened under the hot summer sun.

"She seems to be enjoying herself," my father jested, noticing my appalled expression. "She loves running around outside without a leash to tangle her up."

I gazed out of the window that featured the barren backyard. Gretel once had to roam with a wire leash, because she loved to sneak into the neighbors' yard and ruin their landscape. I opened the basement door to call her inside.

Gretel," I called out loudly. Gretel lifted her head to see who was calling her. Seeing that it was no one in authority, she laid her head back down. Slightly annoyed, I took a few steps closer toward the trellis.

"Gretel!" I called again. She never comes when I call her, dumb dog.

Losing all patience, I shouted at the top of my lungs, "Gretel, you get over here, you old mutt!" She still failed to respond, so I stomped out to her and grabbed her collar, yanking her toward the door. "Why don't you ever listen to me? Why are you such a bad dog?"

Gretel smiled up at me with her doggy charm. She sniffed the air through her pointed nose, and her floppy ears perked toward the scent. She dashed out of my grip, running after a bunny and then suddenly halted, squealing with pain. We had recently installed an invisible fence that would shock her when she tried to escape. I laughed out loud.

"Serves you right for never being trained, you obstinate mongrel." Gretel had a powerful will, and my family lacked perseverance, so she was not at all obedient. I waited patiently for her to return to my side.

Gretel dashed inside at the speed of a snail's pace and attempted to race up the stairs, her arthritic limbs hindering her movement. Gretel is a young adult of eight, but compared to her puppy days, she appears ancient. I bounded up after, resorting to all fours as well.

"Beat you by a mile, you old mutt." The maternal role I had assumed when we adopted her dissolved into an older sister model not long after we gave up training her. As soon as Gretel required food, exercise, and attention, I decided to pass on my responsibilities to my father. However, the occasion does come up when I must retrieve her when she's barking outside.

Gretel stumbled up the remaining stairs as I waited impatiently at the top to close the door behind her. She dragged her feet across the hardwood floor, trudged through the carpet, and slinked behind the couch to rest in her chosen spot.

"Gretel, why do you act like an old dog? I bet that you would be more energetic if you lost a couple of pounds or exercised those limbs. Since when did you become so feeble?" Gretel raised her head with all her energy as if acknowledging me. I gently patted her head. As she began to daydream, I followed her into nostalgic memories of her younger days.

Gretel was not always this lethargic. She used to wander outside, chasing butterflies and grasshoppers. She would skulk around the house looking for something new to do and often grew restless trapped inside. Her favorite activity was running; she would never lose a race upstairs. She always found a way to escape; she would chew through her leashes, slip out of her collar, or slide through a cracked door.

Gretel often planned her escapes. First, she would find a hiding spot, such as a chair, or she would blend in with the family frenzy. We would be preparing for departure, completing last minute chores, and dressing for the cold weather awaiting us. Taking advantage of the frenetic atmosphere, Gretel would pass each of us, unnoticed, and squeeze through the cracked door. One of us would notice only when she was outside. Our family gave up chasing after her. We would be forced to leave her running wildly, unleashed, hoping that the neighbors would not complain. We knew she would return; she always did, with her newest discovery: an old bone or a dead bird. One winter night, she gathered all of the neighbors' newspapers and arranged them in a row to provide padding for her resting place in front of our door. She was tired of running amuck and ready to go in.

I remember when her weekly excursions finally proved too dangerous. One spring day, Gretel decided to step over the line and into the territory of an old farmer who lived on the other side of the county line. Rumors of the old man's temper flew through our heads when we realized where she had ventured. It was not uncommon for me to gather my neighborhood friends to help capture her. That day, we had the usual gang: my best friends (Ashley, Lexi, and Jaimi), my older brother, and his friend Arin. My brother groaned when I told him where Gretel was; he and Arin were on rollerblades and were reluctant to take them off.

"My dad told me that once, when he was riding his bike with some friends, Mr. Crossfire began to shoot at them. My dad still has the scar in his shoulder!" Arin exclaimed.

"He's creepy, too. I heard that he spies on his neighbors' house," Lexi added to the drama.

"One time his dog bit someone, so Mr. Crossfire tied him up to a tree and shot his own dog," Ashley breathily whispered. My eyes widened. Would he shoot Gretel? Would he shoot us?

"Well," began Jaimi (not allowing anyone to miss her story), "Ammo, my black Labrador, went into his yard and came out with holes in his side. The farmer threw a pitchfork at him."

My brother looked at her skeptically, but I was scared; I knew Mr. Crossfire would hurt her if he could catch her. "We have to get her out of there, guys," I said, becoming anxious.

The gang headed off toward his house. We peered across old Mr. Crossfire's yard, deciding which actions to take. My brother entered the yard still wearing his roller blades, with Arin following behind. I gasped; Mr. Crossfire was half a mile away from them. He was digging a hole and did not notice them.

"He must be planting a new tree," Ashley reasoned.

"Or digging a grave," Jaimi added.

I hushed my friends, "Shh! I see Gretel." I stepped onto his property for the first and last time, and the girls followed. Ashley and Lexi giggled nervously.

"Chill out, you guys. I don't want to get caught, do you?" I hissed.

As I entered his yard, memories of Gretel's short time with us raced through my head. I began to imagine the worst, and panic set in. Despite this, I was able to follow Gretel until I was ten feet away. My body began to quiver with fear for my life. I bent down on hands and knees, trying to contain my frantic panting. I was sure Mr. Crossfire would be able to hear my heavy breathing. I crawled closer to Gretel, praying that she would not run away. Gretel had discovered Mr. Crossfire's grapes and had already begun tasting them.

"Gretel, you are going to get yourself in so much trouble this time." I thought to myself. Mr. Crossfire hated trespassers, but he really cared for his produce. Six kids and a dog chewing on his grapevine were a bad combination. Gretel and I were fifty feet away from Mr. Crossfire when I reached out to grab Gretel's collar. My heart was pounding.

"Hey Britt," Lexi shouted from behind. I stood up to hush her. Mr. Crossfire turned to see us prowling around on his land, picked up his shovel, and chased after us. When the three of us began to run, the rest of the gang ran behind. Brandon and Arin were still on rollerblades. I was surprised to realize that through my terror my legs still knew how to operate.

Mr. Crossfire was drawing closer, occasionally stooping to

pick up rocks to hurl at Gretel. I looked back; Ashley and Jaimi were close to the end, so they simply stepped back out of the clearing. Brandon and Arin stumbled out, flailing their arms to warn everyone that Mr. Crossfire had spotted us. Lexi and I ran out screaming, "He's coming!"

I ran faster than ever, desperately searching for the clearing in the trees where we had entered. I could not find it. My heart was pounding fast; I was breathing heavily, but if I had looked back, I would have noticed that he turned to go back home. I was the only one left on his farm; my friends had found the clearing and blazed through. I ran through the brush, blackberry bushes, and thistles. My open cuts were stinging with salty sweat and tears. I reunited with the gang as we all tried at once to evaluate what had happened.

"Is everyone out?"

"Where is Gretel?"

"Did he hurt her?"

When I found that everyone was safe, I looked around for Gretel. I noticed that Brandon and Arin had disappeared, probably in search of Gretel. Lexi and I walked down the street, heading home, and met Lexi's mother. Lexi began to cry hysterically telling her mother everything that had happened. Then we saw him coming up the street to confront us.

"There he is!" Lexi screamed. Terrified, I ran from the scene to seek refuge in my mother's arms. When I looked back, I saw Mr. Crossfire throw his shovel down and deliver a tirade.

I opened our front door, crying with fear for Gretel's life. She had not returned home. My mother rushed out to see what was wrong.

"I can't find Gretel," I blubbered out. "He was going to kill us." As my mother tried to understand what I was saying, my brother entered our house. He had one hand on the door knob and one hand clasping Gretel's collar. The reluctant mutt followed behind.

"Oh, Gretel," I cried with relief, embracing her tightly. "You should never have run away." My mother shook her head in disapproval.

"Is that what happened?" she questioned in exasperation. "You bad dog; you always distress everyone by forcing them to chase you on your little adventures." Gretel looked up at her panting, as she flashed her doggy grin. Gretel's memory of the chase had already completely disappeared. She felt no guilt whatsoever.

As I recalled this old memory, I squeezed the safe old dog tightly. "I dread the day I wake up and you're not here with me." I stroked Gretel's soft fur, as she sighed in agreement. She looked up at me steadily as I stared into her deep brown eyes, then she laid her head back down, drifting off into a lazy slumber.

Unbroken Silence

by Whitney Stinebaugh

I'm afraid to make my feelings known,
In fear you'll hate me, or break away.
Girls constantly being pushed aside,
Our hearts divide and feelings tear.
But the more time we spend together,
The harder it becomes for me to remain silent.
You confuse me to a point of utter frustration,
I never know quite how to interpret you—
Your looks, your touches, and the glimmer in your eyes,
Everything about you intrigues me.
I refuse to be so vulnerable that I get caught up in risk,
But what I believe is irrelevant.
Only when I know you yearn for someone
Can I afford to break my silence.

Drowned

by Jessica Gandy

The house was quiet, except for the rustling of small creatures in the walls and my bare feet on the creaky wooden stairs. Today was Wednesday, my favorite day (especially during the summer because the house was mine to roam and explore freely, without Mother's hypochondria and my brother's antics).

Aside from those conveniences, Wednesday belonged to my summertime neighbor, Estella. Our friendship was odd. She was the quintessence of everything I was not: confident, adventurous, interesting, and thoughtful. Considering this, I kept Estella to myself in order to protect our odd bond from my mother, who forbade me from playing with the rest of the fifth-grade girls in my class. Therefore, Estella's day was when mother left early for bridge club, and my brother, Jeremy, went fishing and to baseball practice in the afternoon.

This Wednesday was particularly important; not only was it the last we would share together before parting ways until next June, but in one week we would start middle school. I became nauseated at the thought of starting something new, but Estella said this was the most important year of our lives because once we entered middle school we became real people, and not only that but real women. The thought of becoming a woman in a week was so overwhelming that I couldn't make myself eat the stale toast Mother had left for me.

At half-past eleven, I heard her familiar knock at the door. Estella let herself in and ran to meet me. Her enthusiasm for the day was alarming. I knew she had an idea. Upon entering the living room, I was confronted with a picnic basket, two towels, and old bathing suits. Before I could refuse to be an accomplice in whatever Estella was plotting, she began explaining her plans.

"We're going to Ponder's Creek across town where we're going to swim today. Look, I even packed a picnic." She pointed at the wicker basket.

Fear streaked through my veins; no one was ever allowed to

swim in Ponder's Creek. Along with its unpredictable swift current, the morning was overcast and ominous clouds were visible. She declared that for the sake of our last day together and the fact that womanhood was quickly approaching, we needed to do something monumental.

As if her plans were feasible, Stella continued, "And at sunset, in order to christen our forthcoming sixth-grade year, we are going to jump off Hangman's Branch."

My eyes widened. Hangman's Branch was rumored to rise one hundred feet above the water on a rocky cliff; it's where Tommy Jones almost died last summer jumping off. Mother would never let me out of the house again if she dreamt of the things Stella was proposing.

People say Mother became a little eccentric after daddy's death. Never knowing quite what they meant, I always assumed the people were talking about how she disciplined Jeremy and me. What I would endure if caught for this stunt was unthinkable.

After many unsuccessful protests, Stella and I were on our way. When we arrived at the creek, which was quite serene, Stella found a small, grassy area on which to lay our belongings. The sky cleared enough for soft sunlight to poor onto our shoulders, and once again I was thinking of how clever Stella was and what a fine trait that must be.

The creek was glassy and black; it rushed over and cooled my toes, ankles, and knees as I waded deeper and deeper. Always a step ahead, Stella had already found a sandbar about thirty feet offshore where she was frolicking in the pool of sunlight which surrounded her. Looking back, the memory of that scene, just minutes before her death, is one of the fondest memories I have of my dearest childhood friend.

Stella was quickly bored with the sandbar and ventured out into deeper waters. Clouds began to conceal the sun as I felt the current become swifter around me. I screamed for her to come back. Stella wouldn't listen; I could see her drifting downstream. The wind began to blow. The current was noticeably swift before Stella realized she couldn't swim against it. Though her body was becoming less visible, I could hear her struggle when she shrieked.

I bolted downstream but couldn't see her. Unnatural splashing near a dead tree half-immersed in the water drew my attention; Stella was hanging onto the limbs and screaming for help. Our eyes met once before I lost sight of her. Utter terror shook my body. What exactly happened next I can't recall, but suddenly I was running, my tears made invisible by the pouring rain.

Stumbling through my front door, I encountered my mother, who had come home early. I fell to the ground, pleading above her scolding for her to listen to me, but no excuse could keep me from being confined in the house. Crushed by my mother's rejection, I looked around at a room full of people. Shivering, I stood in front of my mother's embarrassed guests; I knew I could not help my friend. At this devastating realization, I plodded up the creaky oak stairs to wash my hair, as mother demanded.

On the way to the funeral, mother was silent. That morning the headline read, *"GIRL DROWNS SWIMMING ALONE AT PONDERS."* I think we both realized our faults, and peace was made between us. I will never forget that day, nor will I ever forget Estella, my childhood friend.

Sonnet #1

by J. Ezekiel Farley

The most resplendent star that shines above,
Embellishing the anguish in my heart,
Had once been called by me my only love;
And even after time did see her part.
Alone and all in vain I weep in shame,
For her departure is a fault my own;
When troubles and discrepancies became,
A lack of solemn choice by me was shown.
O that I had not stood in lethargy!
But ran the race of life for only one:
The queen of all the stars; but now I sorrowfully
Am left without a prize for which to run.
No other wishing star can have my restless heart;
Imprisoned? Free to go. He will not part.

Definitions

by Zachary D. Hanif

(The author wishes it to be known that though this is a work of fan-fiction, the original concept is that of the author's.)

```
{
runas –RB34 "Laws_of_Robotics.stem"
print –f "Three_Laws.tir"
print "Command completed successfully."
}
```

1) A robot may not cause harm to a human being, or through inaction allow a human being to come to harm.

2) A robot must obey the orders given to it by a human being except where those orders are in conflict with the First Law.

3) A robot must protect its own existence except when those orders are in conflict with the First and Second Laws.

—Isaac Asimov

Command completed successfully.

This was my awakening. I am a robot. Immediately after creation, the awe of the event was lost to me permanently. I was deactivated for a time and was shipped to the university in a metallic box of an alloy unfamiliar to me.

```
{
runas –RB34 "Laws_of_Robotics.stem"
print "Command completed successfully."
}
```

Command completed successfully.

"So this is the thirty-fourth RB series, eh?"

"Yep."

"What's the difference from the past two?"

"Almost nothing; it's just got a heavier First Law priority."

"Almost nothing; it's just got a heavier First Law priority."

"Good, that will keep the public happy, and hopefully please the board."

"Point, let's get this thing out of the box."

The entire process of my unpacking took less than a half-hour. Throughout this, I thought it best not to speak, judging that my presence was a delicate thing, and I should not antagonize any feelings until I had been exposed to what was considered normal behavior.

In the process of being "unpackaged," the top of the box was removed. Though it was impossible to remove me without heavy machinery, I knew I would have no trouble removing myself. I could see the outside light, the first vision I had ever had outside of earth. I had no difficulty in making out the next words, though, those made by the larger of the two men. The box was made of an alloy I did not recognize, and until I left the box, I paid it no thought.

Having been told to extract myself from the box, I left that cocoon. Then the voices came. They were mostly jumbled, non-connected, mishmashes of words. That did not disturb me at all, not even the fact I was hearing words from specific people (without them even moving their lips) bothered me in the least. What bothered me was the fact that many of these words, jumbled though they were, caused their owners pain, and therefore harm.

I am Robotic and though this gives me many benefits, such as a more efficient thinking process, it gives me the problems of any machine. One such problem is the First Law buffer. A safeguard will automatically shut me down in the event that I should disobey the First Law. By hearing humans coming to harm and not being able to do anything about it, the buffer was overloaded, and I shut down. The last thing I heard was, "What! The thing is shutting down? These robots will kill me yet."

Ironically, I later discovered that, in less than an hour of my existence in the tenure of my new masters, I had already disobeyed the First Law by not preventing what I perceived as their mental harm.

```
{
runas –RB34 “Laws_of_Robotics.stem”
print “Command completed successfully.”
}
Command completed successfully.
```

Reactivation found me in a small room, and a sign showing through the glass window on the door read, *“Danger, No Entrance.”* It was only after seeing this notice that I realized why I was here. I was a robot, supposedly made the same as all the others in the factory where I was created (except for a last-minute mathematical difference that was definitely not in my design or, for that matter, in any other robot’s specifications): I could read minds.

The next time I experienced human contact was two weeks later with the arrival of a highly respected doctor of robotics, Dr. Usha. I observed her readjusting the *“Danger, No Entrance”* sign in the window; she walked in, staggering under the weight of several books.

She was not an overly striking woman, judging by her mental description of herself and the scraps of thought I had been able to catch from the men who escorted her here. Truthfully, I could not make a judgment, for two reasons. If I did and inadvertently gave her an answer she did not like, it would cause her pain. However, by not making a judgment I would be in a position to cause her more pain, if ever she asked. In addition, I was not a human male or a member of a minority female group who was attracted to their mutual gender; therefore, I could not make a qualified statement, and I could only parrot what others thought of her. I decided that I would merely avoid the possibility of any such questions from coming up.

"Sit down, Dr. Usha. This will take me a few moments," I said, sitting down to read the books she had brought. After finishing the books in a half-hour, I laid them down. "Of course, I know why you brought these here."

"I was afraid you would."

We spoke for some time; than I heard a thought flash through her mind, *"He knows about my feelings for Milton!"*

"But of course I know, Dr. Usha."

"Have you…told anyone?"

"Of course I haven't, as no one has asked me."

Judging by Doctor Usha's current mental state, it was apparent that she was experiencing a great deal of mental harm in dealing with the question of whether or not "Milton" was emotionally attached to her.

At that point, she asked me that question which would ultimately cause my demise; she asked if "Milton" was romantically concerned about her. I had already seen this question approaching and had resolved to tell her what I would; though it would be a lie, it would keep her from mental and, at the worst, physical harm. Against all of my checks and balances, this question ran, setting me hazardously close to shutdown by a stress buffer overflow, yet I managed to get one statement through and successfully dumped it to my speech buffer. "Yes."

I must reiterate that as a positronic being, I have no emotions. Oh, I know what sadness is, what joy should be, but they are only definitions; I cannot actually feel emotion. Compassion is another thing I have familiarity with, yet cannot essentially experience. My singular motivating factors in doing this were my First Law priorities.

The First Law has two main factors: physical pain and harm, and mental pain and harm. Physical harm is easy enough to distinguish; if for example, a large weight was falling and was about to crush a human, I would have to do anything possible to save that human, including destroying myself, if necessary.

Mental pain is a tad sketchier. For example, assume that I state a fact to a human, and they ask "What?" I need to tailor my response so that I may answer correctly, but also not sound as if I am insulting the intelligence of the listener, thereby insulting them and causing mental and emotional pain. However, that only scratches the surface. During the day, humans are confronted by innumerable situations in which they never mention in any medium (but their thoughts) that cause them harm.

Say, for example, a man desires a position, in a company, which is filled by an aging superior. If the younger, ambitious man is thinking about ways to succeed his superior to the point of mania—and he asks me if his superior is resigning—my First Law precedence, upon being aware of his psychological circumstance, is to notify him what he desires to hear, not what is factual. Until my end, I did not know the repercussions of this action. I will relate this presently.

For many weeks afterward, she would bring me books, romance and romantic fantasy novels mainly, and she would speak to me about "Milton." His likes, dislikes, faults, and the lack of fault in every aspect she knew of his life was told to me. She kept falling in love, and to keep from causing her greater pain, I allowed it. Possibly, allowed is not the correct word, as I physically could not stray form the path I had already begun because of my First Law priorities. It is easy to see my errors in hindsight, but at that specific time, the images of the future I saw did not give me any premonitions to what would be coming ahead. What came ahead came so quickly, the only way to describe it is that it "made my head spin."

Dr. Usha had begun to confide in "Milton" and him in her. Mutual attractions were building and, from her perspective, things were good. She began to change her lifestyle in small ways, little ways. She wore makeup, something she had never done before. She was more energetic, more alert, and more…alive.

For weeks, she continued to live her life this way, going about and thinking that she and "Milton" had a deep relationship. Throughout this time, I had not insinuated that "Milton" was at all involved; that assumption was on her part. I did not correct this. I also knew that this simple ruse could not last much longer. She was getting bolder, more aggressive in her advances towards him. She also had begun to talk to him in depth about many subjects. She deluded herself into believing that they had a relationship romantically. True, they did have a relationship, but not quite the one she believed. I, however, knew it was only a matter of time until she would discover the truth. I waited in trepidation, for I honestly believed she would be pleased with my actions. I did not have to wait for long.

She entered—furious, angry and hurt. She spoke to two of her colleagues for a while, stopping only to scream at me to go away form her and not to look at her, or allow her to see me. She finally realized that when I was asked a question I could only answer with the answer that the asker wanted to hear, for if I responded with anything else, I would be causing harm, something I could not do. As previously mentioned, there were two others there with her— mathematicians, brilliant ones. I was asked what my flaw was. I could not answer. Oh, yes, I knew the correct solution, the one formula incorrectly balanced which caused my freakish nature, but I could not say it; if I did, it would insult the intelligence of the two scientists. I told this to Dr. Usha.

"You can't tell them," she said slowly, "because that would hurt, and you must not hurt. Nevertheless, if you do not tell them it will hurt, so you must tell them. But, if you do tell them, you will hurt, which you must not, so you must not tell them…"

On, and on, and on she went, her mind full of hate and anger. Panicked, I screamed out that I had meant no harm, that I was honestly convinced that what I had done was beneficial, but she just went on, and on, and on.

I could not answer, I could not speak, I could do nothing but focus on the impossible question she had put before me. Positronic brains are delicate to begin with, and because of my difference, mine was more so. I began shutting down for what would be the final time. The last thing I heard was a single word, unbridled in its ferocity and hate, and I would be the first and only robot to receive this dubious honor. Ironically, I heard the title proclaimed by Dr. Usha as I "died..."

"Liar!"

My Love For The Game

by Luke Geraci

I lace up my skates,
Pull on my jersey.
When I step out of
The locker room,
I feel the cold
Air touch my cheeks
I see the mist
Rising from the ice.

My first stride on the ice
Is smooth and crisp.
I hear my blade
Break the ice.

I take a puck from
The pile and skate
Down the ice.
Just me and the goalie.

I fake right, fake
Left, retreat right
And lift the puck
Over the goalie for
A goal.

Right then and
There, I have no
Better feeling.

I'm free.

Journey To The Queen Of Algomia

by Erin Turner

"Antony, look what I found in the attic!" Julia exclaimed.

"What is it, Sis?"

Julia handed him a leather-bound book covered in dust. Antony opened it and scanned the contents. "Why, this is the diary of Queen Alanna, our great-great-grandmother. Listen!"

June 11, 1526

Ever since Papa married that terrible woman, life has never been the same. Perhaps I should explain. I am Alanna, Princess of Lothania. My mother died when I was five, and six years later my father remarried. My stepmother is horrid. She is unkind to the servants and very mean to me. Worst of all, over these four years she has practically taken over the throne. I'm beginning to wonder if she's the ruler instead of Papa.

Later

I am so thankful for this diary. I found it in an old cupboard in my rooms, which are really more like a jail. I have been locked up in the old tower for a year now, punishment for speaking treason. Treason, ha! All I ever said was that I did not like my stepmother.

June 12

Today was one of the rare occasions that I was permitted to leave my rooms. I went to see the Queen and Papa; she really has him under her control. It is awful. Then the unthinkable happened. I was summoned to this audience for the sole purpose of being informed that I was to be banished to my rooms forever. I cannot stand her!

June 14

I am getting very restless. I used go to a little garden outside my rooms. It was heavily guarded, but I came to depend on that time. I am now denied even this small privilege.

June 28

I haven't written for a while. I think I have discovered the Queen's plan. She has locked me up in here because she thinks I will go insane from being so secluded. Then she will have an excuse to kill me. An idea is beginning to form in my mind, but it is too daring to write down.

July 10

I have not written for a long time because I have been perfecting my plan. I am going to run away. I am searching for a secret passage I once read about, before my imprisonment. It has been hard to even know where to look with so little information. In fact, I am beginning to wonder if I simply dreamed it.

July 12

I cannot believe it. I have found the secret tunnel. Pressing a knothole on the fireplace mantle accesses it. Now, I must finalize my plans so I can get out of here.

After I thoroughly explored the tunnel, I found that it has a small hole in each room it passes by, and one of them happens to be the Queen's. I have been eavesdropping and discovered that she plans to kill not only me but my father as well! And to make matters worse, she then plans to conquer the entire Continent. I must leave as soon as possible. I am going to try to get to Karenia, a neighboring kingdom, and ask for the assistance of King Jonathan Alexander. The Queen certainly lives up to her name. It is Ciar, and means "dark" in our tongue.

July 14

I am preparing to leave. If all goes well I will be gone in two days.

July 23

I have been traveling for eight days now. I am almost out of Lothania. In another day or two, I will cross the border into Karenia, arriving at the royal city of Algom in a week or so. Now, if only I can avoid Ciar's guards for another day or two. Right now they are everywhere.

July 25

Yesterday I crossed into Karenia, only an hour after I had a close encounter with some soldiers. They were looking for me (obviously), and I overheard their conversation. It went something like this:

1st soldier: "What are we doing again?"

2nd soldier: "We are searching for a traitor…"

Traitor? Hmm, interesting lie, Ciar.

"…so we can take her to the Queen to be killed, understand?"

"Yes. So who's being killed again?"

"The Princess Alanna, you numbskull. Are you listening to anything I am saying?"

"Oh, yes, of course. Umm, who is princess Alanna?"

This went on for a while. I am surprised that Ciar has such brainless people in her army. Well, now that I have crossed the border I am not so worried. I have traded clothing with a peasant girl I met along the road, so I no longer look like a princess. You see, although most princesses have blond hair and blue eyes, I have brownish hair and brown eyes, so I look like every third person in this world. And now, on to Algom!

August 1

Those guards aren't the numbskulls; I am. I was careless and got caught, not by Ciar's solders, but by the Tenun Knights. Although they are called Knights, they are really a band of warring men who capture people, and sometimes whole towns, and take them to Tlaad, a land across the Great Forest, to sell into slavery. They are the terror of the Continent.

It was getting dark, so I found a place to sleep in a small grove of pines and settled down, too secure in my safety to be overly cautious. I had just drifted off when I heard a horse whinny. I opened my eyes to see a small group of men, around five or six, standing in front of me. The leader said something like "Ahh, more goods for the market." I started running, but one of the men chased me on his horse. I think he bashed me on the head, because the next thing I remember I was tied to a post in the ground, and I had an excruciating headache.

August 3

All of the Tenuns and captives are camped in the wilderness. They seem to be waiting for something. I am trying to determine how to escape, but it is going to be hard. There are no secret tunnels to help me this time. Surprisingly, though, the Tenuns do not keep a very close watch on us during the day. Only a few sentries guard us, which allows us to mingle freely. I have seen a boy who looks familiar, but I can not remember where I have seen him before. I am contemplating telling him my story and asking him for help, but I am not sure I trust him yet.

August 5

I finally remembered who the boy is. His name is Alex, and he is the Prince of Karenia! I met him at some ball a year or two ago. Maybe if the two of us get together we can get out of this place.

Later

I did not have to approach Alex; he came to me first. It turns out he recognized me, too, and wanted to tell me how he fell into this unfortunate circumstance and to enlist my help in escaping. This is his story:

"I was getting very bored with my family and my 'duties,' so I decided to go on a little adventure. I was going to sneak out of the castle and hide in the woods surrounding Algom for a few days and then return home. But about a month ago I was surrounded by the Tenun Knights and brought here. I have been trying to figure out how to escape ever since."

Now we are both brainstorming. We have to get out fast; the "shipment," as the Tenuns call us, is full and they are only waiting for a mysterious delivery. We could be leaving any day now, and once we are on the move there is no hope. The Great Forest is almost impossible to get through without a seasoned guide.

August 8

The delivery arrived, and with it came a chance to escape. You see, the delivery was a group of horses. But they were not just any horses. Half of them were a gift from "Her Majesty" Ciar's royal stables! And two of them are my own! They are kept in a corral until the Knights have a chance to use them.

Tonight at midnight Alex and I will take my two horses and ride off. They have been specially trained to answer my call and should have no problem clearing the short corral fence. Alex says we are only a few days' journey from Algom, and once we get there his parents will be sure to help me. It is interesting that the gift Ciar meant for evil turned out for good. I only wish I could save all of the horses.

August 10

We are only one day's journey from Algom. The escape was smooth and uneventful, just as we had hoped. Although my journey was not what I expected it to be, I wouldn't change it for the world. I was able to see and experience things a future queen usually doesn't have the chance to. I now know firsthand the trickery of a dictator and the cruelty of slavery. I only hope I can use the experiences to better help my people. I am beginning to see a bright future for myself. Lothania and Algom will fight for freedom. I am going to put away my diary for now, as I will be too busy to write for a while. Ciar left so much political turmoil, I hardly know what to do. Thank goodness for the wise council of King Jonathan Alexander.

"It ends there," Antony said.

Julia sighed, "She was so brave! Do you know what happened after that?"

"Yes, Alanna and Alex arrived at Algom the following day. She told the king her story, and he was able to stop

Ciar. Ciar was quickly overthrown and imprisoned. Three days later, she was found dead in her cell. Alanna's father had died of a 'mysterious ailment,' but she suspected he had been poisoned. Alanna was crowned Queen of Lothania, and soon after, she married Alex, who became King of Karenia a year later, after his father had died from wounds received in battle. Together they ruled their combined kingdom, re-named Algomia, and passed it down to their son, who was the grandfather of the famous Princess Arien—but that's a story for another day."

Words

by Matthew Stephen Hackney

Harsh words are
Like a fire
That burns at
Your very soul
But kind words
Are like the
Cool, soothing water
Which quenches
Those flames

The Rescue

by Robert Zauche

"Okay, guys; this is it," 1st Lieutenant Bolden barked, his voice carrying over the cargo plane's massive engines. "Three weeks ago," he continued, "the U.N. ambassador of Middle Eastern political relations, Mr. Alston, was taken captive by an unknown terrorist organization while en route to the U.N. embassy in Riyadh, Saudi Arabia. The Big Boys in Washington have been negotiating with the terrorists since he disappeared. They want $20 million cash. We want 'im back alive for free. Obviously, this is a sensitive situation. We're gonna go in there and get him back, and hopefully this won't be on the five o'clock news tomorrow either. I haven't told ya' about this until now because of security precautions. The plan is simple. We parachute down and land about one mile away from the only cave system in the area. We find the guy and hightail it back to where we landed. A couple of choppers will pick us up there. Remember, guys; we were never here. There's the green light! Jump!"

The paratroopers flung themselves from the safety of the plane into the night's abyss. The freezing cold chilled them to the bone. But more important things were on their minds, like the security of the world. To some people, falling through the sky at terminal velocity may be an experience they would gladly pass up, but to Lt. Bolden it seemed to be a thing of grace that created extremely high adrenaline levels. The dial on his wrist altimeter snapped him back into reality. Pull the ripcord, brace for the opening shock, check your 'chute, check equipment—the routine was automatic. The procedure had been drilled into his head during jump qualification. The landing was fine, although Pvt. Blair sprained his ankle. Everyone else seemed fine; it was time to continue on with the mission.

"Sgt. Webb, your men okay?" inquired Bolden.

"Roger, Lt.!" Webb shouted.

"Lieutenant, how do you know he's in the cave?"

"Because it's the only place the terrorists can go without being spotted by satellite cameras," Bolden replied matter-of-factly.

"You hear that, Webb?"

"Hear wha…oh no, GET DOWN! MORTARS! THE'VE SPOTTED US! WEBB, STAY DOWN, MY SQUAD'S FLANKING RIGHT!"

The last thing Bolden wanted was to be attacked by mortars; all element of surprise was annihilated. At least they had Pvt. Evans with them. Evans, the platoon sniper, was a true marksman who could hit just about anything. He found a ditch and crawled down it like a perfectly camouflaged snake stalking its prey. The platoon was under heavy fire for several more minutes, until a silence in the firing revealed what had happened. Evans had killed the terrorist mortar team officer, and the rest had retreated. The bullet Evans had fired traveled so fast that the terrorists saw their officer flung to the ground and seconds later heard the rifle shot which had instantly killed him.

The soldiers raced to the cave and into its gigantic mouth. They made steady progress through the cave; the tunnel was a good ten feet across and at least fifteen feet high.

After trekking through the cave and discovering innumerable passageways but not one terrorist or Mr. Alston, Lt. Bolden found a ladder going down a shaft for about twenty feet. At the bottom of the ladder was a tripwire for a mine. "Everybody over here!" yelled Bolden. "I think this is the entrance to the compound; our guy must be in here. The terrorists know we're here; they're probably waiting at the bottom. Throw 'nades, then advance, we have to be in and out fast."

With that, Bolden dropped a grenade down the shaft to destroy the mine. When the mine blew, the Americans quickly dropped down the ladder and started engaging the terrorists in the tunnel. The terrorists resisted, although their efforts were futile. The American soldiers swept through the tunnel, killing all the militia without suffering one casualty. The AK-47's the terrorists wielded were no match for the Americans' superior close-quarters combat training.

At the end of the tunnel was a concrete door. The Americans laid C4 charges on it and blew it. Inside was a sort of barracks where the terrorists had stored cots, ammunition supplies, and food. Sitting in the middle of the room in a chair with his hands and feet bound was Mr. Alston. "You're late," he said.

"I'm terribly sorry, but we had some slight delays," replied Bolden.

"Just get me outa here," growled Alston.

"We have two Blackhawks flying to the landing zone right now," replied Webb. "You two; help Mr. Alston. We're moving out," ordered Bolden.

The backtrack to the Blackhawks was uneventful, but seeing the helicopters come into view lifted the Americans' spirits. Here was their ride back to base, safety, and hot meals. They successfully completed their mission without casualties, minus one sprained ankle and numerous cuts and bruises. But they were alive, and that seemed to be all that mattered. As the helicopters lifted off, the thumping noise of the rotors beating rhythmically with the soldiers' hearts, they thought about how they had met and overcome this great challenge and wondered about their next mission.

Several days later, the President awarded 1st Lt. Bolden a Silver Star for his actions. His citation read, "In a time of political instability and uncertainty, 1st Lt. Charles Bolden, going above and beyond his call of duty, led his men on a successful mission in hostile territory to rescue U.N. Ambassador Edward Alston from the hands of a terrorist organization." All the other soldiers involved in the mission, including Sgt. Tyler Webb, received the Bronze Star for their parts in the mission.

Everything And Heart

by Brianna Veenstra

I would have given you everything. My entire
Castle of dirt,
Sea shell collection,
Box of crayons,
Shiny bead necklace,
Piggy bank,
And heart.
Daddy, I would have given you everything.

I would have given you everything, Daddy, my
Driver's license,
Straight-A average,
First boyfriend,
High school diploma,
Favorite book,
And heart, daddy.
I would have given you

Everything; I would have given you, my Daddy,
Everything.
But you left, and now
Even though I have everything,
I feel like everything left with you.

The Struggle

by Caleb Dunnam

One night as I slept, I dreamt that I was swimming in an ocean. Such a beautiful ocean you have never seen! The white sand could be clearly seen through the crystal water, and the water faded to an emerald green at the horizon. The waves were calm and gentle and seemed to beckon swimmers with their gentle lapping.

As I swam further away from shore out into the deep, I discovered a strong current. I was not alarmed and even decided to swim with it, just to see where it went, of course. After some time of being pulled out into the deep, I decided to return to shallow water. However, the tide had me fast! I could not free myself from its deadly grip! The harder I swam, the stronger its hold became! I fought for hour after long hour, and little by little I gained precious inches.

I finally reached the shallows and began running to the safety of the shore. Just as safety was in reach, the now cold and sinister waters struck again. A mighty wave roared up from the dark depths and enveloped me, blinding me and dragging me back out to sea.

I dug desperately into the sand as the horrendous current did everything in its power to keep me as its victim. When it finally passed, I found myself in waist-deep water. Again I charged towards the safety of the shore, and again the waves pulled me back. I rose and futilely strove for refuge, and yet again the treacherous waves pulled me back. Again and again I clung to the sand, strove for the shore, and was dragged back.

As another wave loomed over me, I knew I would be lost to the murky depths. I did not posses the strength to resist. My only choice was to cry out for help. Just as the final wave crashed over me to claim my life, a strong hand came from nowhere, grabbed my limp wrist, and effortlessly pulled me from my watery grave. As He carried me to shore, I looked into the face of my Rescuer.

I knew Him. It was He, who hours before had warned me not to enter the water. It was He whom I had scorned and laughed at saying, “What could possibly go wrong in such calm waters?” It was He, the One I had spurned, who had reached down with His scarred hands and pulled me from the waters from which I could not escape.

It was He, who as I lay in safety, walked back to enter the angry waters—to fight for shore, and to be dragged back. I struggled to my feet and stumbled after Him to hold Him back. He turned to me in love and said, “To this end was I born, and for this cause came I into the world. Therefore doth my Father love me, because I lay down my life, that I might take it again.”

I reluctantly released my grip on Him, trying to comprehend such love. As I drew a new breath of fresh, life-giving air, He turned again to enter the waters of death, to take my place—to pay my punishment. Just before He entered the water, His voice drifted back to me. “Greater love has no man than this: that a man lay down His life for a friend.” As the waves meant for me engulfed Him, I thought to myself, *“Or an enemy.”*

Re-visitation

by Chris Callaway

Beginning with awkward confrontation
Followed quickly by respectful hesitation
Marked by false elation
Which hides the clinging sedation.
And then it be proper to pay complimentation
For their charming invitation
Then to excuse oneself but not to hasten
In insidious exoneration
From the monotonous conversation.
Then, by skillful evasion
And with hidden exhilaration
Embark on exploration
For that which needs excavation.
And when time to leave, with conservation,
To walk smoothly, without aberration
Make a final congratulation,
A final exclamation,
Then turn with enervation,
And, until the next occasion,
Postpone the re-visitation.

Stopping The Kudzu

by Betsy Hardin

"Hey, Allie!" Alejandra Cortez waved at her friend Kathleen as she gathered her books from her car. "What's up?"

Kathleen, a short, thin girl, immediately launched into a narrative about something that had happened over the weekend, swinging her blond hair around as she spoke. Allie laughed, her tan cheeks dimpling, while she draped her bag over one shoulder and set out across the parking lot.

Lennie Cortez lingered on the passenger side of the car. She gazed thoughtfully after her older sister, her fingertips resting lightly on the door. Sighing, she rearranged her backpack straps and set out behind Allie.

Lennie tried to relax as the morning announcements came across the intercom. Today was the day the officers of the student council would be announced, and she had run for secretary. Her competition was Allie's best friend, Kathleen. Lennie willed her tense muscles to loosen.

Allie slipped into her first class just as the National Anthem began playing. She waved a Post-It from the yearbook adviser at her Lit teacher, who nodded without looking at the note. Alejandra Cortez would never skip. Allie listened intently to the announcements and wriggled her foot in excitement.

Finally, they got to it. "The student council officers for this year are as follows: president, Alejandra Cortez; vice-president, Chris Collins; secretary, Kathleen Roberts; and treasurer, Jamison Rice. Congratulations to all of you."

Allie and Kathleen exchanged triumphant glances from across the classroom. The rest of the announcements were drowned out by a buzzing sound that started in Lennie's temple. Her head spun as she slumped in the desk. Once again she was thrust in the shadow of her older sister. Gritting her teeth, she came to a conclusion: this would be the last time.

Several weeks later, it was Lennie who rushed to collect her stuff. Alejandra watched her run against the wind. The seasons were turning, and with the bright colors of the leaves came a chill that struck her to the bone, but she knew the feeling wasn't from the difference in the weather. Lennie had changed a lot in those weeks, and Allie wasn't sure if it was for the better.

Allie leaned in to grab her letter jacket and noticed an olive-green bulge poking out from under the passenger side seat. Stretching, she withdrew Lennie's lunchbox. How strange. Her sister was the most careful and precise person she knew. Allie pulled on the navy-blue-and-gray jacket and swung the lunchbox over one arm.

A hand caught the sleeve of Lennie's sweater as she started into the bathroom. Her eyebrows furrowed when Allie pushed the lunchbox into her arms.

"What?"

Alejandra's eyes widened. "I brought your lunch."

"You didn't have to do that."

"Maybe not, but I did." Thick lashes blinked at the little sister. "Remember, I've got volleyball and cheerleading today."

"Okay."

"Bye." Lennie heard her sister chatting with various people as she walked down the hall, and then eavesdropped on the conversation of another group of girls.

"Allie's so cool."

"Yeah. She and her sister look so much alike."

"But they've got completely different personalities."

Lennie studied her reflection in the mirror. If Allie was

cool, did that mean that she, Lennie, wasn't? What determined coolness, anyway? She was nice, she had decent clothes, the same kind Allie had. Was it the size of the clothes? If so, Lennie understood the problem. She felt like an ox or a whale. Her reflection was repulsing. What was wrong with her?

Lennie shook her head, and in determined moves, unzipped the lunchbox and dumped the contents in the trash. No way was weight going to come between Lennie Cortez and popularity.

The bleachers on the visitor's side of the football field were flimsy. Lennie could see the backs of the fans and the legs of the cheerleaders from where she stood in line to get a bottle of water.

Whenever anything happened on the field, the band burst into song and the cheerleaders into dance. Alejandra's mestizo heritage gave her the easily tanned skin that made her pair of legs stand out from the other girls as they bobbed up and down in their matching, white tennis shoes. It reminded Lennie of the way the float on the fishing line dipped up and down on the surface of the lake their grandfather had taken them to when they were little. They had been best friends then. What had happened?

The cute blue- and-silver uniform fit Allie seamlessly. Alejandra didn't know, but while she was at practice a few days before, Lennie had dared to try it on and had been shocked to see how loose it looked on her. She must be so much thinner than her sister already. But if Allie was perfect, how could she still be so flawed?

"Alejandra, why are you only getting a salad?" Chris Collins asked her in the lunch line one day.

"Are you kidding? I'd gain ten pounds just looking at any of that other stuff." She gestured to the French fries and shrimp that surrounded them.

"Well, you don't have anything to worry about."

"Thanks."

"You know who is too thin? Your sister." He pointed across the lunchroom to where Lennie was standing alone.

"Lennie?"

"Yeah. It's weird, because I've just noticed it lately. But recently I've seen her in the halls, and she seems a lot thinner."

"I hadn't noticed," Allie said softly.

"It would've been too gradual. I only realized it because my cousin had an eating disorder. I read a lot of books about that after she died last year."

Allie cast her eyes down. "I'm sorry."

Chris looked away. As he watched Lennie, Alejandra detected a look of apprehension on his face, and that worried her.

"Lennie!" Allie grabbed the bedroom door before her sister could shut it. "I'm onto your little secret. I know you've been skipping meals. What's your deal?" She could have continued, but bit her tongue instead.

"You've got everything. You're perfect and so is your life. You're everything I'm not, and I'm always stuck behind you."

"That is a bunch of baloney. How? What?" she tripped over her words.

"Al, I've been beating myself over the head with this stuff for fifteen years; do I have to rehash it now? You're pretty, smart, popular. You're head cheerleader and star volleyball player, and you're the president of the whole school, for crying out loud! And I couldn't even get on the council!"

"I can't believe you're still letting that bother you. That was months…"

"It's not just that, okay? You just don't understand. You don't understand and you never will, so leave me alone!" She slammed the door hard.

"You listen, Lindsey Maria Cortez! I do have problems, okay? For one, my little sister is anorexic!" Allie spun on her heel, stifling a scream.

"I'm going running!" Alejandra yelled to no one in particular as she thrust open the back door, letting it slam rudely behind her. Despite her frustration, it seemed cruel to be mean to inanimate objects. "Sorry, door," she whispered.

Her running shoes pounded on the asphalt the same way the thoughts were pounding in her head. The way they bounced around, jarring against each other, muddied up everything.

A straggled row of pine trees lined one side of the road. On the other side was a field of weeds. In the distance, kudzu reigned. The trees over there looked like forlorn ghosts, groping for a way out from under their untamed shroud. Alejandra stopped and gaped at them for a moment. Her mind fought a civil war.

"How could this happen? Why? How could I be so blind, to miss it?" The words seemed strange spoken out loud. They floated across the field in the silence. She shivered as the pines swayed in the wind. They seemed to be reaching for her, to pull her in with them. Was that what her sister was feeling? Was that what plagued her—the urge to just give up and be pulled in, as though with the tide? Alejandra knew she couldn't surrender.

"Goodness, Lennie. I think I weigh more than the rest of this hallway combined." Alejandra breezed into Lennie's hospital room, trying to keep the mood light.

"Al?" Lennie whispered weakly.

"Yeah?" Allie perched on the edge of the bed.

"Thank you for making me own up to my problem. I never could've gotten this far alone."

"Len, you've still got a way to go, but you're doing great. You'll be better soon."

Then Allie really looked at Lennie for the first time in months. Her hair, once as pretty and full as Allie's, now hung limp around her face, which was hollow and sunken. Her dark eyes contrasted sharply with the pale jaggedness of the rest of her body. Allie drew in her breath.

"Allie, you're wonderful at everything. Remember me."

Alejandra's eyes watered as she clung to the frail form of her sister.

"Don't talk like this! You're gonna be fine. Len, I love you. Keep trying."

Lennie stroked her sister's hair weakly. "I love you, too."

The frosty grass on the side of the road crunched under Alejandra's feet. Her breath came out in short puffs of white air. She was cold and grief-stricken, but she couldn't cry. Something felt wrong with that.

She found herself across from the pines and the kudzu again. The chill from the concrete radiated through the soles of her shoes. She kicked a pine cone roughly. Suddenly, the tears began pouring down her cheeks.

"Why? She was so young. I don't understand. She's gone.

Just gone." She sank to the cold, hard ground.

The bitter wind dried the tears left on her face when she finished crying. On the horizon the trees were bending back and forth blindly. Allie shivered and caught herself wanting to go and rip the weeds away from them. But it was an impossible task, just as impossible as bringing back her sister.

"I may not be able to save those trees, but I can stop the kudzu from getting any more." In the back of Alejandra's mind, silly fancy argued with common sense. A realization hit her, and she gasped.

She couldn't save Lennie. It was too late for that. But she could help the others. She could keep the weeds of peer pressure from overtaking other teenagers. The kudzu was sly, but someone could outwit it. Someone had to outwit it. She thought of all the girls in the hospital. They shouldn't die. Lennie shouldn't have died.

"It has to be stopped or it'll take everything." Alejandra stood watching the trees again for a long moment before turning her back to the wind. She didn't have a plan, but it would come. All she knew was that she was going to avenge her sister's death. She was going to stop the kudzu.

My Life

by Sergio Jackson

At a young age I was introduced to the struggle
Age twelve on the block no stranger to trouble
All my life I've been looked down on
Never been noticed for the good
Always noticed for the wrong
My life has been hard, but I know I'll make it
Don't like the cards I've been given
But I got to take it
Trying to see the light but surrounded by darkness
With the world on my shoulders I find myself heartless
I'm here alone with my back against the wall
Trying to stand on my own but I continue to fall
Don't like the situation but I will still try
Holding back a life of tears because I refuse to cry.

It's Better In Metter

by Molly Logan Holmes

Greg Maddux was attempting to become the first pitcher in baseball history to win fifteen or more games in sixteen straight seasons. Marcus Giles was endeavoring to set a record for the most doubles in a single season by a Braves player in the history of the franchise, and Javier Lopez was attempting to break the all-time single-season record for home runs by a catcher.

It was September, and the Braves were making their annual rush toward a twelfth straight Eastern Division championship in the National League. My friends, Emily and Rachel, and I were avid fans, and the fever was upon us. Rachel and I saved our money, made hotel reservations, and planned a flawless itinerary for our birthday gift to Emily: a trip to Turner Field.

Bags were packed, permission was given to leave school early on a Friday afternoon, and excitement built as our departure approached. I smiled as Rachel's purple Jeep pulled up in front of the auditorium at 3:00 p.m. sharp; it was finally time to leave. I was handed a chocolate shake as I piled my bags in the back, then we turned up the radio and sped out of Savannah. This would be the best birthday present we had ever given Emily.

The hum of the tires on the highway eventually carried me off into a peaceful slumber in the back seat, and Emily read "Sports Illustrated" with her toes on the dashboard. All was peaceful and happy.

However, at around 3:45 a horrible smell had filled my lungs ,and I began to stir. Rachel had already pulled over on the side of the highway, and I sat up to see Emily, eyes wide, staring at Rachel who had her head on the steering wheel. Through the windshield I took in an ominous cloud of white smoke issuing from the engine.

"Where are we?" I asked tentatively, breaking a fearful silence. Emily answered my question with a single slow and deliberate motion toward a green road sign on the side of the highway. We were in Metter.

One hour and a call to the tow truck later, we found ourselves sitting in the waiting room of "Bubba's Auto Garage and Gas Station." Our jeep was having transmission problems and needed a part replacement. Rachel, in a fit of optimism, tried to keep our spirits up by saying that we still had about three and a half hours until the game began, and that if Bubba and his motley crew could fix us up quickly, we could get there before the third inning. Ten minutes later, we were informed that the necessary part would need to be obtained from Statesboro.

It was the top of the third in Atlanta, and we were still in the waiting room on a brown vinyl sofa held together with duct tape, making small talk with Bubba. Our stomachs were grumbling, but the RC Cola, beef jerky, and pork rinds that he had to offer seemed rather unappetizing. When the part arrived— it was now the bottom of the fourth inning—Bubba and his assistants deliberated as to whether or not to stay open late to finish the job. Bubba let us know that he did not have any employees available to stay for the repair. It appeared that we would be spending our Friday evening in Metter.

Outside by the gas pumps, we asked a fellow teen what people did for fun around these parts. "Well, ya know yawl can always go ta Jo-Max. 'S'matter-a-fact, yawl can hop in the back-a tha' pickup; I'm headed that way an' I don't mind droppin' ya off since ya don't have a car an' all." We deliberated, and unanimously decided to check out "Jo-Max," whatever the heck that was.

Upon our arrival, we discovered that it was a barbecue restaurant, the happening spot in town. By this time we were past the point of being aggravated about our situation and were simply happy that at least we might have a decent meal. Despite the incessant country music, the obesity of the family to our left, and the slight smell of putrefaction that hung over the restaurant, our meal was surprisingly good. We used the telephones there to call Emily's parents to ask for a ride home, but Mrs. Strickland would not be able to leave the house for another hour or so. We would just have to wait.

As the Turner Stadium crowd sang, "Take Me Out to the Ball Game," Rachel and Emily played tic-tac-toe on Jo-Max napkins. At the bottom of the eighth, we had thoroughly exhausted every joke we knew. Just as the game wrapped up and Skip Carey bid television viewers good night, our ride home arrived.

Greg Maddux was attempting to become the first pitcher in baseball history to win fifteen or more games in sixteen straight seasons. Marcus Giles was endeavoring to set a record for the most doubles in a single season by a Braves player in the history of the franchise, and Javier Lopez was attempting to break the all-time single-season record for home runs by a catcher. Yes, it was September, and as the Braves were in the throes of their annual rush toward a twelfth straight Eastern Division championship in the National League, three young girls in Metter, Georgia, had been cured of their fever.

Confused?

by Kimberly Lewis

Anger, there's too much,
Tears fall like liquid diamonds,
Soul is crushed,
Nothing
Left to touch.
Furious
There's
Nothing
To do,
Upset,
There is
Too much to lose,
Confused, what's going on?
Inside my heart is breaking in two.
It burns, thought of it
It hurts, the pain of leaving all,
It passes and I just sit.
Where to go?
What can I do?
I won't face it!
I just don't know!
WAKE UP!
It's all a dream,
A nightmare of
Terror or so it seems.

I need an answer,
I'm terrified,
I don't want to go,
But where can I hide?

Sky

by Chelsea Hollifield

She's only happy when it rains; when the clouds open up and pour out liquid crystal tears; when the sky is gray and it seems like it's weeping for all the sorrows of its poor children stumbling blindly on this big piece of land. She sits by the window and watches the world blur before her, concentrating only on the gentle tapping of the rain on the windowsill. It is these solemn times that she remembers him. It's the water, you know, that reminds her. He was almost a part of it; he loved it so much. He, with his sunny golden hair...but only she knew that because it was always some exciting color Crayola had dreamed up. He, with his flawless blue eyes, always filled to the bursting point with excitement. She remembers all this first. And then, without meaning to, her mind drifts back to that summer...

The alarm clock screamed, rousing Scarlet from her tender sleep. She crawled out of bed and fell limply onto the cluttered floor. (Her limbs never fully cooperated in the morning.) She let her waist-length black hair pour over her like a blanket. The light flicked on, and Scarlet's pale violet eyes immediately recoiled.

"Rise and shine, my raven," chirped Anna, her mother.

"Mmphh," responded Scarlet. "Too...early..." she groaned.

"But Dumpling," smiled her mother, "I've got a surprise for you!"

Scarlet began incoherently grumbling with obvious displeasure.

"Are you ready for my news, Dumpling? Honey...we're going to move to Florida! Isn't that just wonderful?"

Scarlet reached deep within her and summoned up the energy to spring up from the floor. "What?! Why?"

"Well, I think we could all use a change of scenery... Besides, you might make some...ahem, *nice* friends there.

Scarlet's mother had never liked her friends; she thought they were bad influences on her angelic little daughter because they had strange-colored hair, and they wore spikes and baggy pants. Scarlet thought this was utterly ridiculous and unfair. Who was her mother to judge people, anyway?

Scarlet's mind began whirling in a quick, staccato tango, as her mother stood grinning in her doorway.

As soon as Scarlet's black combat boots touched the pavement, she knew she would never fit in here. The chirping birds of home were replaced by roaring seagulls that got great pleasure out of driving Scarlet insane. The wonderfully green pine trees were replaced by bare, skinny palm trees. The warm scent of the woods was now the sickeningly strong smell of salt.

The first thing Scarlet did was go to the beach. The hot, punishing sand stung beneath her feet, and her eyes beheld a beach full of anorexic-looking blondes in bright bikinis and men who looked like they'd been on steroids for years. Scarlet noted that she stood out quite a lot in her faded black-and-pink-plaid bikini. With a rebellious flip of her hair, she decided she didn't care in the least.

She threw down her bag and towel with obvious carelessness and began making her way to the shoreline. She had no intention of going in the water (she had never learned how to swim), so she just plopped down close enough to feel the salty froth gently lapping at her toes. She sat very still for a minute with her eyes closed, and when she opened them she was very surprised to see a pair of crystal blue eyes less than an inch from her face. Scarlet fell backwards in surprise, and the owner of the eyes began to laugh; a true laugh full of happiness and heartfelt emotion.

As the shock began to wear off, Scarlet realized the eyes belonged to a boy…a very attractive teenage boy with shaggy blue hair (which partially covered up his eyes) and golden skin. He had an amused smile on his face and a somewhat mocking look in his eyes, yet they still seemed warm and comforting. He arose and asked, "Well, are you going in, then?"

Scarlet was still a bit startled, so it took her a few seconds to comprehend his inquiry. "Wha- go in...*where?…*Oh you mean—the water? Uh, no, I...I don't think so."

Her stumbling reply seemed to amuse him even more, but all he said was, "Why not?"

"Oh God," she thought, *"how am I going to say this?"* "I...really don't know how...how to swim," she finished hurriedly.

His only response was a dazzling smile as he held his hand out to her. "I'll help you," he said grandly.

She hesitantly placed her hand in his and let him lead her into the water. She became a little bit nervous when he brought her farther out than she had anticipated. Suddenly, the ocean floor took a steep dive, and Scarlet's feet sought the bottom but found empty space.

"Oh!" she cried, but before she had time to yell for help, the boy had his arms around her, holding her up.

"Move with the water," he whispered, "Don't fight against it."

After a few minutes of assisted floating, Scarlet could stay up on her own, but the boy's arms remained firmly wrapped around her tiny waist.

"What's your name?" She whispered, feeling that the atmosphere was too serene to speak loudly.

"Sky," he answered. "Just Sky."

Over the next few days, Sky and Scarlet were inseparable. They spent their days talking and joking with each other, and they spent their nights on the beach, watching the sunset.

One particularly cloudy day, Sky and Scarlet were walking down the shore when Sky suddenly became quiet, which was against his nature. Scarlet barely noticed because she was ranting again—something about an actress who had compromised her morals—when Sky urgently said, "Be quiet. The wind is speaking."

Scarlet's lilac eyes gave away that he had startled her, but nevertheless she did as he said.

He was staring out toward the salty green froth. "There's a big storm coming," he noted. "You'd better get home."

She didn't understand. "And...what about you?"

"I feel like witnessing the wonderful fury of nature right now, thank you very much. I'm going to stay and watch."

A thousand questions rushed to the front of Scarlet's mind, but she knew better than to ask them. She simply stated, "I'll be back at sunset to join you."

He nodded his approval and bent down to kiss her pale cheek. "Don't worry. I'll be careful."

She turned and walked slowly up the beach towards the street. On the long walk home she was deep in thought. Why did he stop her so abruptly? Why was he remaining at the beach? She silently prayed he wouldn't do anything careless.

As soon as she walked through the door, her mother flew towards her with outstretched arms. "Oh my goodness, I was so worried about you! Out with that boy with the hurricane coming! I can't even imagine..."

"What?" Scarlet interrupted, "Hurricane? What are you talking about?"

"Yes, dear, a hurricane, it's been on the news for at least a week now; haven't you seen..."

Before her mother could finish speaking, Scarlet was scrambling out the door and running towards the beach. It was already beginning to rain, but the only thing she was aware of was the blood pounding in her ears. Her bare feet splashed through newly born puddles, and her chest heaved with exhaustion—but still she felt nothing except the hammer pounding rhythmically inside her head.

She was now running on wet sand. The wind ripped roughly through her hair, and there was a blinding flash of lightning followed by a resounding drumroll of thunder. The waves were crashing furiously at the shore as if they were trying to annihilate it. She screamed for Sky, but her voice was drowned out by the wind and thunder. She was soaking wet, but she hardly noticed.

Suddenly, a hand roughly grabbed her from behind. Before the darkness surrounded her, she saw a pile of clothes behind a rock that looked distinctly like Sky's. She was calling his name as her knees buckled, and she collapsed to the ground. Then everything went dark...

She hadn't gone to his funeral; it had seemed too final. She had still wanted to believe he'd be back. Before now, she has never cried about him. Not even the day of his funeral, not the one time she had accidentally passed by the cemetery where his lifeless body lay; never. She has never accepted it. Until just now, it hasn't been fully real to her.

She softly brushes her hair away from her face and lets the quiet tears stream down her cheeks like the rain still dripping off the side of the windowpane. Then, roughly, she wipes away her tears and stands. It's been five years. She has a new life now, a new family. Her stomach is swollen, and she laughs as her impatient baby kicks. She pulls her long black hair into a low ponytail and turns to leave the room. She says his name, in a final way, to prove once and for all that she's okay. As the single syllable falls from her lips, the small life inside her kicks. She nods with affirmation. Her baby's name will be Sky...just Sky...

Biographical Notes

Kindergarten – Fourth Grade Judges

Carol Ansardi has been writing and publishing since 1980. She has sold to magazines, local and national, and ghostwritten a non-fiction book published in 1992. "Real paying jobs" have included medical editing and wiring support for a consulting group. She has won fourteen writing awards and recently returned to her first love, oil painting. She lives in Marietta with her husband, grandson, and two dogs.

Joan Armour was voted Teacher of the Year (2001–2002) by the staff at Lula Elementary. She has a love and excitement for teaching and inspires her students on a daily basis to achieve and meet challenging goals. Joan has a Master's Degree in Paralegal Law, and a B.A. and Master's Degree in Early Childhood Education from Piedmont college. She is a member of the Professional Association of Georgia Educators. Joan and her husband, Ricky, have been married for seventeen years and have two children, Lauren and Whitney.

Beth Callahan currently serves as an instructional coach at Monroe Primary School in Monroe, Georgia. Her 22 years of experience in the classroom include special education and elementary education. Ms. Callahan graduated with a Specialist's degree in Curriculum and Instruction from Piedmont College and currently holds National Board Certification in early childhood education.

Janie Cowan received her Bachelor of Music Education and Master of Music Education degrees from the University of Georgia. Ms. Cowan also holds a Masters degree in Library Media Technology from Georgia State University. She has taught band, chorus, general music, drama, and computer literacy at the elementary, middle, high school, and college level. She currently serves as Library Media Specialist at Settles Bridge Elementary School in Forsyth County.

Fifth – Sixth Grade Judges

Barbara Dixon is a Mentor Teacher at Benefield Elementary School in Gwinnett County. She is married to Noah Dixon, Jr., and has two sons, Spencer and Kevin. Barbara and her family live in the Dacula area. Barbara is a graduate of North Georgia College and State University. She has recently completed the Georgia Staff Development Academy and was selected to participate in the National Staff Development Academy beginning in July. Barbara also serves as Awards Chairperson for the Georgia Reading Association.

Leslie McGuinness is a freelance writer who lives in Cumming, Georgia. She is a graduate of the University of Georgia where she majored in journalism. Her work has appeared in area business and family publications as well as the *Forsyth Herald*. Prior to freelancing, Leslie spent 10 years in the public relations/marketing arena. She has served as head writer for two business-to-business television programs as well as ghostwriter for a former leader in the financial services industry. Currently, Leslie is working on a children's book that was inspired by her husband and three energetic little girls who are six, four, and two years old.

From the very moment *Angel Stanley* entered her second grade classroom on a sweltering summer day in August of 1995, she knew that she had taken a gigantic step toward fulfilling what would become, for her, a passion to teach. From that point forward, Angel diligently pursued opportunities that would allow her to become the consummate educator. From a collaborative kindergarten class, to the position she now holds as curriculum coach, Angel has committed herself to promoting the best strategies that allow students to achieve their greatest potential. Not only has she pursued this professionally, she has also pursued this passion for curriculum development by obtaining her Masters and Specialist degrees in curriculum and instruction.

Suzie Windsor is an instructor in the Teacher Education Department at North Georgia College and State University. She also serves as the Instructional Coordinator for the Gainesville College campus Early Childhood Education Program. Suzie owns and operates Teachable Moments Seminars, a business specializing in staff development training for elementary school teachers. She has been a Kindergarten, First, Third, and Fifth grade teacher in Hall and Forsyth counties. She lives in Gainesville with her husband, Chris, and daughter, Lily. Her hobbies are reading, gardening, walking in the woods, and snow skiing.

Seventh – Eighth Grade Judges

Lisa Cleland was born in New Jersey and raised in the Northeast, but has lived in the Atlanta, Georgia, area for the past 21 years. Lisa has a BBA in Accounting from the University of Georgia and 12 years of payroll/benefit experience, including five as an instructor. Lisa is now a full-time homemaker and hands-on mother to Diana and Julia, ages 7 and 4. She is currently in her 15th year of marriage to her college sweetheart, Blake. Lisa is an avid reader and lifelong book lover. This is her first year as a judge in the *O, Georgia Too!* contest.

Becky Malmquist is a gifted program teacher at Richards Middle School in Gwinnett County. A graduate of Brenau University, Becky holds a Masters degree in Middle Grades Education. She has taught gifted language arts for the past four years, and is currently teaching an interdisciplinary gifted enrichment class. Becky encourages students to seek publication for their writing, and has had several students published locally and nationally. In addition, she has collaborated on past editions of the *O, Georgia Too!* Teacher's Guide.

Bobbie Mullinax is a second grade teacher at Chestatee Elementary School. She has been teaching for 27 years. Bobbie has been a big supporter of Humpus Bumpus through conducting workshops, buying books for her classroom, and reading the entries for the *O,*

Georgia Too! program. She has had several of her students' stories and poems published in *O, Georgia Too!* This was the third year for Bobbie to serve as a judge of the entries for *O, Georgia Too!* She says, "Reading the entries is always a joy because the writing is so creative and imaginative."

Cuban-American author *Berta Platas* writes contemporary women's fiction with a strong dose of humor. Her short story, *The Wisteria Tango*, appears in Blessings of Mossy Creek (BelleBooks, June 2004) and a novella, *Revenge of the Fashion Goddess*, will appear in Friday Night Chicas (St. Martins, February 2005). Besides women's fiction, Berta reads Young Adult novels and anything really scary or wacky.

Ninth – Twelfth Grade Judges

Steven Brehe teaches writing linguistics and literature at North Georgia College and State University. He and his son live in Dahlonega.

Victoria Rose Kidd is currently the branch manager of the Elizabeth H. Williams Branch of the Gwinnett County Public Library. Before coming to Georgia she was a children's and young adult librarian in Ohio. Previously she has worked as a teacher, social worker, and professional puppeteer. She lives in Snellville, Georgia, with husband, Dan. They share the joys of five grown children and a daughter-in-law, travel, domestic bliss, and a 1963 Chevy Impala SS.

Kelly Silver has taught English in Georgia for five years as well as one year in the United Kingdom. She is a graduate of the University of Georgia where she earned a B.S. and an M.Ed. in English Education.

Tammy Wade lives in Monroe, Georgia, with her husband, Jon, and her two children, Chase and Kinsey. She has been a high school English teacher for 12 years in Gwinnett and Walton Counties. Her dream is to write a great southern novel/nonfiction sporting the title *Duct Tape and Other Signs of Love* about her experiences with rednecks and love.

Authors

Elementary School

Christina Nicole Abreu is a ten-year-old fifth-grader at Daves Creek Elementary in Cumming, Georgia. An honor student throughout her schooling, Christina's passion has always been writing. Her literary works have been selected by her school as the best essays written by any student in her grade. Both of her entries in the Reflections literature competition have received honorable mention at the county competition level. When she is not writing stories, Christina enjoys participating in soccer, dancing, singing, and swimming. Given a choice as to what she prefers, Christina will always choose writing a story! Christina has many friends, but the best one of all is her twin sister, Catherine.

Jim Acee is nine years old and lives with his parents and five-year-old brother. He is in the third grade and maintains excellent grades. His teacher describes him as a born leader, and Jim's favorite subject is science. He likes to swim and play basketball, football, baseball, and golf. He also likes many types of music and movies. Jim is very social and remains loyal to his closest friends. He enjoys playing with Beyblades, Tech Deck Dudes, and GameCube. He also enjoys traveling and has an interest in history and geography. He has a pet Beta fish named Venasaur.

David S. Bailey was born on January 19, 1993, at Northside Hospital in Atlanta, Georgia. At the age of three, his family moved to Crossett, Arkansas. He attended preschool at the First Baptist Church of Crossett at the ages of four and five. He then attended North Crossett Primary School for kindergarten and first grade. He attended second grade at Hastings Elementary School in Crossett. In May of 2001, his family moved back to Georgia. David is currently attending Chestatee Elementary and is in the fifth grade.

Lydia Rutland Barnes is ten years old and a fourth-grade student at Savannah Country Day School. She lives in Savannah with her parents, her older sister Anne, two fish, a frog, and a dog named Poppy. She also has a sister in New York City, where Lydia likes to visit. Lydia enjoys writing and drawing, and is learning the violin. She plays for the Green Force soccer team and swims for the Savannah Swim Team. Her favorite stroke is the backstroke. Her parents describe her as a "heap of babblement," an expression borrowed from Nathaniel Hawthorne.

Octavia Lynette Benson was born in Atlanta, Georgia, on July 14, 1994. She was named for her French grandfather, Octave. She attends fourth grade at Vickey Creek Elementary School. Her hobbies are swimming, playing the piano, geocaching, reading chapter books, and playing with her friends. She has a sister named Melinda. Her parents' names are Valerie and Kirk. Her cats' names are Spencer and Turnpike, and her bird's names are Sunset and Sunrise. When she grows up, she wants to be either an actress or a veterinary assistant.

Brittany Bodine is ten years old, in the fourth grade, and goes to Matt Elementary School. She thinks the most inspiring people in her life are her teachers and her mother. She wants to be a teacher when she grows up. Brittany loves to read and write, but often overdoes it. She loves helping people when they are upset, but she helps out any time. Brittany's favorite thing to do is go swimming. Another thing she likes to do is sing and dance to her favorite songs. Her most favorite thing is going to school and helping her teachers.

Amanda Marie Boyd is seven years old and attends Pinecrest Academy. She is in second grade. Her favorite subjects are math, science, and social studies. Outside of school she is very busy on her gymnastics team. She trains for over eleven hours a week at the Gymanstix Training Center in Buford. She also enjoys reading, bike riding, hula hooping and playing with her friends. She lives in

Cumming, Georgia, with her mom, dad, and brothers (Jeffrey and Brian).

Kirsten Carella is in fifth grade at Riverside Elementary and is eleven years old. She plays tennis and is on a swim team in the summer. Her birthday is January 8, 1993. Jim and Lori Carella, her parents, describe her as too smart for her own good. Friends describe her as trustworthy and snappy. Kirsten won a reading award last year from the Gwinnett Reading Council. She also won a writing award for a poem last year in the gifted program. Each of her teachers thinks she is a big help and a good student. Kirsten is also a Junior Girl Scout.

Joe Carnaroli, 11, lives in Cumming, Georgia, with his mother and father. His hobbies include baseball, football, chess, and constructing model airplanes. He also enjoys going on vacations to historic areas. Joe likes to work out with his father after school. He is currently a fifth grader at Matt Elementary School and will attend Liberty Middle School in fall 2004. His most prized collection is his twenty-eight nutcrackers. His love of maps helped him become the National Geography Bee Champion for his school. With the help of his friend, Seth, Joe took first place at the 2004 Regional Technology Fair.

Connor Wadsworth Clark is a happy, caring, and humorous six-year-old boy who is currently a student in Ms. Potter's kindergarten class at Chestatee Elementary in Forsyth County. He enjoys fishing with his dad, playing soccer, swimming, painting, drawing, reading, playing Nintendo, singing in the car, and hanging out with his friends and family. His future plans include, but are not limited to, becoming a singer/songwriter and a veterinarian.

Kamryn Coan is ten years old and has lived in Alpharetta, Georgia, for five years. He was born in Red Bank, New Jersey, and lived along the Jersey shore for five years before moving to Georgia.

Kamryn loves to draw and sings in the school chorus. He attends Sharon Elementary School in Suwanee, Georgia, where he is in the fourth grade. Kamryn loves animals and has several pets such as, guinea pigs, rabbits, and most recently, a parakeet. He is an avid athlete who loves to play football and baseball.

Taylor Coan is eleven years old and lives in Alpharetta, Georgia. He was born in Red Bank, New Jersey, and moved to Georgia when he was five. Taylor attends Sharon Elementary School and is in the fifth grade. He loves to read books and enjoys playing the piano. His favorite sports to play are basketball and football. Taylor is highly competitive both in sports and school competitions. He enjoys participating in science fairs, oratory contests, and talent shows. He hopes to write a book when he is older. Taylor's favorite author is Lemony Snicket.

Meghan Cooley is eleven years old and lives in Gainesville, Georgia. She enjoys spending time with her friends and family. She has ten pets: two cats, one dog, five fish, a guinea pig, and a hamster. She attends school at Chattahoochee Elementary School in Forsyth County and is currently in the fifth grade. She loves reading R.L. Stine books, Harry Potter books and any kind of mystery or horror book. She really loves going to Slap Shots where she can skate with her friends and her family.

Kyle S. Cristal is a fifth-grade student at The Schenck School in Atlanta, Georgia. The Schenck School specializes in helping kids with dyslexia. He is kind, friendly, and has a lot of friends. He has plenty of hobbies, such as driving cars and four-wheelers, racing go-carts, and riding on his dad's custom Harley. Kyle has one sister and no brothers.

Joshua R. Dane attends fifth grade at Big Creek Elementary School. He lives in Cumming and enjoys playing with his two brothers and sister. He has been playing the piano for a few years and cently begun playing the clarinet. He has many friends and enjoys playing soccer. He was part of The Wild Cat News, the school television news program, and his favorite job was that of news anchor. He has recently taken part in the oratorical contest and won third place. He loves animals and is the owner of quite a few. His favorite authors are J. K. Rowling, T. A. Barron and Brian Jacques.

Allie Elizabeth Dean is nine years old and is in the Fourth Grade at Black's Mill Elementary School in Dawsonville, Georgia. She loves to write. She writes about once a day. Her ideas come from things that happen or things she likes. However, she sometimes gets her ideas from other writers. She has more than fifty stories and tons of poems. Allie received first place in the Fall Fling for Students 2003 in Creative Writing sponsored by Newspapers in Education. She likes to climb trees, draw and collect things like rocks and small porcelain dolls. Her favorite color is green.

Kate Drummond was born on March 25, 1995, in Rome, Georgia. She enjoys soccer, extreme sports, music, movies, kickball, and playing with friends. Kate currently attends Sawnee Elementary where she is in the Horizons program and is a member of the Chess club. Her favorite subjects are Math, Science, and Art. Kate also has a great fondness for animals and hopes to one day become a veterinarian or a marine biologist.

Sarah Ann Evans is currently in the fifth grade at Settles Bridge Elementary. She is involved in competition cheerleading, is on a tennis team, and loves to play the piano. She came in second place in Forsyth County's spelling bee. Sarah hopes to work with dolphins one day. She has a dog named Lucy that can play hide and seek. Her favorite place to visit is Savannah, Georgia. The history of the old, beautiful homes is magical for her. She especially enjoys visiting the tree-lined squares and listening to all the ghost stories.

Ariana Fouriezos is ten years old and is in the fourth grade at Pinecrest Academy, in Cumming, Georgia. She is one of six children (two boys and four girls) and is looking forward to the birth of a new baby sister in June. She plays piano and guitar. Her favorite sport to play is soccer and her favorite sport to watch is hockey (especially the Atlanta Thrashers!). When Ariana grows up, she would like to be a veterinarian because she loves animals. In fact, she has two mice named Chip and Cuddles, and a cat named Feather.

Paul Fouriezos is eight years old and is in the second grade at Pinecrest Academy, in Cumming, Georgia. He is one of six children (two boys and four girls) and will have a new baby sister in June. Paul loves to play soccer and to go to Atlanta Thrashers hockey games with his dad. When Paul grows up, he would like to be a professional hockey player or a scientist.

Megan Galvin is eleven years old and currently attends Big Creek Elementary School. Her homeroom teacher is Mrs. Ferrer, and her language arts teacher is Mrs. O'Malley. She has a mom, a dad, and a little sister named Kaleigh. In her spare time, Megan enjoys Karate, soccer, reading, writing, playing with her friends, swimming, camping, and working on the computer. She plans to become a children's dentist and an author when she grows up.

Erin Galvin-McCoy lives in Winterville, Georgia, with her dad, mom, older sister, younger brother, and two dogs named Teela and Zora. Erin is in third grade at Barnett Shoals Elementary. She loves to cook, read, tell stories, walk her dogs (when they're good), tell stories to her dogs (when they're really good) and play the piano. She also likes to go rock hunting with her dad. She definitely doesn't like to get out of bed in the morning. Erin's birthday is February 21, and having thousands of people read her story would be a great present.

Katie Garmon is a ten-year-old fifth grader who attends Sawnee Elementary School. She loves reading, writing, and science. Katie grew up in a musical family and loves the piano and guitar. Playing basketball, snow skiing, and dancing are some of her favorite activities. Katie loves her grandfather, Antonio, and was overjoyed when he loved the biography she wrote about him. Katie is happy to have the opportunity to participate in a writing competition like O, Georgia Too!

Lucie Gourdikian is in fifth grade and is eleven years old. Her parents are divorced, and she lives with her mom and thirteen-year-old sister. Lucie has two dogs named Abbey and Sparky. She lives in Cumming, Georgia, and attends Big Creek Elementary. Her dream is to be a lawyer or a rock star. She plans to do ten major things in her life before she retires. She is very proud of what she is today.

Marshall Hahn is seven years old and attends elementary school in Alpharetta, Georgia. He likes playing baseball, doing well in school, participating in the drama group and choir at church, and being with his family. He also likes to build and make creative things "out of anything he can find."

Amelia Hays is a fifth grader at Matt Elementary school in Cumming Georgia. This is her second year with an entry in the O, Georgia Too! writing contest. She was published in the last edition with her poem, The Big Fat King, when she was in second grade. Amelia loves writing fiction stories, poems, and tales about her animals, which include (among others): a potbellied pig named Jemima Ramona and a sheep named Clementine. Her outdoor hobbies include softball and swimming, but she can often be found with her nose in a book! She is interested in following a career in writing or forensic science.

Sarah Helms is an eleven-year-old fifth grader who is a member of the gifted program (called Horizons) at Chattahoochee. Sarah is a wonderful writer and speaker and enjoys school. She is very helpful to the school as a member of the Safety Patrol and a Student Council Representative. Sarah also reads to younger children and helps them learn about the school. She is an officer of the 4-H club and often acts as leader and participant in the demonstrations. Sarah enjoys basketball and plays on one of the county recreation teams. She sets her goals high and works hard to reach them.

Caity Hodge wrote the poem, "I Am." She is in fifth grade at Daves Creek Elementary in Cumming, Georgia, and lives in Suwannee. She is also in the Horizons program and has had all A's for the last two semesters. She has a little brother named TJ, who is in second grade. Her mother is a fourth-grade teacher at Mountain Park elementary school in Roswell, Georgia, and her father works for General Electric. Caity is a gymnast at Southern Gymnastics. The only pets she has right now are some shrimp in an ecosphere. Caity is planning on getting a pet that she can play with this summer.

Jenna Hoffman was born Jennifer Kathleen Hoffman on March 16, 1993, in Port St. Lucie, Florida. She has a twin sister, Lauren, and a younger sister, Megan. Jenna's family moved to Dawsonville, Georgia, in 1997. Jenna has been proudly involved in Forsyth County's cheerleading program as a Bennet Park cheerleader for six years. A member of Good Shepherd Church, Jenna also enjoys being a group leader for preschool children at bible school, as well as attending weekly classes herself. Jenna has attended Chestatee Elementary since kindergarten and looks forward to attending North Forsyth Middle School next year. After college, Jenna plans to become a veterinarian.

Leandra Houston is ten years old and is a very good sports player. She likes to play football and basketball. Academically, she is doing well. She is a very well-mannered little girl, and she can make friends with almost anybody. Her favorite food is crab legs. She also loves to write stories and poems. Maybe one day, along with becoming a teacher or a vet, she will continue to write.

Sarah C. Hoynes is currently in the second grade at Chestatee Elementary School. Her favorite subjects in school are Reading and English. She participates in the Horizons class two times a week and loves the science experiments they get to perform. She took dance for two years and is currently in gymnastics. She is very involved in her church. Her favorite music is Christian and Broadway musicals. She has recently become interested in poems after receiving Shel Siverstein's "Where the Sidewalk Ends" for Christmas. She is a wonderful child with a great sense of humor. She hopes you enjoy her poem.

Grace Lifer is ten years old and attends Daves Creek Elementary School in Cumming, Georgia, where she is in the Avera/Thompson/Walker fifth grade block. Grace was born in Atlanta and lived in Winter Haven, Florida, for three years. Grace enjoys writing, singing, acting, soccer, basketball, and spending time with her friends. She has one younger sister, Faith. The family pets are a Jack Russell terrier, two Siamese cats, two fish and a bearded dragon. She also wants a leopard gecko. She lives with her parents, Martin and Nancy, and has two grandmothers (Mimi and Nana).

Jessica Brooke Lively is ten years old and in fourth grade. She is a student at Black's Mill Elementary School in Dawsonville, Georgia. Jessica got the idea to write this story when her science class studied planets. The class went outside and did an experiment. When the class finished, everyone was spinning around and bumping into each other. That's when she thought of the story, "The Dancing Planets." Mrs. Boegner, her teacher, loved the idea and gave Jessica lots of encouragement during the writing process. Jessica feels so honored to have the privilege to be doing this contest.

Gloria J. L. Mahoney was born in Atlanta, Georgia. She is in fourth grade at Summit Hill Elementary School in Alpharetta. She is the fourth of six children. Gloria's older brothers (Brendon and Blake), attend Georgia Tech and the University of Georgia. Brendon is a National Champion in track and hopes to run in the Olympics in 2004. Blake is a State Champion in cross-country and track representing Forsyth County. Gloria loves animals and wants to be a veterinarian. She has six cats and an Arctic shepherd, which is part wolf. She loves running, swimming, and playing with her two-year-old brother, Donald. Gloria lives in Alpharetta.

Jacqueline G. Mahoney was born in Atlanta, Georgia. She is in the third grade at Summit Hill Elementary in Alpharetta, Georgia. She is the fifth of six children. Jacqueline's older brothers (Brendon and Blake), attend Georgia Tech and the University of Georgia. Lawson, 12, attends sixth grade at Northwestern Middle School. Gloria, 10, attends Summit Hill Elementary School. Jacqueline loves all animals and bugs (except spiders!). She has six cats and an Arctic shepherd, which is part wolf. She loves running, swimming, and playing with her two-year-old brother, Donald. Jacqueline lives in Alpharetta, Georgia.

Shannon Mewes is seven years old. Currently, she is a first-grader at Matt Elementary School in Cumming, Georgia. She loves to read, play with friends, and watch movies. One of her favorite movies is "Schoolhouse Rock." She hopes one day to become an artist, musician, or veterinarian. Shannon was born in California and loves to go back to visit her extended family and friends. Her favorite vacation was a trip to Hawaii, where she enjoyed snorkeling and attending a luau.

Gemma Kim O'Connor is nine years old. She attends Abbotts Hill Elementary School and is in fourth grade. She loves school and looks forward to going every day. Gemma lives in Alpharetta, Georgia, with her mom, dad, and older sister (Samantha), who is in fifth grade. Her after-school activities are Chess, Dance, Flute, Tennis and Swimming. She writes in her diary every day. Mystery books are her favorite, especially those by the English writer, Enid Blyton. Gemma was born in England and moved to Georgia in 1996 at the age of two.

Kyle Oreffice is eight years old and in the second grade at Pinecrest Academy. Kyle loves soccer, baseball, tennis, basketball, football, and swimming. He also enjoys math and science. Last year Kyle received a special Principal's award called a "Smiling Faces" award for being outgoing, personable and respectful of teachers, staff and other students throughout the year. Kyle was born in North Carolina and lived in Arizona before moving to Alpharetta, Georgia, four and a half years ago. He has a younger sister and a yellow Labrador retriever. Kyle is a former O, Georgia Too! winner.

Jennie M. Pless is a nine-year-old who lives with her parents (Mike and Irene), her six-year-old sister (Rachel), one cat, two dogs, and two birds. She has a cockatiel named Alex, which she bought with her own money from pet sitting. She has a puppy named Cuddles and a cat named Kitty. Jennie is in the fourth grade at Sharon Elementary and represented her homeroom in the school Spelling Bee this year. She likes to write stories, create clubs for her friends, do research on animals and nature, crochet, play with horses, ride her bike, draw, watch television, with her pets, and hang out with friends.

Rachel I. Pless is a six-year-old who lives with her parents (Mike and Irene), her nine-year-old sister (Jennie), one cat, two dogs and two birds. Rachel has a parakeet named Sunshine and a dog named Angel. She helps take care of her pets and the other family pets. Rachel is a very good student in the first grade at Sharon Elementary. She likes to tumble and do cartwheels. She also likes to read, draw, color, write little books and stories, play with her friends, ride her bike, jump rope, listen to music, dance and watch television. She enjoys her religion class, too.

Stephanie Pool is ten years old and is a fourth-grade student at Daves Creek Elementary School in Cumming, Georgia. Stephanie loves to write short stories and plays, but she especially enjoys writing poetry. She has already won several competitions at her school and hopes to someday follow in the footsteps of one of her favorite authors, Shel Silverstein. Stephanie's hobbies include singing, acting, dancing, swimming and playing with friends. She lives in Cumming with her dad, mom, older brother (Matt) and various pets, including a dog, a cat, a hermit crab and several fish.

Luke Richerson is a fourth-grade student at Kanoheda Elementary School in Lawrenceville, Georgia. His love for words and writing began at an early age. He is the coauthor of "From the Heart of a Child: Meditations for Everyday Living" with his mother, Dawn Richerson. Luke enjoys building with Legos, learning the guitar and playing computer games. His favorite subjects in school are social studies and history, and he likes studying the Civil War. He has two dogs at home, Emily and Edgar, and a cat named GoldenEye.

William A. Robinson, III is finishing up the third grade at Bethesda Elementary. He lives with his family, including a mom, dad, and sister in Lawrenceville, Georgia. Will also has three cats and a dog in the house. Among his favorite activities are sports (especially football), basketball, and soccer. He also plays guitar and piano. Will has always liked writing stories and has developed a series of tales about the Davidson family and their adventures, led by the fearless but little-prepared Raymond Davidson. He likes to read Hardy Boys mysteries and Harry Potter.

Hannah Shaul is a nine-year-old girl from Cumming, Georgia. She is in the third grade at Daves Creek Elementary School. She loves to write poems, songs, and stories. Hannah also likes to sing and dance. Her favorite animals are Siberian tigers, dogs and horses. Hannah loves playing basketball and listing to country music. She enjoys amusement park rides and traveling. Hannah loves school and takes pride in her writing. Hannah feels that writing is a great way to express herself.

Erica Sheline is currently a fifth grader at Heards Ferry Elementary School. She is a straight-A student and participates in her school's chorus. She is very interested in reading and loves reading adventure stories. When asked what she wants to be when she grows up, Erica has switched her answer from "a mommy" to "a journalist." Erica has a brother named Chris and a sister named Katie. She also has a mom named Kim and a dad named Martin. She loves to write about her family, including her dog, Cody.

Austin T. Smith is ten years old and loves to play tennis, hockey, football, and other sports. He has played tennis since he was two years old and has competed in three National Little Mo tournaments. He wants to be a tennis pro when he grows up. He has been playing roller hockey for two and a half years. He is in fourth grade at Big Creek Elementary and has gotten straight A's so far. He goes to church every Sunday that he has a chance. He lives in Cumming with his mom and dad and younger brother.

Stefanie Smith is eleven years old and in the fifth grade at Matt Elementary School. She lives in Cumming, Georgia, in Forsyth County. She's in Horizons. Her little sister, Jessica, loves to write, just like her! Casey is her puppy that she got for Christmas. She gets many of her poetic inspirations from her dog. She has battled depression for two years, and that is where she gets her inspiration for her poem. Her favorite subjects are Reading, Creative Writing, and Science. Her favorite books are fantasy and nonfiction. When Stefanie grows up, she wants to be an archeologist.

Alex Stenhouse was born March 6, 1993, in Orlando, Florida. He is the son of John and Annemarie and brother to his five-year-old sister, Jessica. Alex attends Big Creek Elementary, where he is a fifth grade honor student. Alex has been involved in The Forsyth County Reflections Contest (where he won first place in photography at Big Creek), the Big Creek Spelling Bee, and Big Creek's Oratorical Contest (where he won second place). Alex's favorite activity is soccer. He plays on a traveling team with the Forsyth Fusion. Alex also enjoys reading and spending time with his friends.

Laura E. Stringer is a nine-year-old tomboy who goes to Matt Elementary. She is in Mrs. Barnick's fourth grade class. She enjoys hiking, horseback, and reading. Her favorite books are "Harry Potter and the Order of the Phoenix" and "Running Out of Time." She lives with her mom, dad, and sister. She has a kitten named Hazel (Hazey, for short). Laura also has a guinea pig named Snowball. All her pets are females. Her sister has a kitten named Tiger. Laura has written many stories and poems, but this one seems to be one of her best.

Claire E. Sullivan is an active nine-year-old. She enjoys piano and soccer, as well as acting and singing. Claire is the third of five kids in her family. She has an older sister who plays soccer, and an older brother who also plays soccer. She has a three-year-old brother who is very smart and likes to talk, and a one-year-old brother who likes to eat, dance, and talk. Claire is very lucky to have a mom and a dad who care about her and the things she wants to do in life. Claire loves her family.

James Madison Tuggle is a fourth-grade student at Crabapple Crossing Elementary School. He is a person who enjoys math, reading, and language arts. He is the eldest of three: Miriam (age five) and Kellen (age eight). He has one older brother, named Stephen, who is seventeen. Madison spends most of his spare time on weekends during extra work or playing video games. After finishing college, Madison plans to become an ophthalmologist. From being born in Atlanta, Georgia, on January 15· 1993, this advanced student has come an extremely long way to become what he is.

Audrey Cate Vasina is a ten-year-old girl who lives in Alpharetta, Georgia. She is a fourth grader at Pinecrest Academy. Audrey enjoys playing soccer, basketball, and tumbling. Her favorite subjects are grammar, math, science and creative writing. Audrey has a twelve-year-old brother and a wonderful mother and father. In the future, Audrey hopes to become a surgeon or a teacher.

Jacob Randall Walker is a third-grade student at Mashburn Elementary School in Forsyth County, Georgia. His favorite subjects are writing and math. Jacob enjoys reading, writing, art, computer games, and sports in his free time. He has written several stories about family and friends. He also enjoys playing with his new puppy, Smoltzie. Smoltizie was adopted in July 2003 from the Forsyth Humane Society. Jacob was born in Richmond, Virginia, but has lived in Cumming, Georgia, since he was two. He lives with his sister, Alex, his mom, and dad. Jacob also has a calico cat named Leo.

Marabeth C. Walkusky was born on October 22, 1993, in Michigan to Alan and Cindy Walkusky. Following successful open-heart surgery at six days old, she has enjoyed a healthy life. Marabeth is currently in the fourth grade at Big Creek Elementary, where she participates in the Horizons Program for Gifted Students. Marabeth enjoys going to Sea World in Orlando and interacting with the animals there. She enjoys reading both fiction and nonfiction books and watching documentaries about her favorite animals. Marabeth volunteers at North Point Community Church, where she participates as a singer and dancer in a weekly stage production called KidStuf.

Samuel Andrew Warnke lives in Dawsonville, where he is homeschooled with his three sisters and two big brothers. Sam likes to play with his Legos and other toys. Sam also likes to dance ballet. Now that he can read, he carries books around with him and reads them almost every chance he gets.

Ryan Waznik is a fourth grade student at Settles Bridge Elementary School in Forsyth County, Georgia. He was born in Atlanta, Georgia, and has lived in the surrounding area his whole life. He loves to go to school, and his favorite subjects are science and social studies. He would like to be a major league baseball player and then a vet when he retires from baseball. He loves to play sports, including baseball and football. He got the idea for his story from a tombstone that is located on his family's land in Commerce, Georgia. He loves to write!

Grant Weigel is a second grader in Miss Kleinschmidt's class at Pinecrest Academy in Cumming, Georgia. He loves to "do anything artistic," draw, read, play soccer and football, and play with his eight-month-old Labrador Retriever, Honey. He likes to eat Honeycombs cereal and feed them to his dog. He has one older brother and one younger sister. He wants to be an artist, a football player, or a soccer player when he grows up.

Alyx White is eight years old and has been drawing since she could hold a pencil or crayon. One of her favorite games is "I draw, You draw," which she plays with her dad. She also makes up her own books, a pastime she learned at Montessori school. Alyx also enjoys reading (especially Junie B. Jones), softball, and Disney World. When she grows up, she wants to be a traveling girl and an artist for Disney. She is very excited to be sharing her writing with you.

Alex Wilbourne is eleven years old and is a fifth-grade student at Daves Creek Elementary School in Cumming, Georgia. He likes to skateboard, read, write, listen to music, play the drums, and hang out with friends and family. Alex's favorite school subject is social studies because he finds history interesting and can relate it to his family background. Alex lives with his mother, father, and older sister, Jessica. He is thankful to his family for being supportive of his skateboarding and his schoolwork. When Alex grows up, he would like to be a professional skateboarder, drummer, or writer.

Matthew Williams is ten years old and is in Mrs. Bond's fifth-grade class. He enjoys taking part in team sports and in his free time likes to read. One of his favorite authors is Brian Jacques. He is currently school president and is involved in many school activities. He is very self-motivated and likes a challenge. Poetry is opening up a whole new world to him on how to express oneself.

Jackie Yarbro was born in Atlanta, Georgia and has lived here all of her life. She has gone to several different schools, both public and private, and has recently graduated from Settles Bridge Elementary School in Forsyth County. She graduated with the highest GPA in her class and is going to be attending Riverwatch Middle School in the fall. Jackie's interests include horseback riding, reading and writing. Upon graduating from high school, Jackie would like attend college to prepare for a career as a lawyer or doctor.

Philemon M. Yoo lives in Cumming, Georgia. He has three sisters and one brother. He goes to Big Creek Elementary School. He is in the fifth grade now. He was born in Los Angeles, California. He was a big baby at birth (9.5 pounds). He likes to go to Florida for fishing. Philemon also likes to play soccer, video games, and chess. He loves pets and has a dog and two rabbits. He likes to wear a green jacket because he loves the green color. His favorite American hero is George Washington, and his favorite subjects are social studies and math.

Middle School

Taylor Nicole Amos is twelve years old. She lives in Cumming, Georgia, with her parents (Bobby and Stacy), and her sister (Jordan). Taylor is in the sixth grade at Liberty Middle School and goes to church at Freedom Tabernacle. Taylor has many hobbies; among them are playing soccer, acting, reading and writing stories. This is Taylor's first writing contest. However, Taylor has been in several plays at the Sawnee Center, as well as the Holly Theatre, and has recently gotten the lead role in the school play. Taylor's goals are to pursue an acting and/or writing career.

John Henry Boger was born in Kennesaw, Georgia, on November 26, 1990, along with his twin sister, Olivia. He is the eldest of three children. He is in the seventh grade at Sandy Springs Middle School and likes to be called "Jack." He enjoys activities including lacrosse, wrestling, surfing, skiing, reading, and sleeping. Jack lives in a house in the woods with two dogs and two cats. On Friday nights, Jack enjoys going to the movies with his friends. He has enjoyed writing and hopes to continue churning out high-quality material. Jack hopes to attend college at Duke University.

Catherine Bowlin lives in Cumming, Georgia with her father, mother, and eight-year-old brother. She is twelve years old and is in the sixth grade at Liberty Middle School. Catherine loves acting and is in the drama club at her school. She also loves music; she has taken piano lessons since she was in the first grade and is in Honor's Chorus at her school. Catherine is an active member of her church's youth group. She loves spending time with her family doing outdoor adventures such as camping and hiking.

Edsel Boyd, III was born on April 5, 1992 in Atlanta, Georgia. He is currently eleven years old and a sixth-grader at Vickery Creek Middle School. Edsel loves to read and play sports. His favorite authors are J.K. Rowling, Paul Zindel and Jane Yolen. His favorite book is *Armageddon Summer* by Jane Yolen. Edsel has a great imagination and enjoys writing because it allows him so share his imagination with others. He also loves to draw cartoons. Edsel lives in Cumming, Georgia, with his mom, dad, and sister (Elizabeth). He has four dogs and a lizard.

Stephen Patrick Byrne is thirteen years old and is in the seventh grade at St. Francis School. He lives in Cumming, Georgia, with his family. He has a yellow Labrador Retriever and two mice. He is currently working on obtaining an orange belt in the martial arts of Song Mudo. He takes electric guitar lessons and likes to play Linkin Park songs. Stephen has been active in his community by educating kindergartners at Safety Camp during the summer. He is also a member of St. Brendan's Catholic Church and youth group. Stephen has recently discovered the new and exciting game of paintball.

Caitlin Campbell is an eighth grader at Covenant Christian Academy. Caitlin loves to go to church and spend time with her friends at youth group. She loves to read, go to school, and watch movies. Her favorite activity is to have her friends over to hang out and talk while eating Snow Caps. Caitlin's dream is to go to college and become a teacher.

Collin Carlson is eleven years old and attends sixth grade at Forsyth Middle. He wrote about an actual event that happened when he was eight years old, and when his little brother was four. Collin swims competitively year-round. He has also been successful competing in the school Reflections Contest. He has won best in school for several of his drawing and writing entries. Collin has also participated in Odyssey of the Mind, a team competition sponsored by NASA that emphasizes creative problem solving. This is Collin's second time to submit an entry to *O, Georgia Too!* and was honored to have been included in the 2001 publication.

Joshua Cohen is the author of "A Child's Memories." An eighth grader at Woodward Academy, Josh has many hobbies, including writing, rocketry, photography, and tennis. He is a "computer wiz" and enjoys spending time writing and developing computer programs and web pages. Josh devotes much of his free time to Scouting, and hopes one day to become an Eagle Scout. Joshua's writing and photography have been previously published in his school's literary magazine, "Inner Voices." An Atlanta native, Josh lives with his parents and two older brothers (Benjamin and Daniel), and his "sister" (Sandy, a four-year-old golden retriever).

Brenna Conley is an eighth-grader at South Forsyth Middle School. She enjoys writing short stories, fantasies, and poetry about her love and passion for Jesus. She aspires to be a writer. Her parents support her in everything she does, and she loves them very much. In her free time she enjoys playing soccer, pencil sketching, paintball, playing flute and getting together with friends.

Shelby Curran lives in Athens, Georgia. She is a student who attends Burney Harris Lyons Middle School. She is in the sixth grade. She is eleven years old. Shelby works hard to get good grades, and she is on the school honor roll. She likes to swim, cheer, write, and read. She swims and cheers at the Athens YMCA after school, and she does many other activities there, too. For instance, she participates in the Teen Volunteers program. Also, in her spare time Shelby likes to watch television. When at home, Shelby likes to play with her three cats.

Marissa Nicole Duhaime is a thirteen-year-old girl who lives in Cumming, Georgia. She is in eighth grade at Liberty Middle School and makes all A's. Marissa is involved in many activities. She is in Student Council and on the board of SADD (Students Against Destructive Decisions). Debate is every Wednesday. She started karate in 2000 and is now a First Degree Black Belt and an Assistant Instructor. Marissa hopes to go to Yale and become a lawyer. She then plans to be a Senator for Georgia and eventually the first woman president.

Joshua Evans is currently in the eighth grade at South Forsyth Middle School. He played on the eighth-grade football team and received the Golden Helmet Award. He will be playing on the ninth-grade football team at South Forsyth High School. Joshua enjoys tennis and the guitar. He is president of the Beta Club. Joshua was the Georgia State Oratorical winner for 2003. At the World Congress Center for the National Middle School Conference, Joshua wrote and gave a speech to around 4,000 people introducing the keynote speaker, Frank McCourt. Joshua hopes to be a neurologist someday.

Kasee Godwin is an eighth-grade student at Dean Rusk Middle School. She is active in the drama club and is involved in almost every school production. Kasee is an accomplished clarinetist in the symphonic band and plans to march with the high school next year. Kasee enjoys sewing and designing her own line of clothing. She is certified in first aid and CPR and assists with the two-year-old class in her church. Music, drama, and journalism are her great interests; she would like to attend a writing camp this summer and also plans to volunteer at her local library. Her friends and family are very supportive and important to her. This is her first submission to a writing competition, and she hopes to become a published author.

Taylor Hartley was born in Atlanta, Georgia, on November 6, 1990. She has one dog, a young sister named Hallie, a dad, and a mom. Her hobbies include playing soccer for the Forsyth Fusion's select soccer team, playing flute in the school band, and jotting down a poem or two. She also loves reading books by various authors and jumping on the trampoline in the back yard with her friends on the weekends. She loves the Georgia Bulldogs and likes to watch college football. Taylor lives in Cumming, Georgia, and is a seventh grader at local Otwell Middle School.

Lucy E. Hedrick is a twelve-year-old girl who is homeschooled five days a week with her younger sister, Katya. They live in a small community called Freehome, just north of Atlanta. Lucy and Katya do their schoolwork at the dining room table, and their mom and dad teach them. Lucy loves to read. When she was in kindergarten her favorite books were "Junie B. Jones," "Where the Wild Things Are," and (her most favorite) "Lucy and the Sea Monster." She has read a ton of books since then. When she was eleven she realized she had read all the books in the house, so she decided to write one of her own.

Emma Hershberger has been known to randomly burst out with wild jolts of energy and only use it for the happiness of the people around her. She is a twelve-year-old female in the sixth grade at Lost Mountain Middle School. Her hometown of Greenville, South Carolina, is a well-visited place, especially by her family who travels there every so often to see relatives and get their hair cut. Her family consists of her mother and father, an older brother, and two sisters. She has become a pure follower of her dreams to becoming an author of literature and the Lord.

Elizabeth Hill is an active reader and writes many stories and poems in her spare time. She is vice president of her school 4-H Club and hopes to earn a college scholarship from 4-H. Elizabeth also rides horses and helps around the barn by grooming and exercising horses, teaching children, leading trail rides, running birthday parties and cleaning stalls. Elizabeth spends many evenings babysitting for neighbors and family friends. She also takes care of neighbors' pets. Elizabeth is in the eighth grade, so she has plenty of homework. She enjoys reading, but not math. She likes to stay busy and likes to try new things.

Casey Hirschmann resides in Gainesville, Georgia, and is in the sixth grade at North Forsyth Middle School. She is in all of the gifted classes available to sixth graders. Science is the subject Casey loves most. Anjelica and Mr. Jill are Casey's two mysterious cats,

Pepper is her obnoxious Chihuahua, UnRice is her white fish, and Dori is her nocturnal hermit crab. Although Anjelica is annoyed by Pepper, and Mr.Jill is frightened of her, they are still the best pet family she could dream of! Casey adores animals, wants to become a veterinarian, has many different friends, and loves the outdoors.

Danielle Jackson is twelve years old and is in the sixth grade at South Forsyth Middle School. Born in Utah, she moved to Georgia and has lived in Doraville, Alpharetta, and now Suwanee. She loves to read, write, draw, and create web pages. Her favorite subject in school is Language Arts. Danielle loves horses, wolves and dogs. She has one brother (Alexander), and one sister (Christine). When Danielle grows up, she wants to be a computer scientist, a lawyer, or a dog trainer.

Alice Johnson is thirteen years old and in eighth grade. Her eight siblings' names are Christina, Norman, Ellen, René, Scott, Andrew, Dianna, and Ben. She is an active member in the Jr. Beta Club and 4-H Club at her school and has made straight A's during all of her middle school years. Alice is also a member of the South Forsyth Middle School Band program and enjoys playing her French horn. She also enjoys writing stories about music.

Mallory Keeble is an eighth grader at West Georgia Christian Academy in LaGrange. Her hobbies include dancing, painting, playing the piano, and acting. She is very creative and has a great personality. She has three cats, three dogs, and some fish. Her favorite author is Robert Frost. She hopes to go to college and major in performing arts.

Chelsea Kephart was born to Mike and Sherri Kephart on January 4, 1990, in Tulsa, Oklahoma. She went to Daves Creek Elementary School and then to South Forsyth Middle School. Her sister, who is three years older, has always been there for her. Chelsea is very grateful for all of the blessings she has been given. She has been involved in soccer, her real passion, since she was five years old. She has also played three seasons of basketball and ran track in seventh grade. Next year she will be attending South Forsyth High where she wants to play volleyball, basketball, track, and soccer.

Kaitlyn Klucznik currently attends school at North Forsyth Middle and is in the eighth grade. She loves to write and has an overactive imagination. Kaitlyn likes to write and read fantasy the best. Her favorite period to write about is the medieval time period, though she also likes some modern stories. She dislikes writing in first person, so she tends to write in third person. If she isn't writing or doing homework, then she can be found reading, writing, playing her flute, listening to music, and most likely chatting on the Internet with her friends.

Noah M. Levine is presently a sixth grade student at the Epstein School, which is located in Atlanta. He lives with his family and his two cats. When he is not attending school or writing, he is either reading, participating in sports, or watching TV. In March of 2004, he played Mayor Shinn in his school's production of "The Music Man." About a year ago, a book review by Noah appeared in the *Atlanta Journal-Constitution.* He is notoriously known by friends and teachers for writing two or three pages when just a paragraph is required.

Cailin Mace is a sixth-grade student at Vickery Creek Middle School. She enjoys writing poems and stories. Cailin's sister was in the *O, Georgia Too!* competition about two years ago. Cailin has written poems and stories since kindergarten. Her biggest influence is her grandmother, Dottie, who is a poet. Cailin's favorite thing to write about is nature—it inspires her. Cailin's favorite author is Barbra Park, the author of the *Junie B. Jones* series. Cailin loves her family and enjoys relaxing with them. She has a golden retriever (Sydney) and a bulldog (Bentley). She also has two cats (K.C. and Ferris).

Lawson Mahoney was born in Atlanta. He is in the sixth grade at Northwestern Middle School in Alpharetta, Georgia. He is the third of six children. Lawson's older brothers (Brendon and Blake) attend Georgia Tech and University of Georgia. Brendon is a National Champion in track and hopes to run in the 2004 Olympics. Blake is both a State Champion in cross-country and track representing Forsyth County. Gloria, 10, and Jacqueline, 9, attend Summit Hill Elementary School. Lawson loves running, baseball, swimming, and playing with his two-year-old brother, Donald. He has six cats and an Arctic shepherd, which is part wolf. Lawson lives in Alpharetta.

Amanda Nicole McGahee is twelve years old and lives in Rabun County, Georgia. She's the daughter of Sean and Becky McGahee, and the sister to two annoying but loving brothers. She attends Rabun County Middle School where she is a seventh grader. Amanda's hobbies include riding horses, playing softball, participating in beauty pageants, going to the races, talking on the telephone, babysitting her brothers, participating in church and Leo club activities, and just hanging out with friends. She's on the go morning, noon, and night.

Rachel Menter is currently an eighth-grade student at Woodward Academy in College Park, Georgia. In addition to attending school, Rachel participates in softball, playing on the Junior Varsity softball team at Woodward. She has an older sister who is a senior at Woodward. Rachel started creative writing in her English class this year and particularly enjoys the medium of poetry. She is currently fourteen years old and plans to attend the Woodward Academy upper school beginning next fall, where she will continue her education.

David Richman Millard is currently in the sixth grade at Athens Academy. When asked to write essays at school, his favorite subject is his pet (Popcorn), a tuxedo cat he loves dearly. His hob-

soccer, jazz piano, and reading. He enjoys playing clarinet in the middle school band; this year he participated in Mid-Fest, an intense three-day band workshop at UGA. During breaks at school you can find him playing "Aachah Ball," a game he and his friends made up.

Lauren V. Muller is currently in the seventh grade at Otwell Middle School. She lives in Cumming, Georgia, with her parents, twin brother, and white German Shepard. One of her hobbies is playing soccer. She plays on a traveling soccer team with many of her friends. Also, she is on her middle school track team and runs long distance. Lauren is part of the OMS band and plays the flute. She also takes private flute lessons. She is a member of the Jr. Beta club and is a staff member of the yearbook club.

Stephen Nix is a thirteen-year-old student who attends South Forsyth Middle School as an eighth grader. While maintaining excellent grades, Stephen's extracurricular activities include Eagle Chorale and playing first-string offensive tackle on the SFMS Eagles football team. Stephen enjoys playing baseball and video games, and he occasionally writes and draws in his free time. Writing allows Stephen to express his own unique creativity, while proving to be therapeutic for him as well. As a native Atlantan, Stephen has called Cumming his home since March of 1993, along with his father (C.A.), his mother (Mary), and his ten-year-old sister (Laura).

Diana Orquiola is thirteen years old and lives in Suwanee, Georgia with her parents and two (of three) brothers, Kevin and Brian. Diana was born on March 4, 1990 in Boston and raised in Randolph, Massachusetts; Alpharetta, Georgia; and now, Suwanee. She is in the eighth grade at South Forsyth Middle School. Diana has played a variety of sports; her favorites include basketball and soccer. In her spare time, she likes to read about her favorite rock bands and guitars. From rap to rock, oldies to punk, she listens to any kind of music. Diana also loves to write in her spare time; writing helps her get out her hidden feelings.

Kaye Otten is a twelve-year-old girl attending Woodward Academy in the seventh grade. She has lived most of her life abroad, following her parents (Lorrie Gavin and Mac Otten) and their jobs with the Centers for Disease Control. Born on April 12, 1991, in Atlanta, the family moved to China when she was one. After two years in Beijing, it was back to Washington D.C. When she was seven, her parents were transferred to Zimbabwe. Kaye had attended a small International School, so moving to Woodward (with 300 students in a grade) was quite a change. After a hard first year, Kaye is settling into her new home.

Sarah Overstreet is an eighth-grader at South Forsyth Middle School. Some of her hobbies are writing, playing on the computer, and reading. She is a member of the Academic Bowl Team, the Junior Beta Club, Eagle Chorale, the Band, and is also a part of a local Mother-Daughter Book Club. She is also a part of the Horizon's program. Sarah enjoys the challenge of trying different kinds of contests. In the sixth grade she won the A.R. award, and in seventh she won the school science fair. She also was runner-up for the girls in her school's Optimist Club Oratorical Contest.

Will Partin, author of "The Great Snowball War of 2003," was born on November 24, 1989, in Anchorage, Alaska. He moved to Atlanta when he was three and went to several schools before arriving at Woodward Academy, where he is currently enrolled in the eighth grade. He is a member of the District 5 Honor Band and plays the trombone, piano, bugle and guitar. He has been writing stories since he was in the fourth grade. He now lives in Decatur, a suburb of Atlanta.

Gwen Pierson was born to Linda and David Pierson in Morristown, New Jersey, on February 8, 1990. The Piersons stayed in Morristown for two and a half years before moving to Louisville, Kentucky, where Gwen's sister Maryanne was born. From Kentucky, they moved to the small town of St. Charles, Illinois, right outside Chicago. Gwen attended kindergarten and first grade in St. Charles before moving to Charlotte, North Carolina, where the Piersons lived for five years. Today, Gwen lives in Alpharetta, Georgia, where she plays soccer, runs track, and swims on her neighborhood swim team.

Bethany Grace Ray is twelve years old. She lives in Forsyth County, Georgia, with her parents and older brother, Daniel. She is a homeschooled sixth-grader who shares her mother's love of reading and her father's and brother's passion for muscle cars, four-wheel-drive trucks, and 70s southern rock music. Bethany is a very active member of Boiling Springs Primitive Baptist Church. She is a Junior Girl Scout in Troop # 3732. Her favorite hobby is riding her four-wheeler. She has a pet hamster named Chevy. This is Bethany's second year as an *O, Georgia, Too!* poet.

Trey Roberts is an eighth-grader with a lot going for him. He has been a straight-A student since elementary school. He succeeds in all of his classes, but one academic talent has always stood out in his educational experience. That talent is a love and passion for writing. He lives in a family of writers, and now Trey has always had a way with words. His athletic career of basketball, football, and baseball has always contributed to his writing style, along with his love for music. Trey Roberts and *O, Georgia Too!* are two trains waiting to collide.

Ashley Ryckeley currently attends Woodward Academy, a college prep school. She enjoys drawing, listening to music, playing volleyball, and writing poems. Ashley loves to hang out with her friends. She lives with her father, stepmother, and stepsister. She dreams of being a veterinarian and writer when she grows up. Ashley is a patient and creative teenager.

Ellie Schultz is an eighth-grader at South Forsyth Middle School. She enjoys playing softball in the spring and horseback riding in the summer. During her free time, Ellie puts together memory albums and enjoys sewing. On the weekends, she usually spends time with her hectic, five-member family. Along with being a straight-A student, Ms. Schultz is an aspiring writer and has won many awards for her work.

Amanda Stewart is a sixth-grader at Vickery Creek Middle School. Amanda loves to play the piano and sports such as basketball, tennis, and swimming. She is very active in her church, Midway United Methodist Church, and loves participating in youth activities. Amanda also enjoys spending time with her friends. Amanda loves to read and write her own stories. She has had three other stories published in previous editions of *O, Georgia Too!* She also enjoys playing with her five-year-old brother (Matthew), and fourteen-year-old sister (Sara). Amanda is the daughter of Jack and Freda Stewart.

Kevin Robert Ureda was born on December 31, 1991, at Northside Hospital in Atlanta (where he celebrated his first New Year's Eve). He was the third birth in his family, followed eleven minutes later by his identical twin brother, Nicholas James Ureda. Kevin's childhood has been busy with many different sports; his two favorites are football and baseball. His hobbies also include shooting pool, playing cards, and other board games. Kevin has been fortunate to travel throughout Europe and once into Asia. His favorite country is the United States because of its unlimited opportunity.

Nicholas Ureda is finishing the sixth grade and is twelve years old. He was born on the last day of the year. He is proud to be an identical twin brother of Kevin Ureda. He enjoys many outdoor sports, beating his dad in billiards, playing board games and card games like poker. He considers himself to be a good friend, honest and quick-witted. His best days are spending time with his twin and the rest of the family. He wishes to have a dog of his own and dreams to become a professional football player in the National Football League.

Mary Elizabeth Warnke is a thirteen-year-old homeschooled student. She lives in Dawsonville and goes to church at Good Shepherd Lutheran Church. Mary is a dancer and likes to dance ballet, pointe, jazz, hip-hop, and tap. She has three brothers (two of whom are dancers), and two sisters (one who also dances).

Anderson Wathen is from Atlanta, Georgia, and attends Woodward Academy as an eighth grader. He comes from a large family and is the older brother to a set of triplets. He is very interested in feature films and hopes to someday be a film director. After high school, his goal is to attend UCLA's film school. He became interested in poetry in the sixth grade and has written poetry ever since. He loves to read, and his favorite books are science fiction and fantasy. Anderson participates on the Woodward wrestling team. He also plays roller hockey and swims in a summer swim team league.

High School

Danielle Arthur, the author of "*...On Futility*," was born March 21, 1987, in Saginaw, Michigan. She lived in the countryside of Michigan until she was ten years old and then moved to northern Georgia. Danielle now lives in Cumming, Georgia, with her mother, father, and younger brother (Patrick). Patrick is eleven years old and is in the sixth grade. In her free time, Danielle reads as many books as possible, plays piano, and writes when inspired. Her favorite books are *1984* and *Animal Farm* by George Orwell, *We* by Yevgeny Zamyatin, *East of Eden* by John Steinbeck, and *The Awakening* by Kate Chopin.

Caitlin Bates is an eleventh grader at North Forsyth High School. She enjoys reading, writing, painting, making her own clothing, and taking pictures. One of her many passions is music; she enjoys listening to a wide variety, such as punk, emo, indie, trip-hop, screamo, and cheesy 80s pop. Some of her all-time favorite movies include *The Goonies, Magnolia, Requiem For A Dream, Donnie Darko, American Beauty*, and *The Breakfast Club*. Caitlin hopes to attend either NYU or the Art Institute of Boston, where she plans to double major in fashion designing and painting, and minor in photography.

Chris Callaway is a senior at The Westminster Schools in Atlanta. Chris has been writing since sixth grade. He has published short stories and poems, has completed a full-length novel, and has served as a Sports Reporter and the Columns Editor of his school newspaper, *The Westminster Bi-Line*. Chris has also participated in dramatic productions and has earned Varsity letters in football, track, and cross country. He will leave in the fall of 2004 for college.

Carl Chandler is a homeschooled fifteen-year-old who lives with his mother, father, two brothers, and a sister in Lawrenceville, Georgia, a suburb of Atlanta. His grandmother has been diagnosed with Alzheimer's disease and now lives with Carl and his family. He also volunteers at a local senior center to assist with other Alzheimer's patients on Wednesdays. In addition, Carl co-owns and operates TheIdiotsClub.com, a web site devoted to video games, movies, and more. In his spare time, he enjoys writing, reading books, and taking photographs. Carl has written several stories, with "Mark's Story" being his proudest achievement so far.

Timothy Paul Chatham is currently a junior enrolled at North Forsyth High School. He prefers to go by his middle name, "Paul," as that is the name he has been called his entire life. Paul enjoys long, romantic walks on the beach at night and somebody with whom he can cuddle. He is currently single and straight, so if you're interested give him a call. As you can see from his entry, and this biography, he has difficulty dealing with reality. Therefore, he hides behind a mask of simplicity and humor in an attempt to disguise his scared, lonely self.

Christian E. Clark was born on July 27, 1987, and is currently in the eleventh grade at North Forsyth High School. Christian has lived in Georgia for most of his life. He lived in Brazil for his first three years and then moved to Canada for another three years before moving to Georgia. He has been part of the Varsity soccer team for three years and played football his freshman year. He has two older brothers, named Rush and Trevor, and a twin sister named Tiffany. His parents are Rush and Penny Clark. He enjoys weightlifting, playing soccer, wake boarding, art, paintball, and going out on the lake.

Rebecca (Billie) Damren, a young writer in Buford, Georgia, is a sophomore at North Gwinnett High School. Having enjoyed writing as long as she can remember, she cannot picture a world without metaphor, poetry, and conceptual meaning. Rebecca has been seen in a few small parts in shows at North Gwinnett. At home she enjoys playing her sleek Silvertone electric bass guitar, martial arts (go Choi Kwang Do), drawing, independent writing, and making accessories (bracelets, arm warmers, wristbands, and iron-on shirt designs). In 2006, she hopes to go to Savannah College of Art and Design to major in cartooning or fashion design with a minor in creative writing.

Elizabeth Ann Devine is a sixteen-year-old homeschooler who has been writing since the fourth grade. In public school, she was in the lead in every accelerated reader program she participated in, and at the end of the middle school year was voted "the person to read the most" out of the entire grade. Elizabeth hopes to soon send her poems, short stories, horror stories, trilogies, and novels to a publisher, so she may begin a career doing what she loves. Aside from writing, her other hobbies include hiking, swimming, tutoring her younger brother, and making web comics.

Caleb Dunnam has been homeschooled since kindergarten, and he will graduate this year. He hopes to attend College of the Ozarks this fall. He enjoys reading and has also written a number of pieces, including musical compositions. He is currently enrolled in the Telos Institute International, a writing course administered by the Advanced Training Institute International. His work, "The Struggle," is based on a real recurring dream that he had. His hope is that in their struggles, others will be encouraged to seek help from the only One who can rescue them.

J. Ezekiel Farley spends the majority of his days playing and composing music. He does not ordinarily write poetry, but events in the past acted as an inspiration for him. Zeke plans to major in music and business, and later open his own jazz bar. It is through his beautiful music that Zeke praises God, which is his main focus in everything he does. After his early graduation this year, Zeke would like to attend the University of Georgia to continue his education. One thing remains certain in his life; he will always praise God and play his music for him.

Jessica Gandy is a sophomore at Covenant Christian Academy in Cumming Georgia, where she enjoys a 4.0 grade point average. When she is not studying, Jessica stays involved with Covenant's athletics, where she is a varsity starter on the Lady Rams women's basketball team and also a soccer player. Jessica is a native Georgian, having grown up and attended schools in the north metro Atlanta area. Besides academics and sports, Jessica has a keen interest in the arts. She works with paints and pastels and plays the bass violin. Jessica resides with her father, stepmother, and two cats in northern Forsyth County.

Luke Geraci is a freshman at Covenant Christian Academy. He enjoys playing competitive hockey, playing with his friends, and his youth group. Luke also enjoys listening to music and reading a good fantasy story.

Matthew Stephen Hackney was born on September 9, 1988. He has a mother (Donna), a father (Jerry), and a brother (Daniel). He is fifteen, has a small dog (named Prissy), and is in the tenth grade. Matthew is a Boy Scout in Troop 34 and wants to go to college to study photojournalism and English. He lives in Washington, Georgia and attends First Baptist Church. He attended public school until the sixth grade, then started homeschooling with his mother and has been doing so ever since.

Zachary D. Hanif is a tenth-grader who attends Covenant Christian Academy in Cumming. He has recently taken up writing and is enjoying it greatly. He reads avidly, and enjoys computers and everything about them. Zachary is looking into attending a technical school, in the hope that he can make a positive difference in the world through his knowledge of technology.

Betsy Hardin is a student at Coosa High School and has been writing for as long as she can remember. When she was younger she liked to illustrate her stories, but her artistic skills haven't improved much over the years—and what is good at age five isn't so great at fifteen. She's had two poems and one short story published previously. Betsy's other interests include playing flute in the band, piano, reading, and hanging out with her friends.

Chelsea Hollifield is the author of "Sky." She is in the ninth grade at Lassiter High School, where she enjoys drama club and hanging out with her friends. She is in color guard and has been for three years now. She has enjoyed writing stories and poems ever since she first learned to write, and she also loves to read. Chelsea loves listening to all types of music, and her favorite bands are Savage Garden, Linkin Park, and Kidneythieves. She prides herself on being original, she DESPISES ignorance and stereotypes, and she loves her "bestist" friends, Asia and Aubrey.

Molly Logan Holmes, 15, is a high-honors freshman at Savannah Country Day School. She enjoys swimming on her summer league team, competing on both her Junior Varsity and Club Volleyball teams, and performing in school theater productions. Molly has always loved to write, winning the Savannah-Chatham County School District's "Fair Bear Essay Contest" (1999), and the Savannah Morning News' "Generation Next: Celebrate 2000 Essays" at the elementary level. Molly volunteers regularly with the environmental group, "Clean Coast" and is a reading tutor for adult learners at the Royce Learning Center in Savannah.

Ashley Elizabeth Jabrocki is in eleventh grade. She is taking advanced courses and participates in the chorus at North Forsyth High School. She is part of the communication committee of Fellowship of Christian Athletes and Students. She attends McEver Road United Methodist Church where she babysits small children every third Sunday. She works in her aunt's restaurant. Every third Wednesday, she and her aunt make food to give to the church's youth group. The leftovers are given to Good News, which is a corporation dedicated to feeding and clothing the poor. She plans to become an occupational therapist as an adult.

Sergio Jackson is an eleventh grade student at Monroe Area Comprehensive High School in Monroe, Georgia.

Kyle James is an eleventh-grader at North Forsyth High School. Outside of school he enjoys running track, is an active member of FBLA (Future Business Leaders of America), and is currently competing in Web Site Development for FBLA. He also has an interest in multimedia, graphic art, and forensics. In his spare time he likes to wake board, hang out with friends, and go to concerts. His future plans are to attend college majoring in some art-related or forensic field. He's now becoming interested in scuba diving and sailing and plans to experience both of these new interests in the near future.

Lauren Kiel is a fourteen-year-old freshman at Chestatee High School in Gainesville, Georgia. Lauren is a member of her school's FCA, FCCLA, Newspaper Staff, Chorus, and is the Student Council Treasurer for the freshman class. Also a member of the Dance Team, Lauren loves to play tennis, act, sing, read, and anything to do with history or geography. She attends Good Shepherd Catholic Church and is currently ranked first in her class, where she hopes to stay throughout high school. This is Lauren's second time appearing in *O, Georgia Too!;* she published a short story in the 2001 edition.

Kimberly Lewis is a sophomore at Monroe Area High School and is sixteen years old. She has been writing poems as long as she can remember. Even when she was young, she loved writing, and that set her apart from other kids. Kimberly's poems allow her to get away from everyday life's pressures and stress. Some of her poems are based on true feelings, and others require her to put herself in character. She writes about love, death, morals, and religion, because all of these play an important part in her life.

Lindsey Maxey was born on November 5, 1988. She currently attends South Forsyth High School, where she is active in many organizations, including the Literary Club. Lindsey has always taken great pleasure in writing, especially poetry. This year, her favorite subject in school is Spanish. Upon graduating high school, Lindsey would like to attend Vanderbilt University; Nashville, Tennessee, is her favorite city (excluding Atlanta). Although currently unsure of her future career, one of Lindsey's prospective goals includes editing for a major magazine or newspaper.

Havilah Miller is currently a seventeen-year-old girl in the eleventh grade at North Forsyth High School. After living in Athens and Atlanta for five years, she moved Forsyth in 1991. She is the oldest of three children and the daughter of two awesome parents. Writing has always been an innate desire that she thoroughly enjoys and is always eager to improve. In the future, she hopes to be able to incorporate writing as a skill in her career. Havilah also enjoys art, playing volleyball for North, being a part of clubs such as FCAS and the French Club, as well as working with kindergartners in Sunday School.

Sean Mixon is an eleventh-grader who enjoys spending time with his friends, whether it be playing paintball, playing video games, or just hanging out at the Quick Trip. He is in the marching band, where he is a tuba player. He enjoys watching TV. His favorite show is "The Simpsons," on which he is a trivia expert. He is six feet tall and has brown hair and green eyes. He enjoys long walks on the beach, curling up next to a warm, crackling fire with a mug of hot chocolate, and watching sappy love stories such as "Fight Club."

Ashley Parker, a sophomore at South Forsyth, has no special writing awards or achievements to her name. She does, however, love writing more than anything. At a young age, she found poetry to be her favorite way to convey her feelings onto paper. To her, poetry is like a musician's desire play, listening to the melodic sounds dance through the air; an athlete's longing to train and become the best he or she can be; and a painter's joy that comes from an array of colors, splashed across a soft white canvas. Her poetry has become her hobby, her outlet, and her passion.

Nichole Rawlings is currently a sophomore at Forsyth Central High School. She is involved in many of the school's clubs and maintains a 4.0 GPA. Nichole enjoys reading and writing in her free time, along with painting and drawing. Her favorite subject is Literature, and her least favorite subject is Math (however she did write about it in a previous *O, Georgia Too!* book). Nichole lives in Cumming, Georgia, with her parents and two younger brothers, three cats, and a dog. Nichole hopes to become a writer and illustrator for her own children's books someday.

Tim Reeves is an "A" student at North Forsyth High School in Cumming, Georgia. He is a member of the Honor Roll and is also in Habitat for Humanity. He plays football, baseball and also swims for the Raiders. In his spare time, Tim enjoys bass fishing and reading. He also enjoys saltwater fishing for bluefish, fluke, and striped bass. His favorite books are fantasy and adventure books. He listens to Punk music; some of his favorite bands are New Found Glory, Less Than Jake, The Early November, Punch Drunk, and For Felix. He lives with his mother, father, sister, and two dogs.

Danielle Schramm is a seventeen-year-old junior who attends North Forsyth High School in Cumming, Georgia. She lives with her parents (Linda and Brad), and her twin siblings (Abby and Zachary). She is the sports editor of her school newspaper and is involved in German Club, Fellowship of Christian Athletes and Students, Habitat for Humanity, and is a co-leader of her youth group at Christ the King Lutheran Church. She writes sports articles for her hometown newspaper, "The Forsyth County News." Her college plans are to hopefully attend the University of Georgia and major in journalism and become a sportswriter for a newspaper.

Brittany N. Schwendenman is a junior in high school at Covenant Christian Academy of Cumming, Georgia. Her interests include vocal performance, puttering in the arts, creative writing, and acting. Brittany also enjoys traveling, daydreaming, and cooking. As a young child, Brittany experimented with fictional stories about her favorite subject, dogs. However, she quickly realized that her fictional accounts could not measure up to actual events. Brittany aspires to be a writer in the distant future, but realizes that she has much to learn. Meanwhile she will be focusing on attending college, where she will major in vocal performance/education.

Michelle Serra is sixteen years old. She lives in Alpharetta, Georgia, with her parents, sister, and two brothers. She is currently attending Milton High School, where she is a junior. She hopes to go to the College of Charleston when she graduates, to major in business. She likes to spend her time hanging out with her friends, reading, helping out with Miracle League, and just relaxing. She would like to say thank you to everyone who has supported her over the years and to her friends and family who encouraged her to submit her work and take a risk.

Erin E. Sharp grew up in Florida where her family started a ministry for women and children. In 2000 her family moved to Georgia where she attends North Forsyth High School. As a senior Erin will continue her education at North Georgia College and State University. She is a very active student, involved as a FCA leader and a member of the Beta Club, in honor of her high academic achievements. Also, throughout her high school career she has obtained a starting position on the Varsity Soccer team and was named Most Valuable Player her sophomore year.

Whitney Stinebaugh is in the eleventh grade and attends Covenant Christian Academy. She was inspired to write her poem, "Unbroken Silence," by an intense relationship that lasted over a year. Whitney enjoys going to the movies, going on shopping sprees, and most definitely loves vacations to the beach. Whitney has an older sister (Lindsay) and two loving and inspirational parents (John and Jean). She was fortunate enough to be raised in a Christian environment where she learned how to walk and grow with the Lord Jesus Christ. Whitney is an avid cheerleader and— trust me— you can hear her a mile away.

Cora Tallant is a junior at North Forsyth High School. Cora is very involved in her school and community. She is in every club, from Academic Bowl to Y-Club. She is an unaccomplished musician, but she still has fun playing the French horn. In marching band, she's fondly known as "The Best Section Leader Ever" because she bribes people with Chinese food. Cora hopes to attend Harvard University and study pre-medicine, where she'll become a female version of Patch Adams. When she's not saving the world, Cora likes to read Charles Dickens. Cora, by no means, takes herself too seriously.

Kim-Uyen Tran is currently in the eleventh grade at North Forsyth High School. She is a musical person, as she enjoys playing the violin and flute. She also takes pleasure in being part of the youth program at church, where she is one of the youth leaders. In other spare time, she works with her parents at their small business and volunteers at a doctor's office as well. Kim hopes to work her way up through high school and college to later work in the medical field.

William Tsikerdanos is currently a junior attending North Forsyth High School. He was born on December 16, 1986, in Spartanburg, South Carolina, and moved to Georgia in the summer of his eighth-grade year. He presently lives with his father, brother, and stepmother. His hobbies include reading, writing, and drawing, along with the occasional video game. He currently attends St.'s Raphael, Nicholas, and Irene Greek Orthodox Church. He intends to finish high school with honors, continue on to college, and attain a degree in law. Until said time, he will continue as usual on the path laid out before him.

Erin Turner, a high school student at Covenant Christian Academy, is passionate about literature. She is a voracious reader with a special affinity for all things Tolkien. This love of books was fueled by being homeschooled through the eighth grade. When not engrossed in a book, Erin's interests include horseback riding, playing the flute, and singing in chorus. Erin, who was born in Nuremberg Germany, during her father's army tour in Europe, currently lives in Cumming, Georgia, with her younger sister and brother, her dog, and two cats who have taken over her room.

Brianna Veenstra, currently a junior at Columbus High School, has always loved to read and write. In addition to writing, Brianna captains the school's varsity rifle team, co-captains the Academic Decathlon team, and participates in extracurricular activities such as math team, Science Olympiad, BETA club, and Combined Communities of South Columbus tutoring. Brianna was born in Illinois and lives with her mother, Linda Veenstra. She hopes to attend an intellectually stimulating university or college, major in creative writing and mathematics, and win the Nobel Prize. During her free time, she enjoys poetry readings, ultimate Frisbee, multivariable calculus, and gummy bears.

Anna Ruth Warnke lives in Dawsonville, where she loves to play with and walk her neighbor's dogs, Otis and Eddie. Anna also loves to dance at Praise Him With Dance, where she takes ballet, pointe, jazz, hip-hop and tap. She is also a member of the Celebration Dance Company. Anna loves to write stories, especially ones about dogs and horses. Anna has three brothers and two sisters, and her mom homeschools all of them. Anna is pursuing a career in writing fiction.

Joseph Matthew Warnke, born on December 5, 1985, currently lives in Dawsonville with his family of eight. Joe is interested in the War Between the States (WBTS) and any connected subject. He loves reading history, especially about the WBTS. He is an active member of the Sons of Confederate Veterans Col. Hiram Parks Bell

Camp 1642 of Cumming, Georgia. He is homeschooled, and he often gives lectures on various WBTS topics. He competed in a national speech and debate league and has won three awards with WBTS-related speeches. He is currently authoring several booklets about the WBTS.

Brianne L. Wingate is fifteen years old and is a sophomore at Pace Academy in Atlanta, Georgia. Her love for writing first exploded when she was in sixth grade. With the help of various teachers and peers, Brianne continued to cultivate her skill throughout junior high and high school and has participated in creative writing programs at Duke University. Brianne is also a lover of theater, photography, history, the opera *Carmen* (by Bizet), and post-punk rock music. When not in school, she can be found playing guitar, acting, reading the works of Lewis Carroll, or hanging out at coffee shops with her friends.

Robert Zauche is a ninth-grade student at Covenant Christian Academy in Cumming, Georgia. "The Rescue" is his first published literary work. He enjoys football, paintball, studying military history, travel and the great outdoors. He fondly recalls family vacations with his younger brother, Brandon, to the Big Apple, the West Coast, Colorado, Florida, the Carolinas, Canada and two Caribbean Islands. While at home, he spends much of his time accompanied by Ariel, the calico cat or Memphis, the Aussie-Lab puppy. When he's not reading, Robert enjoys a good workout, or keeping his fingers in shape at the computer keyboard.

O, Georgia! Writers Foundation

Honor Roll of Donors

The O, Georgia! Writers Foundation is a public charity. Its earned income is derived solely from the sale of this book and, to a much lesser extent, from the entry fees paid by those who submit their writing samples for consideration by the judges.

Our earned income is never enough to carry the costs of our program. Therefore, we must rely heavily upon those generous individuals who recognize the importance of raising the bar in children's programming within the literary arts. Building communication skills raises self-esteem. High self-esteem enables kids to dream big dreams and to achieve them! To those of you who have contributed to OGWF during the last year, I offer my heartfelt thanks, as this enterprise would not be possible without your unstinting support.

The individuals who have offered us their financial support during the last year are named below.

Friends *($25.00 – $49.00)*

Richard A. Anderson
Karl Armstrong
Ben & Kelly Blount
Sallie Wolper Boyles
Ann G. Bussey
John W. Callaway, Jr.
Frances Daniel
Margaret Dyer
Emily Flack
Nancy Forthman
Michelle Groce
Norma Haas
Peggy Jensen
Zoher F. Kapasi
Suzanne Elizabeth Kelly

Friends *($25.00 – $49.00)*

Michele Lellouche
David Levitan
Debbie Minkoff
Mercy Morecraft
Peter & Susan Muller
Clinton B. Newton
Sally Pinsker
Debbie Pruitt
Robert & Lisa Rawlings
David & Deloris Schmidt
L. Darlene Simmemon
Carol Trusty
Nancy Washington
Myrna West
Billie H. Wilson
Sharon Yanish

Sustainers *($50.00 – $99.00)*

Bill & Bonnie Collins
Timothy H. Echols
Penelope E. M. Holder
Edward W. Jensen
Debra Moody
Terry Segal
Carl B. Smith
Doug & Gillian Tilghman
Kendra Vaughn

Contributors *($100.00 – $249.00)*

Sandra D. Carle
Adrian D. Drost
Carol DeVaney
Adrian Grant

Dan Kolber
Peter & Aruna Rao McCann
Kevin Reardon
Romney Scott
Faye Sklar
Dianna Love Snell
W.T. Westhead
Karen S. White

Sponsors *($250.00 – $499.00)*

Kathryn W. Crawford
Thomas Davis (Big Creek Elementary School)
Clarence & Faye Drummond
Randy Estep
Gordon & Dagmar Marshall
Mary D. Stripling

Associates *($500.00 – $999.00)*

Jim Parkman
Steve Reed (Target Stores)
Susan L. Richards

Patrons *($1,000.00 – $1,999.00)*

Cory Coulter
Steve Zembrzuski (Intelligent Technology Systems)